Teaching and Learning in Further Education

This third edition presents the most up-to-date picture of teaching and learning in colleges in the UK. It has been fully revised in order to capture the considerable changes that have taken place since the second edition was published. These changes relate to all aspects of college activity. At the same time, the fundamental principles that help teachers to develop their students' knowledge and skills provide an important and much-needed platform of stability. This book introduces readers to those principles and to a wide range of strategies that can be used to support the learning of an increasingly diverse body of students.

Further education colleges provide education and training to more students than any other institutions in the post-compulsory sector in the UK. Drawing on a considerable research base, this book places FE teaching and learning in its historical, social, economic and political contexts to help readers to better understand how practice in colleges has evolved.

The book explores:

- the changing context, structure and funding of the FE sector
- the nature and range of FE students and staff
- the range of curricula and qualifications
- teaching and learning theories and strategies
- the assessment and recording of achievement
- continued professional development
- support available to FE teachers.

For this new edition, particular emphasis has been placed on the following topics:

- workplace, work-based and work-related learning
- e-learning and the use of new technologies
- the impact of 14- to 16-year-olds in college
- the development of new full-time vocational programmes
- collaboration between FE and higher education

- marginal groups in college, including second language learners and asylum seekers
- developments in assessment and individualised learning.

Full of practical activities and case study examples, *Teaching and Learning in Further Education* helps the reader to consider differing student needs and how these might best be served. It is essential reading for lecturers, tutors, managers and teaching assistants in further and higher education. Throughout, case study examples help you to consider differing student needs and how these might best be served. They also provide an opportunity to reflect upon how the changing policy context of FE impacts upon students, programmes and institutions. Practical activities are also included, which can be used as catalysts for questioning your attitude and approaches to work in FE.

Whether you are embarking on a career or already teaching, this book will help you review your approach and understanding of the process of teaching and learning in further education.

Prue Huddleston is Professorial Fellow and Director of the Centre for Education and Industry at the University of Warwick.

Lorna Unwin is Professor of Vocational Education at the Institute of Education, University of London.

Teaching and Learning in Further Education

Diversity and Change

Third Edition

Prue Huddleston and
Lorna Unwin

Routledge
Taylor & Francis Group

LONDON AND NEW YORK

First published 1997
Second edition published 2002
Third edition published 2007
by Routledge
2 Park Square, Milton Park, Abingdon, Oxon OX14 4RN

Simultaneously published in the USA and Canada
by Routledge
270 Madison Ave, New York, NY 10016

Routledge is an imprint of the Taylor & Francis Group, an informa business

© 2008 Prue Huddleston and Lorna Unwin

Typeset in Garamond Three and Gill Sans by
Florence Production Ltd, Stoodleigh, Devon
Printed and bound in Great Britain by
TJ International Ltd, Padstow, Cornwall

British Library Cataloguing in Publication Data
A catalogue record for this book is available from the British Library

Library of Congress Cataloging in Publication Data
Huddleston, Prue.
  Teaching and learning in further education/Prue Huddleston and
Lorna Unwin. – 3rd ed.
     p. cm.
    Includes bibliographical references and index.
  1. Continuing education – Great Britain. 2. Adult learning – Great
Britain. 3. Teaching – Great Britain. I. Unwin, Lorna II. Title.
LC5256.G7H76 2008
374.941 – dc22   2007025735

ISBN10: 0–415–41350–8 (hbk)
ISBN10: 0–415–41349–4 (pbk)
ISBN10: 0–203–93847–X (ebk)

ISBN13: 978–0–415–41350–3 (hbk)
ISBN13: 978–0–415–41349–7 (pbk)
ISBN13: 978–0–203–93847–8 (ebk)

Contents

Figures

Preface

This book differs from many other texts on teaching and learning in further education (FE) colleges as it argues that teachers need to understand the wider context that helps to shape their professional activities. Teaching in an FE college in the UK is a very demanding job. At first glance, it would seem that the FE teacher shares few of the advantages enjoyed by colleagues in schools and universities. Unlike schools, colleges are open to their students from early in the morning to late at night, often at weekends, and throughout the traditional summer holiday period from mid-July to early September. Unlike universities, colleges are open to people of all abilities, from adults who may be learning to read and write to those who are technically highly skilled and, again increasingly, to those who are following undergraduate and postgraduate courses. Some school pupils aged 14–16 are also now spending up to three days a week in colleges throughout the UK, a move which has significant implications for curriculum design, student support, and teaching styles.

There is, therefore, a heterogeneity about the student body, structures and curricular offerings in FE colleges which would send some school and university teachers running for cover. That very diversity, however, helps make FE colleges stimulating and exciting environments in which to work as a teacher.

Change is the name of the game in education and training in the UK, particularly in England. Since the second edition of this book was published in 2002, colleges have had to cope with substantial changes to qualifications, assessment procedures and funding regimes. As authors of a book that seeks to present a comprehensive analysis of the FE sector, we face the challenge of trying to be as up to date as possible. We acknowledge, however, that given the way in which successive governments, particularly in England, seem intent on reorganising some aspect of the architecture of education and training every few months, some of the initiatives covered in this book may have been further amended or even withdrawn in the time it takes for the manuscript to be published. All colleges struggle to incorporate externally imposed change in such a way as to cause as little disruption as possible to their students and staff, but change is endemic and, therefore, many staff will find themselves under unwelcome pressure at various times.

Working in any sector of education means we must be prepared for change and periods of upheaval, much of which may be imposed from outside our sector or organisation. However, the majority of FE teachers still spend much of their working day focused on helping their students to learn, to progress and to achieve. Throughout this book, we have tried to portray the realities of college life in order to emphasise that FE teachers must be capable of adapting to many different situations and circumstances. In any one day, an FE teacher will employ a range of strategies, moving from a traditional didactic style in one lesson to being a facilitator of group work in another, from the company of mature adult students to a group of disaffected 14-year-olds, and from teaching and assessing in the college classroom to the variable conditions of the industrial or commercial workplace.

This book has been written primarily for people who are embarking on a teaching career in colleges of further education and for those already teaching who may wish to review their approaches to and understanding of the process of teaching and learning. It may also be of use to managers in FE and to people working in organisations that have a relationship with FE colleges. Researchers engaged in studying FE colleges and post-compulsory education and training more broadly may also find this book a useful resource for information and potential research topics.

The book is divided into three parts: Part I: Further education in context; Part II: Teaching and learning; and Part III: Professional development. Part I has been fully revised to take account of changes to the way in which FE is structured, the student body and curricula and qualifications. Chapter 1 pulls together the different facets of the FE world to show how colleges are funded and the external constraints that govern the ways in which they can go about their business. Chapter 2 examines the nature and scope of the FE student population and introduces the reader to some real students whose needs and expectations pose challenges for teachers and support staff. It also describes the different types of staff found in colleges and the multi-skilled nature of teachers. In Chapter 3, we discuss the rich diet that comprises the curricular and qualification offerings found in FE colleges, from basic skills workshops through to higher education courses.

Part II focuses on teaching and learning. Chapter 4 explores the relationship between teaching and learning, drawing on a number of theoretical approaches that can help teachers reflect on their work and be used as a basis for examining the challenges they encounter. This underpinning theory is continued in Chapter 5 where we present a number of strategies for use in the different teaching situations found in a college. Part of the chapter highlights the increasing importance of e-learning and the use of information and communication learning technologies. In Chapter 6, we focus on assessment and recording achievement.

In Part III, we see that, as in all teaching, regardless of the sector, professional educators never stop learning about their work and spend a great deal of time reflecting on how to improve and develop their competence and levels of creativity. In Chapter 7, we discuss the concept of the reflective practitioner as it relates to both teachers and students, and the extent to which teachers can also function as researchers. As a result of the increased recognition of the importance of FE colleges to people's life chances and the UK economy, more research is being funded. We discuss some of the findings of the latest research studies throughout the book and highlight the work of some key projects. The possibilities for continued professional development are examined in Chapter 8, and Chapter 9 provides information about the organisations and resources upon which FE teachers can draw for support in their work. At the end of the book we indicate further reading material for each chapter that will help you extend your understanding of some of the complex learning and teaching concepts covered in the book.

In each chapter, we have included sets of questions and activities for you to consider. We have boxed these under the heading 'Reflections' and hope that you will find time to use them as catalysts for questioning your attitudes and approaches to your work in FE and for discussion with colleagues.

This book has been written in the spirit of sharing rather than preaching and, as such, reflects the philosophical basis of much of the teaching and learning that occurs in FE colleges. Our ideas come from our own experiences of teaching in colleges and, more recently, of working with FE professionals in a staff development and research capacity. We hope the book provides you with some useful and relevant information and ideas but equally we hope it provides enough challenging material to make you say, 'I think I would tackle that situation differently' or 'I can come up with a better way.'

Abbreviations

ALI	Adult Learning Inspectorate
AoC	Association of Colleges
APL	Accreditation of Prior Learning
AS	Advanced Subsidiary
ATL	Association of Teachers and Lecturers
BERR	Business, Enterprise and Regulatory Reform
BTEC	Business and Technology Education Council (merged with the London Examinations Board to become EDXCEL in April 1996)
CBI	Confederation of British Industry
CCEA	Council for the Curriculum, Examinations and Assessment (CCEA in Northern Ireland)
CoVE	Centre of Vocational Excellence
CPD	Continuing Professional Development
CPE	Continuing Professional Education
CPVE	Certificate of Pre-Vocational Education
DCSF	Department for Children, Schools and Families
Delni	Department for Employment and Learning Northern Ireland
DfES	Department for Education and Skills
DIUS	Department for Innovation, Universities and Skills
DTI	Department of Trade and Industry
EBP	Education-Business Partnership
EIS	Education Institute Scotland
ETLLD	Enterprise, Transport and Lifelong Learning Department (Scotland)
ELWa	Education and Learning Wales
EMA	Education Maintenance Allowance
ESF	European Social Fund
ESOL	English for Speakers of Other Languages
FE	Further Education
FEFC	Further Education Funding Council
GCSE	General Certificate of Secondary Education

GCE	General Certificate of Education
GFE	General Further Education
HE	Higher Education
HEI	Higher Education Institution
HEFCE	Higher Education Funding Council (England)
HEFCW	Higher Education Funding Council Wales
HNC	Higher National Certificate
HND	Higher National Diploma
IB	International Baccalaureate
ICLT	Information and Communication Learning Technologies
IFP	Increased Flexibility Programme
ILA	Individual Learner Account
ISR	Individual Student Record
LEA	Local Education Authority
LEC	Local Enterprise Company
LSC	Learning and Skills Council
LLSC	Local Learning and Skills Council
LLUK	Lifelong Learning UK
LSDA	Learning and Skills Development Agency
LSW	learning support worker
MSC	Manpower Services Commission
NATFHE	National Association of Teachers in Further and Higher Education
NEET	Not in Education, Employment or Training
NIACE	National Institute for Adult Continuing Education
NQF	National Qualifications Framework
NVQ	National Vocational Qualification
Ofsted	Office for Standards in Education
OU	Open University
PGCE	Postgraduate Certificate of Education
PIU	Performance and Innovation Unit
QCA	Qualifications and Curriculum Authority
QCF	Qualifications and Credit Framework
QIA	Quality Improvement Agency
QTLS	Qualified Teacher, Learning and Skills
RDA	Regional Development Agency
SCRE	Scottish Council for Research in Education
SFC	Scottish Funding Council
SFEC	Scottish Further Education Funding Council
SHA	Secondary Heads Association
S/NVQ	Scottish National Vocational Qualification
SQA	Scottish Qualifications Authority
SSC	Sector Skills Council

SSDA	Sector Skills Development Agency
TA	transactional analysis
TEC	Training and Enterprise Council
TS	teaching strategies
TVEI	Technical and Vocational Education Initiative
UCU	Universities and Colleges Union
UNAC	Undeb Cenedlaethol Athrawon Cymru
VLE	Virtual Learning Environment

Part I

Further education in context

Chapter 1

Where will I teach?

Nature and scope of further education

This chapter describes the shape and scope of the complex and shifting landscape of further education (FE) in the UK. Part of the chapter presents an historical review of the structural changes imposed on FE by central government over the past 20 or so years. Teaching and learning are situated activities that are profoundly affected by the contexts in which they occur. At the same time, teachers and learners also shape and change the contexts in which they work and study. This chapter is intended to help you gain a better understanding of the nature of the context in which you teach in terms of how your college is being affected by internal and external pressures and the role colleges play in a broader educational landscape. In writing a book of this nature, we are faced with the challenge of trying to keep up to date with educational change in the UK, and particularly in England where government ministers seem to have an almost pathological desire to invent as many new policies as possible during their (often) very short term in office. In the five years since we wrote the second edition of this book, the content of this chapter has changed radically, and we know that in the time that passes before someone reads it there will have been new policies invented and some agencies may have come and gone. We want to stress, however, that while FE teachers work in a dynamic context, much of what they do still involves the age-old process of helping people to learn and achieve their ambitions.

Both Scotland and England have been carrying out full-scale reviews of their colleges. The difference in 'ownership' and timescale of the Scottish and English reviews is significant. The Scottish review was announced in June 2005, by Jim Wallace, then Deputy First Minister in the Scottish Parliament and Minister for Enterprise and Lifelong Learning, but he was quick to point out that while his officials would provide support, the review would be organised and carried out by colleges themselves with their associated stakeholders. The review is still underway. In England, the Secretary of State for Education and Skills (at that time, Charles Clarke) commissioned Sir Andrew Foster, former Chief Executive of the Audit Commission, to undertake a review of colleges. While Foster consulted college staff, his review was very definitely 'owned' by government. His review was completed within one year (DfES, 2005a).

One consequence of the Foster Review is particularly notable. In 2007, the '157 Group' was established by 22 principals of the largest and most successful colleges. The group's name refers to a paragraph in the final report of the Foster Review, which argued that:

> This review could result in a greater involvement of principals in national representation, in particular those from larger, successful colleges where management capacity and capability exists to release them for this work. There is a strong need for articulate FE college principals to be explaining the services they give to society and how colleges can make a significant contribution to the economy and to developing fulfilled citizens.
>
> (DfES, 2005a, para 157)

This development is significant in that FE colleges are now very much in the limelight in terms of public policy, having spent many years off the educational radar, unlike universities and schools which have been much more successful in making sure both government and the general public understand the value of their activities. Of course, achieving greater visibility is not necessarily a good thing, particularly if colleges are expected to share the main burden in terms of helping the UK increase its skill levels, while, at the same time, providing a home for thousands of 14- to 18-year-olds who the schools cannot or are disinclined to teach. One reason for ensuring the FE voice is heard in all areas of the UK is that colleges are now having to come to terms with the establishment of National Skills Academies, an idea first proposed in a 2005 White Paper (DfES, 2005b). The aim is to have 12 academies by 2008 covering a range of occupational sectors including, for example, Fashion Retail, Financial Services, Construction, and Food and Drink Manufacturing (see: www.nationalskillsacademy.gov.uk). The academies are sponsored by leading employers working with Sector Skills Councils (SSCs). Some might have premises, but all will seek to share and develop courses with other providers, including Centres of Vocational Excellence (CoVEs) in colleges. They represent a long-standing desire by successive governments to make education and training, and particularly FE colleges, more responsive to employer needs. Readers will need to locate such developments within the broader historical and contextual framework which this chapter seeks to provide.

This book uses the term FE to encompass colleges that provide education and training for learners from the age of 14 upwards. The lower age limit has dropped to 14 since 2002 when the Department for Education and Skills (DfES) in England introduced the Increased Flexibility Programme for 14- to 16-year-olds (IFP). The aim was to provide vocational learning opportunities for young people who otherwise would be studying full-time in schools for their GCSEs. The IFP is organised and delivered by partnerships of schools, colleges and training providers at local level. Following this initiative, Scotland, Wales and Northern Ireland have all introduced similar programmes. As a result, there has been a significant growth in the numbers of 14- to 16-year-olds in FE colleges throughout the UK, posing considerable challenges for teachers, support staff and managers. This development raises issues related to teaching and learning in colleges and we will examine them in more detail throughout the book (see Lumby, 2007). The vast majority of students in FE colleges are still, however, over the age of 16, and colleges are the biggest providers of post-16 education in the UK.

Part of the complexity of the FE landscape is the range of institutions designated as colleges. Currently, in England, there are 253 General FE (GFE) and tertiary colleges, 102 sixth-form colleges, 16 specialised designated colleges (mainly for adults and some with residential facilities), 17 agricultural and horticulture colleges, and 5 art, design and performing arts colleges. In Wales there are 27 GFE colleges and one sixth-form college. In Scotland, there are 43 FE colleges and in Wales 2/. In the autumn of 2007, the 16 FE colleges in Northern Ireland were merged to create six super-colleges. These figures are subject to change because, much more so than in the case of schools and universities, colleges are subject to merger and even closure. For example, in England, the current total number of 393 colleges has dropped from a figure of 429 in 2000, largely as result of mergers. In 2005/6, there were 3.63 million students in colleges in England enrolled on courses funded by the Learning and Skills Council (LSC). Latest available figures for Scotland show just under 400,000 students in FE, while for Wales, the figure is around 250,000 and for Northern Ireland, just under 90,000. The majority of FE students across the UK are over the age of 19 and studying part-time, but the full-time 16- to 19-year-old students outnumber those of the same age group found in schools.

The vignette in Figure 1.1 provides details of how a small GFE college in England is organised and funded. During 2006, the LSC made a dramatic reduction in terms of the level of funding it allocated to adults aged 19 and over and switched its focus to the 14–19 age group. All colleges in England were affected by this. For the college shown in Figure 1.1, the cuts meant that the numbers of adult students studying part-time fell from 9,174 in 2005/6 to 3,550 in 2006/7. As a result, the college had to make some teaching and support staff redundant and had to close some of its centres offering personalised learning opportunities.

The title 'tertiary college' was originally given to institutions providing both vocational and academic courses for the 16–19 age group, which combined the functions of a further education college and a sixth-form college in areas where schools did not offer sixth-form (post-compulsory) provision. There are some 50 institutions in England classed as 'tertiary'

South-east Derbyshire College is a general tertiary FE college based in the small town of Ilkeston and covering the semi-rural districts of Amber Valley and Erewash. The first table shows the number of staff employed by the college. Colleges calculate their staff numbers using a formula known as 'full-time equivalents' (FTE).

Group	Full-time	Part-time	Total
Teaching Departments (including technicians)	90	55	145
Teaching support services (libraries)	4	4	8
Other support services (welfare, admissions and careers)	7	5	12
Administration and Central services	61	40	101
Premises	13	10	23
Other (research)	0	0	0
Total (FTE)	**175**	**114**	**299**

Based on numbers as of May 2007

The second table shows the numbers of students enrolled at the college. The part-time column includes people who come to the college for off-the-job training as part of a government-supported work-based learning programme such as Modern Apprenticeship.

Student numbers

Group	Full-time	Part-time
14–18	1,101	271
19+	173	3,279
Total	**1,274**	**3,550**

The college offers courses across a wide range of subject areas as the next table shows:

Figure 1.1 South-east Derbyshire College

Subject areas

Social sciences
Physical sciences
Humanities
Languages
Art, design, media and music
Engineering [light], motor vehicle and electronics
Construction trades – wood and brick
Care, social care and early years
ICT
Business
Sport and Sports Science
Beauty Therapy
Public Services

Courses for full-time students lead to qualifications including AS/A2 in a range of subjects and vocational qualifications from Foundation to Level 3 in 20 subjects. The college also runs an 'Enrichment' curriculum for 16–19 year old full-time students.

Courses for part-time students lead to National Vocational Qualifications [NVQs] in a wide range of subjects, and Higher National Certificates and Dipolomas in engineering and business studies. Taster courses for progression to NVQs and Advanced Level qualifications are also offered to adults. The college runs a range of vocational programmes for 14–16 year olds who have been excluded from local schools.

Funding streams

The college receives funding from the following sources:

- LSC participation grant for learning
- LSC standards grant [objective specific]
- Tuition fees collected from learners and employers
- European Social Funds [social inclusion work]
- Single Regeneration Budge [SRB] and similar grants [social inclusion in deprived communities]
- Work based learning payments
- Work based training levy from Construction Industry Training Board and JTL [electrical]
- HEFCE [via University franchise arrangements]
- Local Education Authority Year 11 contract
- Compulsory sector for 14–16 vocational programmes

Given the complexity of these funding streams, colleges have to employ financial managers who are alert to the different sources of funding and who can make the most of the opportunities on offer.

Figure 1.1 (cont.) South-east Derbyshire College

colleges. For example Richmond-upon-Thames College describes itself as follows on its website:

> Building on its traditional role as the borough's sixth form provider, the College's primary focus is full-time students aged 16–19 and their preparation for University, training or the workplace. Operating within a wider setting, it aims to contribute to adult, HE, employment-based and 14–16 provision, working, wherever appropriate, in collaboration and partnership with other institutions (see: www.richmond-utcoll.ac.uk).

The existence of different types of college in England has been the subject of debate over many years and their respective levels of achievement in terms of student outcomes and retention rates are regularly compared (see RCU, 2003). Achievement and retention rates in tertiary colleges have been found to be at least as successful as those of sixth-form colleges and better than GFE colleges at all levels, apart from the lowest entry level (DfES, 2005a). These comparisons are, of course, problematic in that they may overlook the differences in student intakes, and the economic and social contexts in which the colleges operate. The main debate tends to focus on whether 16- to 19-year-old full-time students are better served by studying in schools, sixth-form and tertiary colleges as opposed to general FE colleges. Sixth-form colleges cater almost exclusively for 16- to 19-year-olds studying A levels and in some areas they compete with both schools and other colleges for students.

Perry (2005: 1) has argued that 'colleges exist in a local infrastructure that is rarely designed, but more often the consequence of historical and organisational factors'. Some of the oldest of the FE colleges have their roots in the Mechanics Institutes of the mid-nineteenth century. Originally intended to provide technical education on a part-time basis for the growing numbers of technicians and craftspeople required by the industrialisation process, they grew and developed during the twentieth century to provide vocational education and training mainly on a day-release basis. For example, Huddersfield Technical College began as the Huddersfield Mechanics Institute in the 1840s, and became a technical college in 1896, whereas Lowestoft College, the most easterly college in Britain, traces its origins to evening art classes held in 1874, and courses in navigation for fishermen began in 1923. As Green and Lucas (1999: 11) note, the growth of the FE sector was 'part of the formation of the modern state in the late nineteenth century, reflecting one of the many aspects of a voluntarist relationship between education, training and the state'.

The 1960s and 1970s saw a considerable expansion in the FE sector, not just within the area of vocational education but also in the development of professional and academic courses. Some of these were on a full-time basis, often for those students who were looking for an alternative to education provided in the school sixth form. In the late 1970s and early 1980s, world-wide economic recession led to a sharp rise in the number of young people in the UK who could not find jobs. The Labour and Conservative governments of the day sought to alleviate youth unemployment by introducing a series of youth training and work experience schemes (see Unwin, 1997). Parallel programmes were also introduced for unemployed adults. Many colleges became involved in these schemes by providing off-the-job training and/or by acting as 'managing agents'.

The FE sector has worked hard to demonstrate an 'inclusive' approach. That is, it has provided mainly non-selective education for everyone who wished to benefit from extended education or vocational training. In many colleges this provision now includes everything from basic education to undergraduate and professional programmes. Most colleges also provide courses for young people and adults with learning difficulties. The 1996 Tomlinson Report (Inclusive Learning) had a major impact on colleges as it turned on its head the existing attitude to provision for learners with difficulties, including disabilities: 'Put simply, we want to avoid a viewpoint which locates the difficulty or deficit with the student and focus instead on the capacity of the education institution to understand and respond to the individual learner's requirement' (Tomlinson, 1996: 4).

The Beattie Committee on inclusiveness in Scotland in 1998 followed Tomlinson's lead. In 2002, the Disability Discrimination Act was extended to educational institutions, placing a duty on them not to discriminate against disabled learners and, where necessary, to provide them with personal support.

Selection does exist in parts of the sector. For example, sixth form colleges are much more likely to specify entry qualifications for A level courses than GFE colleges. In 2003/4, the proportion of students in GFE colleges in England in what are termed 'widening participation' postcodes (that is localities with poorer families and low rates of participation in higher education) was 29 per cent compared to 25 per cent of the general population. The figures for school sixth forms and higher education were 19 per cent and 20 per cent respectively (DfES, 2005a). Colleges are multi-faceted organisations, on the one hand providing for the needs of their local community, and on the other hand for a growing regional, national and, in some cases, international student clientele. At the start of their third century of existence, colleges are now opening their doors to young people between the ages of 14 and 16 who have been excluded from school and/or those who it is believed might progress more effectively in a college environment. In her 1997 seminal report on FE, Helena Kennedy declared that 'Defining further education exhaustively would be God's own challenge because it is such a large and fertile section of the education world' (Kennedy, 1997: 1). Felstead and Unwin (2001: 107) in an analysis of further education funding argued that colleges in England were trying to fulfil four key aims:

- to respond to the government's economic agenda to improve basic and intermediate skill levels of young people and adults and increase their participation in education and training;
- to fulfill their role as the main provider of sub-degree post-compulsory education and training at local level;
- to continue to provide a wide-ranging curriculum which bridges the vocational/non-vocational divide;
- to continue being a 'second-chance saloon' for young people and adults who want to return to learning.

In addition, many colleges are engaged in higher education (HE) provision in partnership with local universities. In Scotland, around 20 per cent of all HE students are actually based in FE colleges, and the majority of part-time HE provision in Scotland takes place in FE colleges (see Morgan-Klein, 2003). Three-quarters of these students are studying for Higher National Certificates (HNCs) or Higher National Diplomas (HNDs). Gallacher (2006: 45) argues that this substantial presence of HE in FE in Scotland has enhanced the status of FE colleges, which are now 'clearly viewed as key institutions in widening access, promoting social inclusion and providing opportunities for lifelong learning'. Field (2004), however, has agreed that deep inequalities still persist for adults who try to enter the more prestigious universities in Scotland via the FE route. In England, it is estimated that 11 per cent of all HE enrolments are in FE colleges (AoC, 2007). Parry's (2005) research has shown that students from FE colleges in England account for 37 per cent of all full-time undergraduates in higher education. Of these, 55 per cent were educated at GFE colleges, 40 per cent at sixth-form colleges, and 6 per cent at specialist FE colleges. College-based higher education is also expanding in Wales (Griffiths, 2003) and Northern Ireland (Osborne, 2003). Despite the increasing closeness of the FE/HE interface, however, Parry (2005: 11) argues that, in England, 'higher education has still to be widely recognised and accepted as a normal or necessary activity in colleges' (see also Harwood and Harwood, 2004).

These developments pose interesting questions about the nature of student and staff identity, about the potential place of research in an FE teacher's portfolio, and, ultimately, about the extent to which the traditional status boundaries between FE and HE will dissolve (see also Duke and Layer, 2005).

Since 2001, colleges in England and Wales have worked closely with higher education institutions and employers to introduce foundation degrees (see Chapter 3 for more details). Scotland is not delivering foundation degrees, preferring to stick with the existing Higher National Certificates (HNCs) and Higher National Diplomas (HNDs) that have been available for many years in the UK, and which have a high satisfaction rating with both students and, crucially, employers. The new degrees may lead to a major change in the status of colleges in England as the 2007 Further Education and Training Bill has proposed that colleges be given the power to award them on their own. At present, the degrees are awarded by universities, though largely delivered in colleges. Universities UK, the membership organisation representing the majority of UK universities, has warned that, by giving colleges degree-awarding powers, the 'UK HE brand' would be diminished, and the House of Lords blocked the proposal at the Second Reading of the Bill. Others, however, including the Association of Colleges (AoC) in England have argued that colleges have proved they can deliver good quality higher education and that they can respond more quickly to employer needs. Parry (2005: 14) has argued that, in the light of the expansion of higher education, the concept of further education has 'become increasingly redundant' and that it should be abandoned 'in favour of an open system of colleges and universities'.

Since 1993, colleges in England have experienced a number of major changes to the way in which they are funded and their relationship with central government. Until April 1993, FE colleges were under the control of their local education authority (LEA) from whom they received the bulk of their funding, the rest coming from central government and other agencies. The 1988 Education Reform Act had given colleges and schools the power to manage their own budgets and thus began to loosen the control of the LEAs. In 1991, the White Paper, *Education and Training for the Twenty-first Century*, announced that colleges were to be given the 'freedom' they needed to play a 'central part in providing more high-quality opportunities' and to enable them to 'respond to the demand from students and employers for high-quality further education' (DES/ED/WO, 1991: 58). In his foreword to the White Paper, the then Prime Minister, John Major, outlined his government's desire to 'knock down the barriers to opportunity', and for 'more choice', in order to 'give every one of Britain's young people the chance to make the most of his or her particular talents and to have the best possible start in life' (ibid., Foreword).

Under the terms of the 1992 Further and Higher Education Act, which followed the White Paper, all colleges, including sixth-form colleges, were removed from LEA control, just as polytechnics and higher education colleges had been in 1989. Colleges became independent self-governing corporations with responsibility for their own budgets, staffing, marketing, course planning and provision. Two new national funding bodies were established for England and Wales: the Further Education Funding Council (FEFC) in England; and the Welsh Funding Council. In Northern Ireland and Scotland, colleges were funded via the Northern Ireland Office and the Scottish Office. In 1999, the Scottish Further Education Funding Council (SFEFC) was established. The removal of colleges from LEA control was part of the Conservative government's attempts to reduce the power of local authorities following the poll tax debacle. Gleeson (1996: 87) has argued that the 1988 and 1992 Acts and a further Education Act in 1994 led to post-16 policy being 'driven by market principles and deregulation' and a break with the 'municipal or public service view of school and further education which linked schools and colleges with LEAs within the spirit of the settlement which followed the 1944 Act'. Reference to the 1944 Education Act is important for it stated, for the first time, that it was a legal duty of LEAs to support FE provision and maintain colleges. The local political constraints on LEAs meant, however, that the funding available to colleges varied considerably from one part of the country to another.

Though free from LEA control, colleges in England soon found that the FEFC was to impose a strict funding methodology which would determine the nature of the courses and qualifications they could offer. Lucas (1999: 54) has argued that 'few supporters of incorporation realised that a move away from the benign control of LEAs would mean so much FEFC regulation and downward pressure'. The creation of a national funding methodology was a central pillar of the FEFC's goal to forge FE into a coherent and more homogenised sector on a par with schools and higher education. What had often been referred to as the 'Cinderella' of the education sector was now expected, virtually overnight, to emerge from the shadows. The months and years following incorporation proved to be both an exhilarating and painful period for FE colleges. Taubman (2000: 82–3) records that following incorporation, 'further education had proportionally more days lost to strike action than any other sector of the British economy'. In their attempts to provide the 'choice' for students and employers laid out in the 1991 White Paper, and to maximise the funding on offer from the FEFC and other bodies, some colleges hit the media headlines for falsifying student numbers and other fraudulent practices (see Shattock, 2000, for a discussion of how this arose). Although it is fair to say that the vast majority of colleges managed incorporation without recourse to bad practice, the imposition, by government, of a market-driven approach across the public services in the mid-1990s encouraged educational institutions to compete in ways that did little to enhance the quality of education and training, nor to ensure that learners gained access to the most appropriate provision.

Just prior to the incorporation of colleges, the government had created a network of 100 Training and Enterprise Councils (TECs) in 1990 in England, Wales and Scotland (where they were called Local Enterprise Companies). The TECs (and LECs in Scotland) were established as employer-led companies whose objectives were to fund, organise and manage work-based training programmes for young people and adults, but also to stimulate enterprise in their local areas. As many colleges acted as managing agents for government-supported training schemes and also as off-the-job training providers for employers and other managing agents, they found themselves in a paradoxical relationship with the TECs and LECs. On the one hand, they depended on the TECs and LECs for some of their funding, whereas on the other they competed with them for customers. Every young person who accepted a place on a youth training scheme was also a potential full-time FE student (see Unwin, 1999).

In 1997, the new Labour government announced that one of its first priorities would be to carry out a major review of post-compulsory education and training structures in England. This led to a White Paper in 1999, *Learning to Succeed*, in which the government spelt out its dissatisfaction with the current arrangements for the funding and planning of post-16 education and training:

> There is too much duplication, confusion and bureaucracy in the current system. Too little money actually reaches learners and employers, too much is tied up in bureaucracy. There is an absence of effective coordination or strategic planning. The system has insufficient focus on skill and employer needs at national, regional and local levels. The system lacks innovation and flexibility, and there needs to be more collaboration and cooperation to ensure higher standards and the right range of choices . . . the current system falls short.
>
> (DfEE, 1999: 21)

The White Paper proposed a massive restructuring of the landscape in England. The responsibility and leadership of post-compulsory education and training (now post-14) would become overwhelmingly centralised, and delivery of programmes and services handed to agencies contracted to the state (see Ainley and Vickerstaff, 1993, for an earlier discussion on the 'Contract State').

Using very similar language to the 1991 Conservative White Paper discussed above, *Learning to Succeed* based its reforms on the need for people to reach their potential by having access to as many learning opportunities as possible. Just as in a host of other policy documents dating back to 1976 when the then Prime Minister, James Callaghan, declared that the education system was failing the nation's economy, this new White Paper stressed the economic imperatives that should drive education and training provision. The FEFC would be abolished and replaced by the Learning and Skills Council (LSC) for England to oversee what is now called the 'learning and skills sector', covering FE colleges, private training providers, adult and community learning, prison education and the voluntary sector. The TECs (though not LECs, which still exist) would be abolished and replaced by 47 local LSCs. The LSC's first chairman, Bryan Sanderson, who had previously been Chief Executive of BP Chemicals, was quick to impress on colleges that his new agency wanted them to operate within a tough business model. He expressed this in a lecture to the Royal Society of Arts soon after taking office in April 2001:

Customers can be disaffected, there can be a high drop-out rate, there may be a mismatch between what the customer wants and what they get, there may be continuous rethinks on policy but none of those things seems ever to really matter because there's probably a belief that the money will come anyway. To be brutal, we in the Learning and Skills Council need to inject a little discomfort into this scenario – fear of the revenue streams suddenly drying up.

(Sanderson, 2001: 23)

The abolition of the FEFC, which had inspected colleges as well as funding them, meant that new inspection procedures were required. The White Paper proposed, therefore, that the Office for Standards in Education (Ofsted) would extend its remit from just inspecting schools to inspecting college-based provision for 16- to 19-year-olds, and that a new Adult Learning Inspectorate (ALI) would be created for work-based provision for 16- to 19-year-olds as well as all college-based post-19 provision. The ALI replaced the Training Standards Council (TSC) which had been inspecting government-funded work-based training in colleges and other training providers. Finally, a new approach to careers advice and guidance was to be introduced. The White Paper announced that the existing Careers Services and organisations responsible for supporting young people more generally (for example, the Youth Service and the Probation Service) would work together under the umbrella of local agencies to be called Connexions. This latter reform had been recommended in a parallel report from the government's Social Exclusion Unit (see SEU, 1999).

The evolving new landscape

In April 2001 the changes proposed in *Learning to Succeed* came into operation. In June 2001, the Labour government was re-elected and further reforms came into force. The DfEE was renamed the Department for Education and Skills (DfES). The significance of this was that responsibility for the Employment Service, which managed the New Deal programmes for unemployed people over the age of 18, passed to another new department, the Department for Work and Pensions. The Regional Development Agencies (RDAs), responsible for raising the capability of the English regions to compete both nationally and internationally, remained under the remit of the Department for Trade and Industry (DTI). The Cabinet Office established the Performance and Innovation Unit (PIU) responsible for researching and policymaking in the area of workforce development and skills. The Cabinet Office also appointed an e-Envoy with responsibility for pushing forward Labour's policy to promote e-commerce and the use of new technologies, while the DTI appointed a new Minister for e-Commerce and Competitiveness. The important point here is that colleges in England, with their wide-ranging interests, have increasingly had to relate to all the government departments that have influence over some aspect of post-14 education and training provision. As we can see, that influence is not confined to the government's education department.

Finlay *et al.* (2006), in their recent study of the LSC, echo Ainley and Vickerstaff's (1993) earlier concern about the role of government agencies. They argue that, paradoxically, 'the apparent devolution of power to intermediary agencies', such as the LSC, has been accompanied by 'a greater centralisation of power as the modernising state confines local public services to being the deliverers of central government priorities'. The pressure to deliver affects everyone involved and, ironically, the intermediary agencies have found themselves subject to constant criticism and interference. Hence, despite having established the LSC, its parent department, the DfES, has sought to restrict any sign of independence. Just as there are aftershocks following an earthquake, the FE landscape in England has continued to be affected by government-imposed changes since 2001 (see Coffield *et al.*, 2008, forthcoming). For example, the head office of the LSC has been severely 'downsized' in terms of staffing numbers and its 47 local LSCs reorganised into a regional structure.

Coffield *et al.* (2005: 651) have summarised the enormity of the LSC's remit:

> The LSC is expected, for example, to cope with all the contradictions and strains caused by responding simultaneously to the following potentially conflicting forces: it must be a centralizing council in order to create more consistency around the country and yet it must allow more local flexibility to cater sensitively for differing needs; the previous heavy emphasis on competition is now to be tempered with more collaboration and partnership working; it is charged by government with fostering both economic prosperity and social inclusion; it needs to balance market forces with the need for regulation; it is under pressure from government to 'deliver' both excellence and equity; it is responsible for planning coherent educational provision for all 14–19 year olds and yet must somehow accommodate the individual requirements of independent, specialist schools and city academies; it is being urged to become more transformational and less transactional, to move from managing contracts to managing a sector; it must reconcile as best it can the values of the labour market with those of the educational system; it is operating a business model while being criticized for not being publicly accountable. It is a tall order.

Devolved government in Scotland, Wales and Northern Ireland has also resulted in further structural change affecting FE colleges. In 2001, TECs and the FEFC were replaced in Wales by the National Council for Education and Training in Wales (known as ELWa, which stood for Education and Learning Wales). ELWa was responsible for all post-16 education and training and incorporated both the Further and Higher Education Funding Councils for Wales. In 2006, ELWa was incorporated into the Department for Education,

Lifelong Learning and Skills (DELLS) within the new National Assembly for Wales. DELLS also covers further and higher education funding. The Scottish Executive, which was established as the newly devolved government for Scotland in 1999, following the first elections to the Scottish Parliament, gave responsibility for FE to its Enterprise and Lifelong Learning Department (ELLD). This has now been renamed the Enterprise, Transport and Lifelong Learning Department (ETLLD) and the Scottish Further and Higher Funding Councils have been merged into the Scottish Funding Council (SFC). In Northern Ireland, the Department for Employment and Learning (Delni) now has responsibility for further and higher education, while the Department for Education looks after schools. The merger of the funding councils in Scotland, Wales and Northern Ireland marks a significant difference to the English context where FE and HE are still funded separately despite the increasing closeness of their relationship described earlier in this chapter.

Following the move to devolved government, Scotland, Wales and Northern Ireland have begun to develop their own distinctive strategies for FE, and for lifelong learning policies more generally (see Raffe, 2007). For example, Northern Ireland (through Careers Service NI), Wales (through Careers Wales) and Scotland (through Careers Scotland) have all introduced an all-age model for careers education, advice and guidance, whereas England continues to deliver different services to young people and adults. In 2003, the government published a Green Paper, *Every Child Matters*, which set the agenda for integrated services for children and young people, including the establishment of Children's Trusts managed by local authorities (HM Treasury, 2003). This was followed in 2005 by an associated Green Paper, *Youth Matters* (DfES, 2005c), which included proposals to return the existing Connexions service (which operated as an independent agency) back to local authority control (see also ECOTEC, 2006). As a result, from April 2008, the existing Connexions service in England will disappear as funding for advice and guidance is returned to local authorities. Guidance provision for adults in England remains the responsibility of the LSC and Ufi (University for Industry – now LearnDirect), but the current arrangements are also being reviewed.

Wales and Scotland also differ from England in that they are much closer to the implementation of post-16 frameworks for credit accumulation and transfer encompassing all qualifications up to and including postgraduate and professional (see Howieson *et al.*, 2002). Furthermore, a Welsh Baccalaureate qualification, which has been in a pilot phase since 2003, is to be rolled out on a national scale from September 2007 (for more details see Chapter 3). For the moment, however, the similarities in the practice of teaching and learning in FE colleges in these three countries and those in England still far outweigh their differences.

Finally, change has also affected the way colleges are inspected. In April 2007, ALI was abolished and its responsibilities absorbed into Ofsted, whose acronym remained the same, but now stands for Office for Standards in

Education, Children's Services and Skills. In Scotland, the HM Inspectorate of Education (HMIE) became an executive agency of the Scottish Parliament in 2001 as part of devolution. Arrangements in Wales and Northern Ireland have, however, remained the same with both retaining the titles of Her Majesty's Inspectorates, though in Wales this is referred to as Estyn.

FE funding

The way in which educational institutions are funded has a major impact on their character. Allocating funding is a highly charged political process and government and its agencies are constantly reviewing their formulae. As shown above, the establishment of the further education funding councils in 1992 was designed to rationalise a system of funding that was highly localised. In 1993, the Audit Commission and Ofsted produced a highly critical report on drop-out rates for 16- to 19-year-olds on full-time courses in English colleges. Titled Unfinished Business, the report highlighted, for the first time, the large numbers of students who were leaving courses before completion (30–40 per cent) and condemned this as a huge waste of public money as well as a waste of students' time and effort (Audit Commission/Ofsted, 1993). The new funding councils were, therefore, charged with designing a more efficient funding regime that would improve retention and achievement rates.

Under this new funding methodology, every student enrolled at a college would attract funding units, the precise number of which depended on the course they were following, the progress made and whether they achieved the intended outcome. This introduced the principle that funding should follow the learner. The FEFC also drew up a list of those qualifications it would fund (known as Schedule 2) and those it would not. Colleges could, of course, provide courses leading to non-Schedule 2 qualifications but it would have to charge students fees for these or get them funded from somewhere else. A further ploy was to repackage existing non-Schedule 2 provision to bring it within the Schedule 2 framework. As Unwin (1999) discovered, this relied on the creativity of college lecturers and curriculum managers. For example, one college lecturer explained that 'flower arranging is off, but floristry is on because we can get that accredited', whereas another described how popular classes in interior design techniques such as stenciling were reclassified under the heading 'Decorative Paint Techniques' (ibid.: 79). Colleges were awarded their funding allocation annually after submitting a strategic plan in which they set out a target number of units for that year (see Felstead and Unwin, 2001). To assist colleges with their funding plans, the funding councils introduced the Individualised Student Record (ISR).

Opinions differ as to the effectiveness of the FEFC funding methodology. McClure (2000) cites performance figures for 1993–8 in England, such as the rise in student numbers, improvements in quality of provision, and increased value for money for the public purse, to conclude that the new regime worked.

Table 1.1 LSC budget 2005/6

	£ (million)	%
Further education	5,160	49.5
School sixth forms	1,783	17.1
Apprenticeships and entry to employment	1,047	10.1
Other programmes	2,147	20.6
Administration	281	2.7

Source: LSC (2006) Annual Report, Coventry: Learning and Skills Council

On the other hand, Lucas (1999), while acknowledging some positive outcomes, argues that the FEFC model led colleges to put financial considerations above the quality of learning. Felstead and Unwin (2001) highlighted the way in which the need to amass funding units encouraged colleges to recruit full-time students to courses that were inexpensive to run. This, in turn, meant colleges were less concerned about local labour market needs.

The FEFC model is important in that it established the government's control over what was eligible for funding. The LSC abandoned the concept of Schedule 2 and Non-Schedule 2, but replaced this with its own approved list. While some of the elements in the list are subject to change, the LSC basically funds colleges to deliver courses leading to nationally recognised qualifications, plus some associated funding to support specific initiatives. It does this through what is called 'Plan Led Funding' whereby colleges submit annual estimates linked to a three-year development plan. The LSC began life with a budget of £5.5 billion. Five years later, in 2005/6, the LSC's budget had doubled to £10.2 billion allocated as shown in Table 1.1. The category, 'Other programmes', refers to a myriad of provision that is usually designed at local level to meet the needs of specific learners and to generate innovative practice.

The LSC's key objectives are to:

- raise participation and achievement by young people;
- increase adult demand for learning;
- raise skills levels for national competitiveness;
- improve the quality of education and training delivery;
- equalise opportunities through better access to learning;
- improve the effectiveness and efficiency of the sector.

Its overall mission is that, 'by 2010, young people and adults in England have knowledge and skills matching the best in the world and are part of a truly competitive workforce' (see: www.lsc.gov.uk). It is interesting to compare this dramatic pronouncement with the much more low-key statement used by the SFC on its website:

The Scottish Funding Council distributes about £1.5 billion in funding each year for teaching and learning, research and other activities in Scotland's colleges and universities. Established in 2005, the Council provides a strategic overview of tertiary education in Scotland to help secure a more coherent system of high-quality learning, teaching and research (see: www.sfc.ac.uk).

A further comparison could also be made with the following statement from the 2005 Foster Review which suggests a somewhat broader vision than that provided by the LSC:

> The need for an outstanding FE college network is not just about national prosperity. It is also about how far countless individuals in this country value themselves, enjoy being who they are and have fulfilling and enjoyable lives.
>
> (DfES 2005a: 11)

In 2005, the average GFE college received a grant of £14 million from the LSC, though some received closer to £35 million, while others received as little as £1 million. This diversity reflects the different size of student intake, with the largest GFE having 45,000 students, while the average has 12,000. The average allocation to a sixth-form college was £6 million, and the sixth-form college intake ranges from a maximum of 7,000 students to a minimum of 570 students. The majority of students (71 per cent) in GFE colleges are adults studying part time, while the majority of students (56 per cent) in sixth-form colleges are 16- to 18-year-olds studying full time. We could ask: Does size matter? Perry (2005), in a paper commissioned by the Foster Review, suggests that, as far as England is concerned, it does and cites the fact that the larger colleges have a better inspection record. He notes, however, that they face the same problems as smaller colleges when it comes to maximising their resources. He argues that a move towards what he calls a 'national brand' might be a creative way forward. This might involve organising colleges in a federated system with one Chancellor in a similar way to some of the community colleges in the United States or some universities, such as London, in the UK. Colleges could then pool the costs of human resource management, IT infrastructure, publicity, and, crucially, the development of teaching resources and curriculum design.

In 2004/5, colleges in England derived some 82 per cent of their income from the LSC, but, according to Association of Colleges (AoC) estimates, this figure has risen to enable colleges to respond to the government's Skills for Life strategy (which aims to improve the basic literacy, numeracy, ICT and language skills of adults in England) and the increasing demands for expanded provision for 14- to 19-year-olds. Colleges receive the rest of their income from a range of activities including charging fees to some adult learners and some employers, from the Higher Education Funding Council (England) (HEFCE) for higher education students, and from the European Social Fund for projects related to deprivation or to increase diversity. The acute dilemma for college managers is how to balance the time they and their colleagues need to spend meeting government demands and targets with the need to chase and develop other income streams. Too often, the national and the local are in conflict. In their report for the Foster Review, King *et al.* (2005: 9) quoted from an interview with a college manager:

> The targets and priorities set by the government, such as increasing the number of learners acquiring basic skills, level 1 and 2 qualifications, are not necessarily the main priorities for our college or where there is strongest demand. Our college, for example, has more demand for higher level qualifications, level 3 and foundation degrees.

Ironically, although government and the LSC constantly insist that colleges should be more responsive to employer demand, they are slow to acknowledge that employers might not want the qualifications in the nationally approved list. As King *et al.* (2005) warn, this might mean that employers will choose to give their business to private training providers who can meet their needs more quickly, and often at a cheaper price.

A long-standing complaint of colleges is that despite serving a larger proportion of 16- to 18-year-olds than schools, they actually receive less money per student. The gap in funding between schools and sixth-form colleges has been almost eliminated, but for GFE colleges, the gap still stands at 5 per cent. The AoC has argued that the funding gap means that 'government spends more money on those young people who need it least', as many students in GFE colleges tend to come from more disadvantaged backgrounds than their peers in school sixth forms or indeed sixth-form colleges.

Colleges also face an equally controversial issue – the funding of adult learners. The National Institute for Adult Continuing Education (NIACE) has drawn attention to Clauses 2 and 3 in the Learning and Skills Act 2000 which specify how the LSC is to differentiate between its funding for 16- to 18-year-olds and those aged 19 and over. (NIACE, 2005) For 16- to 18-year-olds, the LSC must 'secure the provision of **proper** facilities' for education, training and organised leisure time activity, but for adults, the word 'proper' is replaced by the word 'reasonable'. NIACE argue that this means that the LSC must meet the needs of 16- to 18-year-olds first and then spend what is left on adults. Given the current emphasis on the government's 14–19 agenda, adult learners in colleges will find they are required to pay higher fees and may also find that provision for them has been reduced. The AoC (2007) has estimated that 570,000 places for adult learners were lost in 2005/6 with further losses predicted.

As a result of the Foster Review, and in the light of the Leitch Review of Skills published in 2006, further changes to the LSC funding model have been proposed. The race is on to raise the UK's game in terms of its competitiveness by radically increasing the number of people qualified to at least Level 2 (see Wolf, Jenkins and Vignoles, 2006; Wolf, 2002 for critiques of this view). In a White Paper linked to the Further Education and Training Bill currently being debated in parliament, the DfES has stated that:

> Funding will be targeted on priority areas and follow the needs of learners and employers – with young people's choices funded in full and increasing amounts of funding for adult learning flowing through demand-led mechanisms – Learner Accounts and Train to Gain.
>
> (DfES 2006b: 65)

The discourse of this statement is highly illuminative as it captures the current government obsession with 'choice', 'demand', and 'targets' as being the drivers that will 'modernise' the public services. The reference to Learner Accounts and Train to Gain is also significant as these are two initiatives, which, if they continue as planned, are likely to have a major impact on colleges in the coming years. Both initiatives dramatically affect the way in which funding for adults flows through to colleges. The concept of Learner Accounts recreates the Individual Learning Account (ILA) initiative launched in September 2000 and closed in October 2001 when the government admitted that it had led to fraudulent practice by a number of training providers who were claiming money for non-existent learners and/or for delivering non-existent courses. The DfES claims that it has learnt lessons from the ILA fiasco and will put much more robust quality assurance measures in place for the new Learner Accounts.

The concept of Learner Accounts and Train to Gain are closely related. In 2002, the government set up a series of regional Employer Training Pilots, funded through local LSCs and the Business Link network, to encourage employees without a Level 2 qualification to seek training (see Hillage et al., 2006, for a critical evaluation). In 2006, the initiative was renamed Train to Gain, and became available on a national basis. Under Train to Gain, money is available to fund individuals so they can obtain their first Level 2 qualification (either NVQ or GCSE equivalents) and to compensate employers (with less than 50 employees) while their employees engage in training, although larger employers can also take part. A skills broker is also funded by the LSC to help the employer and employee decide on their training needs and arrange suitable training. A Learner Account is set up for all individuals who achieve a first full Level 2, on enrolling for a Level 3 course, or on being recommended for a full Level 3 course by an Information Advice and Guidance adviser or Trade Union Learning Representative. On becoming an account holder, the learner receives a membership card and an account number and is entitled to a discount on the cost of a Level 3 course at any LSC sponsored provider, with the discount set to reflect the national fee rate set by the LSC for that year

(37.5 per cent fees and 62.5 per cent public funding subsidy in 2007–8). Shortly after enrolment on a course, the learner receives their first account statement setting out their own financial contribution, the state's financial contribution, and other financial contributions, for example, from their employer.

In his foreword to the 2006 FE White Paper, the then Prime Minister, Tony Blair, wrote:

> We must set a new ambition to tackle once and for all those skills weaknesses. The colleges and training providers that make up the Further Education sector are central to achieving that ambition. There is much to be proud of in our Further Education system, with some excellent colleges. But at present, Further Education is not achieving its full potential as the powerhouse of a high skills economy. This White Paper sets out the reforms needed to realise that potential. They build on the public sector reform principles we have applied in other services, including more choice for customers, tailoring services to meet individuals' needs, encouraging new, innovative providers to enter the market, and robust action to tackle poor quality combined with more autonomy for the excellent. Our reforms will renew the mission of the Further Education system, and its central role in equipping young people and adults with the skills for productive, sustainable employment in a modern economy.
>
> (DfES 2006b: foreword)

Older members of staff in colleges may, at this point, be feeling a distinct sense of déjà vu, particularly if they can remember the 'responsive college' movement of the 1980s. The language here, however, is much harder and the statement carries the added threat of bringing in 'new, innovative providers' to compete with colleges.

Responsiveness, collaboration and the curriculum

Anyone who has worked in or carried out research on FE over the years will have witnessed the dynamism that characterises much of the sector. Colleges are constantly changing and adapting to new demands and circumstances. A major part of being responsive involves collaboration with a whole host of organisations and communities, some of whom, particularly local and regional government agencies are also in a continued state of flux. The following statement from the website of South Birmingham College reflects this dynamic reality:

> South Birmingham College students come from every walk of life and from all age groups. With over 1,000 courses available to choose from, South Birmingham College will give a fresh start for those looking for a

career change, career advancement or for the simple pleasure of learning. You can study full-time or part-time, during the day, in the evenings or at weekends. Qualifications include – BTEC, GNVQ, NVQ, C&G, RSA, HNC and HND, Access to Higher Education, Foundation Degrees and the essential GCSEs. At Digbeth in the heart of the city, we have unrivalled provision and facilities in a wide range of courses including Media, Multimedia, Business and Professional Studies, ICT and Trade Union Studies. In Balsall Heath we have totally refurbished our premises to allow for a superb learning environment within a Women's Academy. The new Centre for the Built Environment in Bordesley Green offers truly outstanding facilities for construction trades. (see: www.southbirmc.ac.uk)

South Birmingham College hosts a Centre of Vocational Excellence (CoVE) in Childcare Training. The CoVE initiative combines recognition of the considerable expertise and experience within colleges, with the age-old desire on the part of policymakers to make them more responsive to employer need. In July 2001, the then Secretary of State for Education and Skills, Estelle Morris, announced that 16 colleges in England could establish CoVEs in one or more specific specialisms as part of the first phase of a £100-million strategy devised by the previous Secretary of State, David Blunkett, for all colleges to have at least one CoVE by 2004/5. By January 2006, 400 CoVEs had been established, set up with a £500,000 grant from the DfES. They include, for example: Accrington and Rossendale College – Construction Crafts, Canterbury College – Travel and Tourism; Cornwall College – ICT Networking Skills; Loughborough College – Sports Science, Exercise and Fitness; and South Birmingham College – Childcare Training. As we saw earlier, these CoVEs will now have to adjust to the arrival of the National Skills Academies.

In her research on CoVEs, Wahlberg *et al.* (2007: 2) found that the concept encompassed a range of different interpretations of what these centres amounted to:

- a *badge*, giving recognition for existing excellence;
- *specific provision*, identified as a particular building, group of staff or bundle of courses;
- a delivery or teaching *mission* reflecting a return to FE's roots with a focus on what is being studied and its vocational relevance;
- a *managerial ethos* defined as reactive planning to demand-led provision (employer demand not student demand);
- a purpose-built *partnership* between specified colleges and private training providers;
- a development *grant* of around £500,000;
- the delivery of *bespoke, Level 3 training courses* to employers.

The CoVE concept recognises that, amid the great diversity of provision within one institution, there will be one or more core subject areas for which it has particular expertise. The initiative is also indicative of the government's decision to retain a sectoral approach to the development and management of vocational education and training that had been developing since the 1960s. In 2002, the Sector Skills Development Agency (SSDA) was launched to lead a 'Skills for Business Network' of Sector Skills Councils (SSCs) to cover the whole of the UK. The 25 SSCs replaced the existing National Training Organisations (NTOs) and were given increased funding by government to deliver an ambitious remit. This would involve identifying the skill needs of their sectors, working with education and training providers to devise new qualifications, collaborating with local and regional agencies, championing the work of their sectors, and raising the levels of skills among the population. Post-school education and training providers are covered by their own SSC, Lifelong Learning UK (LLUK), which replaced the Further Education National Training Organisation (FENTO) in 2005. As a result of the 2006 Leitch Review of Skills, the SSCs have been given even stronger powers and responsibility, and the SSDA is to be replaced in 2008 with a more powerful Commission for Employment and Skills. For colleges in England, the most significant shift has been the decision to place SSCs in the lead role with regard to the design of the new diplomas for 14- to 19-year-olds and the recommendation that only those vocational qualifications approved by SSCs should be eligible for government funding.

The SSCs also represent a now dominant theme in the current government's approach to post-14 education and training: that it should be 'employer-led' (for critiques, see Unwin, 2004; Keep, 2005; Ryan *et al.*, 2007). This phrase permeates government documents and ministerial speeches. Given the origins of many colleges, as described earlier in this chapter, it could be argued that such an approach poses no problem for the FE sector. The reality, however, is that many employers do not want to 'lead' the design of qualifications and many struggle to define their training needs. Some employers take a very short-term approach to training and would like to abandon qualifications, while others regard training as equating to a few hours of induction on the job. At the other end of the spectrum are employers with long and proud histories of close cooperation with education through their professional bodies or local arrangements.

College staff

From the above description of the nature and scope of FE, it is clear that staff in colleges are faced with many competing demands on their time and energies. Those who manage the system are responsible for multimillion-pound businesses. They are accountable to different funding bodies, to local and national employers and to the external inspectorates for the quality of education and training provision. These pressures may appear contradictory at times: for example, the need to provide excellence in vocational education and training at the same time as driving down costs and increasing student numbers. As one FE lecturer we spoke to put it: 'It is impossible to put a financial value on people's learning needs and achievements.'

Employment patterns within the sector have changed in recent years with an increase in part-time staff, more flexible contracts, and the introduction of non-traditional teaching hours, for example at weekends. New contracts issued by colleges outline very different terms and conditions of service from what one might expect for a teacher in a primary or secondary school. Edwards has suggested that 'the trends towards multi-skilling and flexibility elsewhere in the economy are also to be found in institutions of post-compulsory education and training' (Edwards, 1993: 48). Hill (2000) reminds us, however, that the 'flexible firm' model has characterised the FE sector for many years due to the need for colleges to supplement their core staff with part-timers as they respond to the changing student market and to government initiatives. The following extract from the employment contract of a main grade lecturer in one of the largest FE colleges in England illustrates the extraordinary range of duties she will be expected to undertake:

> Formal schedule teaching, tutorials, student assessment, management of learning programmes and curriculum development, student admissions, educational guidance, counselling, preparation of learning materials and student assignments, marking student work, marking examinations, management and supervision of student visit programmes, research and other forms of scholarly activity, marketing activities, consultancy, leadership, supervisory, administration and personal professional development.

The reference to 'research and other forms of scholarly activity' signals an interesting extension to the workload of FE teachers, one that is discussed in detail in Chapter 7.

Although many staff in colleges belong to trade unions, national terms and conditions no longer exist. This means that colleges differ as to how many teaching hours they expect lecturers and support staff to deliver, with an estimated variation of between 720 to 1000 hours (Flint, 2005). Colleges in Wales and Scotland appear to be more uniform than those in England. Overall, pay rates for lecturers in GFE colleges fall below those for teachers in schools and sixth-form colleges.

Staff are being required to take on new roles so that in addition to a teaching and tutorial role they may have significant administrative duties (see Avis et al., 2001). Some FE lecturers may also have responsibility for promoting and marketing their courses. They may be expected to counsel students. Many staff have budgets as well as their course teams to manage. The introduction of distance, open and e-learning systems has required some staff to take on the role of authors as well as developing new techniques for working with flexible pedagogies.

Edwards refers to the blurring of roles between 'lecturers and tutors, administrators and technical staff' (Edwards, 1993: 48). There are hybrid support tutors who, rather than acting as traditional teachers, provide self-study support to students and are responsible for recording prior learning or achievement. A new or established teacher in the FE sector may be working on a number of part-time contracts in different institutions. The future workforce could comprise freelance professionals moving between colleges in response to demand for their expertise. This unpredictability in employment reflects the way in which the organisation of work in the wider society is being restructured, but the FE sector has been particularly affected by uncertainty since the mid-1990s. Avis (1999: 251), building on the work of a number of commentators (for example: Elliott, 1996; Hodkinson, 1997; Randle and Brady, 1997; and Ainley and Bailey, 1997) on the increasing problems faced by FE staff as a result of marketisation and managerialism, highlights the following areas for concern:

• loss of control;
• intensification of labour;
• increase in administration;
• perceived marginalisation of teaching;
• stress on measurable performance indicators.

Gleeson and Shain (1999: 558), however, argue that 'the influence of markets and managerialism is as much a contested as a controlling one', and that, 'While there is evidence of deprofessionalisation and casualisation in FE . . . here also exists competing forms of resistance and response from lecturers and senior managers which challenge the hegemony of managerialism at college level.' As in any other profession, FE teachers are subject to the controlling tendencies of managers and to the restrictions placed on their actions by external agencies. The extent to which FE teachers are able to exert their professional identities will differ from college to college and will also be influenced by the status of their subject area, their level of confidence in their ability, and the degree of support they receive from colleagues and managers. It is worth remembering that FE teachers still spend much of their time with students and, as Bloomer (1997) argues, 'it is an individual matter as to how far teachers decide to exert agency and thus take control of their work situation'.

In their study of staff satisfaction in 80 colleges in England, Davies and Owen (2001: 8) found that staff were much more likely to feel valued within a college that had 'an embedded culture of continuous improvement – rather than one of blame – which encouraged bottom-up initiatives within a clearly understood framework'. Such colleges might be said to have embraced the concept of the 'learning organisation', which has been much promoted since its emergence in the late 1980s (see Jones and Hendry, 1994). Within such organisations, work is organised along flatter as opposed to hierarchical lines in order to devolve responsibility and encourage greater sharing of knowledge and skills. Employees, at all levels, are encouraged to learn and develop continually. A key test of whether a workplace can be said to have the characteristics of a learning organisation is the way in which it treats newcomers. Lave and Wenger (1991) conceptualise workplaces as 'communities of practice' in which skills and knowledge are passed on from one generation to the next, thus ensuring that the community continues to thrive. Trainees or apprentices begin as 'legitimate peripheral participants' who, under the guidance of more experienced workers, gradually progress to become full participants in the community. The use of the term 'legitimate' is significant because it recognises the importance of a trainee's peripheral status. In other words, trainees need time to develop their skills and should not be expected to function as productive workers until they are ready.

The staff in FE colleges come from a diverse set of backgrounds. Some will have academic qualifications and others with professional qualifications will have perhaps become teachers after a substantial career in business or industry. There will be those who have qualified through a craft or technician route, who have spent a considerable time on the shop floor or training apprentices. In addition there is a range of support staff: kitchen assistants, laboratory technicians, audio-visual technicians and learning support. There will also be clerical and administrative staff and those responsible for student services. Robson (1998: 588) argues that 'the very diversity of entry routes into FE teaching . . . creates, in sociological terms, a weak professional boundary' and, thus, weakens the profession's overall standing (see also Robson et al., 2006; Wahlberg and Gleeson, 2003; Avis and Bathmaker, 2006). She adds that most FE teachers, who deliver technical and vocational subjects, retain strong allegiances to their first occupational identity (as formed in industry or commerce). Moving into a college can, therefore, be a stressful experience if those preformed occupational identities are threatened or disregarded.

Noel has shown that FE colleges in England continue to be segregated workplaces in terms of gender and ethnicity (for a report on Scottish colleges, see Riddell et al., 2005; Ducklin and Ożga, 2007):

A horizontal division into male and female areas of learning and teaching is combined with a vertical division in which men hold the most senior posts. Women, and black staff, are over-represented in part-time, hourly-paid posts. Black staff are concentrated in certain curriculum areas – Basic Skills, English for Speakers of Other Languages (ESOL) and, although less frequently, in Maths and Science. They too are underrepresented in management.

(Noel, 2006: 154)

The following advertisement appeared on the website of West Herts College in the South of England. It shows how one colleges has tried to encourage people from a range of backgrounds to apply for jobs:

It's not just our students who come from all walks of life

At West Herts College, were actively ma king wider access to education a reality. Serving more than 10,000 students across four campuses, we help people from all walks of life to realise their full potential through a broad and evolving range of academic and vocational courses. And it's precisely because our students are such a diverse mix of people that we strive to ensure that our workforce is drawn from all sections of the community. We welcome the different backgrounds, skills and experiences of our people, and appreciate the individual contributions they make to college life. What can you offer? Following a recent Ofsted report that recognised our achievements and highlighted our 'outstanding capacity' to continue improving, this is a great time to join us.

The job titles below are taken from newspaper advertisements for college vacancies. We have deliberately chosen them, rather than the standard advertisements for lecturers in specific subjects, as they illustrate the complexity of teaching and learning in colleges:

- Widening Participation and Basic Skills Manager
- Team Leader – Employers and Marketing
- Head of Enterprise Services
- Lecturers for Additional Learning Support
- Curriculum Co-ordinator for Essential Skills
- E-learning Manager
- Manager, Open Learning Centre
- Chief Executive
- Lecturer – Employability Programmes.

The growth in staff with responsibility for 'learning support' reflects a number of issues: the increasing emphasis in colleges on flexible and student-centred learning; the need to improve retention and attainment levels; and the recognition that lecturers need help in the classroom to support students with very mixed abilities. Colleges also have to make provision for students with disabilities and learning difficulties. In their investigation of the nature and scale of learning support in colleges in England, Robson *et al.* (2006) adopted the following definition for the role of the learning support worker (LSW):

> The definition of a learning support worker that was adopted for this investigation is any member of staff employed in an educational context who is not on a teaching or training contract but who provides support to learners through direct and regular contact with them. We do not include staff that hold other designated roles (such as librarians, technicians, careers advisers or sign language interpreters).

Robson *et al.* (2006) found that in addition to providing support to students with disabilities or learning difficulties, LSWs were supporting: learners to improve their basic skills; those on English for Speakers of Other Languages (ESOL) courses; learners with histories of non-attendance at school; learners whose behaviour is deemed to challenge the system; and learners who have particular blocks in learning. Colleges differ in the way they utilise LSWs. Robson *et al.* (2006) found that some colleges employed no LSWs, while others employed them in significant numbers. In terms of profile, they found that 80 per cent of LSWs were women and of the total number of LSWs working in colleges in 2003/4, 20 per cent were employed on full-time contracts. Unlike classroom assistants in schools, who tend to have comparable terms and conditions across the country, the pay rates of LSWs range from just above the minimum wage to approaching a basic lecturer's salary. The range of duties undertaken by LSWs also varied from college to college. LSWs are clearly providing a very valuable service, but their presence in colleges raises challenging questions about the boundaries between their interaction with students and that of the lecturers.

Getting qualified

Since September 2001, all new teachers employed to teach in an FE college in the UK have had to possess a recognised teaching qualification based on national occupational standards controlled by LLUK. The qualifications are delivered in a variety of ways through partnerships between colleges and universities. In September 2007, LLUK introduced a new compulsory introductory qualification for all new entrants teaching publicly funded programmes in the post-school sector to give them a 'threshold status' to teach. Staff for whom teaching will be their main role will then be required to progress to a full teaching qualification, which grants the status of 'Qualified Teacher, Learning and Skills' (QTLS). The qualifications are credit-based and form part of the evolving national credit and qualifications frameworks covering the whole of the UK. All teachers and trainers will also be required to complete 30 hours of continuing professional development (CPD) every year.

The introduction of a compulsory teacher training certificate for FE teachers based on competence-based occupational standards has been highly contested by many people including FE teachers themselves and academics researching the sector (for a review of the history, see Lucas, 2004; Noel, 2006). The arguments about the suitability of the approach connect to much broader debates about the appropriateness of the competence- and standards-based model introduced in the UK in the 1980s (see Raggatt and Williams, 1999, for a history). Lucas (2004: 15), while welcoming the introduction of compulsory qualifications for FE teachers and a more coherent approach to teacher training, has questioned whether the standards-based model is adequate for a profession that operates across distinctly different learning contexts servicing the needs of a very heterogeneous population of learners.

LLUK (2007: introduction) claim that their occupational standards are adequate to capture this diversity of professional practice:

> Not all standards will necessarily relate to all teaching roles. Rather they supply the basis for the development of contextualized role specifications and units of assessment, which provide benchmarks for performances in practice of the variety of roles performed by teachers, trainers, tutors and lecturers within the lifelong learning sector.

The standards are based around two types of role: teacher; and teacher-related. The latter role covers LSWs and also people who act as assessors for competence-based qualifications, but do not teach. The standards are organised into six overarching domains:

Domain A	Professional values and practice
Domain B	Learning and Teaching
Domain C	Specialist learning and teaching
Domain D	Planning for learning
Domain E	Assessment for learning
Domain F	Access and progression

These domains are presented in more detail in Chapter 4.

Mandatory standards-based qualifications are also being introduced for college principals from 2008 (LLUK, 2006).

The UK is very different from many other European countries in the way it approaches vocational teacher training, in that people wanting to teach vocational specialisms have to attend the same generic training courses as teachers of general education. The reasoning is that whether one is teaching bricklaying or French, the principles are the same. In some other countries, notably Germany and Finland, the concept of vocational pedagogy is taken much more seriously. The expansion of dedicated vocational pathways, CoVEs and the

National Skills Academies in the UK is likely to bring this issue much more to the fore in future years.

Inspection and governance

As we have seen, the FE sector has undergone a period of rapid and continuous change in recent years. Colleges face increasing pressures in terms of funding, accommodation and resources in a climate of increased student enrolments and output-related performance indicators. The extension of vocational education to 14-year-olds and the increasing presence of this age group in colleges has meant that the inspection process has also expanded. In Scotland, colleges are inspected by Her Majesty's Inspectorate of Education (HMI) on behalf of the SFEFC. In Wales, HMI (known there as Estyn) inspects colleges on behalf of Elwa, and in Northern Ireland, HMI inspects colleges on behalf of the Department of Education. From April 2007 in England, the whole of colleges' provision has been inspected by Ofsted through a system of annual assessment visits and full inspections every four years. A new four-year cycle of college inspections began in September 2005. Annual assessment visits review college performance using students' achievements and other data and help determine the basis and timing of the next inspection. Those colleges graded inadequate are currently subject to a full reinspection within two years of this judgement being reached. Those colleges averaging good or better grades in the previous inspection are subject to a 'light touch' inspection. Ofsted inspects colleges against the following themes: effectiveness of provision; capacity to improve; achievement and strategy; quality of provision; leadership and management. It uses the following grading scheme:

Grade 1　　Outstanding
Grade 2　　Good
Grade 3　　Satisfactory
Grade 4　　Inadequate

Colleges have to address the following questions:

1　How effective and efficient are provision and related services in meeting the full range of learners' needs and why?
2　What steps need to be taken to improve provision further?
3　How well do learners achieve?
4　How effective are teaching, training and learning?
5　How well do the programmes and courses meet the needs and interests of learners?
6　How well are learners guided and supported?
7　How effective are leadership and management in raising achievement and supporting all learners?

As well as publishing information on completion rates for all courses, colleges are required to publish the actual destinations of all their students who achieved qualifications in the previous teaching year. Colleges are encouraged to use these destination data to spot patterns and trends and as a basis for evaluating student experience.

In 1992, when the Conservative government took colleges out of LEA control and made them corporate bodies, it meant that 'Governing bodies and college principals were required to change their modus operandi almost overnight' as they switched from a 'service philosophy' to 'one akin to entrepreneurialism' (Shattock, 2000: 89). Colleges were now required to recruit the majority of members of their governing bodies from the private sector, as these people were expected 'to impose a proactive market orientation on colleges that had previously been reactive and bureaucratic' (ibid.: 91). This policy has since been questioned following a series of financial and mis-anagement scandals which were widely reported in the national media from the mid-1990s onward. In 1999, the Labour government changed the regulations on college governance to create governing bodies which had a better balance of representation from business and the community. Gleeson and Shain (1999: 553), however, note that college governing bodies in FE 'remain largely self-selecting organisations accountable only to the Secretary of State, and not to the communities they serve'. They argue that it is impossible to separate the problems of FE governance from wider debates about democracy, inclusive management styles, deregulation and, crucially, the role of FE itself. For FE teachers, however, the nature and style of their college's governing body will affect their professional life, and having some knowledge and understanding of the way in which their college is governed could be helpful.

Conclusion

This chapter has stressed that FE colleges are large, complex and heterogeneous organisations. They are busy, dynamic places of learning with shifting populations composed of students of all ages, and they are constantly called upon to respond to the demands and ideas of government. As we write, further change is in the air in England. Just after we were handing over the manu-script of this book to the publishers, Gordon Brown took over from Tony Blair as Prime Minister of Great Britain and Northern Ireland. On his second day (28 June 2007), the new Prime Minister announced that the DfES was to be abolished and two new departments created to cover education: (a) the Department for Innovation, Universities and Skills (DIUS); and (b) the Department for Children, Schools and Families (DCSF). The big question for all who work in colleges, is 'Where does FE sit in this new configuration?' Earliest indications are that the work of colleges will be divided between the new departments, with 14–19 activity coming under the DCSF and post-19, including the implementation of the Leitch Review of Skills, under DIUS. n addition, it is being suggested that the funding of all 14–19 education will revert to local education authorities and, hence, there will be a return to some of the pre-1992 funding arrangements described earlier in this chapter. Apprenticeship programmes for 16- to 25-year-olds will come under DIUS, but Young Apprenticeships (for 14- to 16-year-olds) will stay with the DCSF. These changes mean that the role of the LSC is in doubt. A further departmental change could also have some impact on colleges as the DTI was also abolished and replaced by the Department for Business, Enterprise and Regulatory Reform (BERR). The innovation and skills remit of the DTI will be absorbed by the new DIUS.

It is too early to speculate on the extent to which these changes will affect the day-to-day work of FE teachers, but, as we will try to show throughout this book, the process of teaching and learning in colleges has weathered many bureaucratic storms over the past hundred or more years. In the following chapters, we examine the implications of the complexities that shape the FE landscape for teaching and learning, and for teachers' attempts to develop their own strategies and ideas for working with learners.

Chapter 2

The student body
Who will I teach?

Diverse student body

One of the distinguishing features of the FE sector has always been the diversity of its student population. Since FE is essentially 'education for all', this is reflected in its student body in terms of age, gender, ability, attainment levels, economic, social class and cultural background and differing learning needs. Teaching in FE presents a set of challenges that are quite different from those presented in primary or secondary education.

The following vignettes illustrate the way in which FE colleges in England, Scotland and Wales serve a wide range of student communities:

College 1 – City College Manchester

A large GFE college operating across 4 sites. It has 20,495 part-time time students, 4,764 full-time students and 850 international students from 50 different countries. The college hosts CoVEs in logistics, media, retail, and health services. It is one of the biggest providers in England of teaching and learning in prisons and detention centres, covering 40 establishments throughout the country. The expansion of Manchester Airport will lead to an estimated 20,000 new jobs over the coming ten years. In response, the college has established the Airport Academy to provide courses and information and guidance for local people who want to gain employment in the industry.

College 2 – Orkney College

One of Scotland's smallest colleges with a main campus in Kirkwall and an annexe in Stromness for maritime studies. The majority (87 per cent) of the 1,923 students study on a part-time basis. Some 33 per cent of students are on higher education courses. Although the majority (80 per cent) of the population lives on the Orkney mainland, the rest of the population is scattered across the outlying islands. For them the college provides courses through a network of outreach centres, mainly located in schools.

College 3 – Coleg Morgannwg

A very large GFE college with premises in five towns in South Wales: Aberdare, Glyntaf, Pntypridd, Rhondda and Nantgarw. It also has three further sites for the provision of adult and community learning. The college has just over 29,000 students. The Rhondda campus is in an area with high levels of social and economic deprivation and receives Objective One ESF funding from the European Union. The college is heavily involved in the economic regeneration of this part of Wales.

Many teachers in FE will be expected to teach across a wide range of programmes that could include basic skills programmes at one end of the spectrum and undergraduate or even postgraduate work at the other. Similarly, the students may range from age 14 to 65 and beyond. At the time of writing, one London college has some 90-year-olds among its student population as well as some 14-year-old pupils from local schools. Some of the 14- to 16-year-olds in colleges arrive there from Pupil Referral Units (PRUs). They may include teenage mothers, pupils excluded from schools for behavioural problems, children who are 'school phobic', and pupils who are awaiting the results of special needs assessments (Culham, 2003; Attwood *et al.*, 2004). These different age ranges are not confined to particular programmes of study. An A level group, for example, will not necessarily include only those of 16- to 18-year-olds as would be the case within a school sixth form.

Students in FE represent an enormous range of different circumstances and any one class or group of students will be heterogeneous in nature. In this sense, the work is real mixed-ability teaching. It is not only the ability of the students which differs, however, but also their motivation, prior experience, expectations and the way in which they are funded. They may also have very different social class and cultural backgrounds and their domestic circumstances may be widely different. Some of the students may be returning to learning after a long break, others may be continuing their education but in a different environment. Others will be attempting to combine full-time employment with part-time study or juggling the competing demands of family commitments and study requirements. Some students may have been 'sent' by their employers or by the State to undertake training. Some students may have physical disabilities; others may have emotional and behavioural difficulties. The teacher in FE has to be sensitive to this diversity in the planning, preparation and delivery of programmes.

The patterns of attendance will vary between full-time and part-time, day or evening, employment release, block release or attendance at individually designed short courses. An increasing number of students are registering as distance learners or open learners. Some students may be attending a college solely to have prior learning accredited for the purpose of acquiring an S/NVQ. Others may never attend the college but will be taught by college staff at their place of employment. For the student who attends college on a day-release basis from work, or the 14-year-old who attends both school and college, there may be difficulties in adjusting to the different environments and different personnel.

The attempts to develop more flexible provision for 14- to 16-year-olds throughout the UK is partly a belated response to the so-called 'status zero' problem. The 'status zero' group of young people, as identified by Istance and Williamson (1996), are those who disappear each year from official statistics at both local and national level (see also Pearce and Hillman, 1998). They have variously been labelled: 'disaffected'; 'non-participants'; 'hard to reach'; 'socially excluded'; 'at risk'; and 'not settled'. The current term used by policymakers is 'NEET' which stands for Not in Education, Employment or Training. In September 1999, Education Maintenance Allowances (EMAs) (up to £40 per week) were introduced in 15 English LEAs to encourage disadvantaged young people aged 16–19 to stay in full-time education and have since been extended to Wales, Scotland and Northern Ireland. Other initiatives at local level do not, however, seem to have had much effect on the 'not settled' who can amount to as much as 10 per cent of the 16–19 cohort in some areas of the country. The *Time off for Study* legislation, introduced in 1998 to give 16- to 18-year-olds in jobs without training the entitlement to a day off per week for part-time study, has been less than successful. This is not surprising for it puts the onus on the young person rather than the employer.

There are also now more opportunities to enter HE via the FE route through the introduction of access programmes, foundation degrees and 'two plus two' degrees. This has introduced a cohort of undergraduates to some FE colleges' student population. On the other hand, there are now more programmes aimed at encouraging people of all ages to improve their basic literacy, numeracy and ICT skills funded under the multi-million pound *Skills for Life* initiative launched in England in March 2001.

The need for FE colleges to market their services more actively both at home and abroad has led to an increasing number of overseas students pursuing courses in British colleges. Some colleges have established overseas offices, or agents, to market their courses and to attract overseas students; others send staff abroad to teach on college programmes. Many colleges are involved in vocational education and training research and development programmes sponsored by the European Commission or by the British Council. These may involve student or staff exchanges and study tours. Overseas students may be studying courses to improve their English language competence; others will be pursuing vocational qualifications.

Colleges now have to cope with a much wider range of student abilities, including those students with learning difficulties. The 1996 report of the Tomlinson Committee's review of FE's provision for students with learning difficulties and disabilities, *Inclusive Learning*, highlighted the need for the sector to make further improvements and to embrace the concept of inclusive learning (Tomlinson, 1996). As Dee (1999: 141) explains, Tomlinson sought to reject the stereotyping of people with learning difficulties and/or physical disabilities. The Beattie Committee in Scotland was established to: 'review the range of needs among young people who require additional support to participate in post school education, training and employment; the assessment of need; and the quality and effectiveness of provision in improving skills and employability'.

In 1998, the FEFC allocated £2 million to support the inclusive learning quality initiative (FEFC, 1999). This was complemented by the provision made to implement the recommendations of the Kennedy Report (Kennedy, 1997), *Learning Works*, which highlighted the need for colleges to widen participation to include underrepresented groups in their communities. In his 2000/1 report, the FEFC's Chief Inspector noted that the development of an inclusive approach to learning was 'increasingly significant within the sector' but that staff were still not being given 'the training or time they need to put college intentions into practice' (FEFC, 2001: 57). Dee (1999: 142) argues that 'inclusion is a process and not an absolute state' and that colleges need to work towards inclusion (see also Bradley *et al.*, 1994). An example of how colleges are trying to be more inclusive is illustrated by the following list of groups of people found in one English college's student magazine and who are encouraged to join courses:

- homeless
- ex-offenders
- people with mental health difficulties
- people from ethnic minority communities
- full-time carers
- women in refuge
- travellers
- care leavers
- single parents on low incomes
- long-term unemployed
- those overcoming drug or alcohol dependency.

Riddell *et al.* (1999), however, have analysed the position of people with learning difficulties within the 'education market' and the 'social care market' and argue that there is still a long way to go before their voice is properly heard and their needs met.

We are very aware that this brief discussion of the FE sector's response to the needs of people with learning difficulties and/or physical disabilities raises far more questions than can be dealt with here. Clough and Barton (1995: 2) point out that people with what were once, and sometimes still are, called 'special needs' are the 'recipients of powerful professional categories' which 'envelop their identities'. There is also considerable debate about whether their needs are best met in specialist provision and the case for integration is by no means fully accepted. Corbett (1997: 171) writing about young people, notes:

> The tensions within the inclusive ideology are evident. At one level, concepts of 'entitlement for all' and quality assurance measures suggest that the most vulnerable young people are no longer to be offered a second-rate education and training diet but are to be assessed and guided in a way that equates with the treatment given to their peers. At another level, they are no longer seen as 'special' or in need of additional protective care, which can open up opportunities for real progression into mainstream developments but can also mean that they become casualties of a market culture in which the weakest go to the wall. If they are included, this means inclusion into a harsh and uncaring economy where there are no favours given, only deals bargained for.

Despite cuts in funding, many FE colleges still offer some provision for adults wishing to pursue leisure or recreational programmes. This adds another dimension to the work of colleges and to the student profile. Many of these students may be studying at outreach centres or in premises away from the main college site. It should also be remembered that there are eight residential adult education colleges in the UK: six in England, one in Wales and one in Scotland.

The FE teacher will be faced with more changes and challenges as colleges address the key priorities of widening participation, inclusion and raising standards. The inclusive college is one which caters for the widest possible student population with an enormous diversity of learning needs, where programmes may be delivered through a range of techniques. The inclusive college has to serve community needs as well as respond to a commercial market.

Student identity, disposition and motivation

The dispositions and motivations of such a diverse range of students will obviously be widely different, and the ways in which students learn will vary in pace and style. This requires a flexible teaching approach from FE teachers in order to provide for the needs of individual learners (see Chapter 5). The teacher will also have a central role to play in other aspects of learning support, for example through guidance and counselling, both on entry to a programme and throughout its duration. Returning learners may also need support not just in the subject being studied but in how to study it. These competing pressures on the FE teacher's time are not easy to balance when the substantial managerial and administrative loads which are inherent in most vocational programmes are added to them.

The proposals set out in the FE White Paper (DfES, 2006b) for a more personalised learning offer, coupled with evolving Qualifications and Credit Framework (QCF), are likely to have a significant impact on the way in which provision in colleges is organised. Teachers and trainers will be required not only to tailor learning programmes more directly to individual learner needs, but to provide advice, guidance and support in helping learners to construct learning programmes from a wide range of possible units.

Every learner and teacher has an individual identity, and some would argue that we all have multiple identities – as we weave in and out of the different areas of our lives, we take on the identity that is most appropriate for the spaces and places we find ourselves in. There is now a large body of research exploring the relationship between identity, personal biography, individual dispositions and learning (see, *inter alia*, Evans *et al.*, 2004; Billett and Somerville, 2004; Bloomer and Hodkinson, 2000). The concept of disposition comes from the work of the French sociologist Pierre Bourdieu, and relates to the way in which individuals have subconscious (or tacit) attitudes to and ways of approaching life (see, Bourdieu and Wacquant, 1992). Our 'dispositions' develop and change as we grow and are affected by a whole range of life experiences. Understanding something of the personal biography of students can be helpful to teachers, though, in reality, there is often little time to garner this information, and, in some circumstances, it would not be ethical or even advisable to enquire too deeply. Being empathetic to our students' circumstances is, however, an important part of being an effective teacher. Just as we might hope our students realise we have lives outside college and that they will have an impact on our life in college, so too should teachers remind themselves that students are only students for part of their waking hours.

Reflection

We now present a series of vignettes of typical students to be found in any college. We would like you to read each one and consider the following questions:

1   As a teacher what perceptions do you have of each of these students and of their learning needs and dispositions?

2   What steps would you take to ensure the students were being adequately supported?

3   How does your disposition towards being a teacher change from week to week, and how has it changed over time?

Jonathan

Jonathan is 18 years old and is taking a BTEC Diploma in Performing Arts as a full-time student at his local college. His school experience was rather negative although he achieved five GCSE subjects with grades A*–C. His parents were not enthusiastic about his transfer to the local college at 16 and would have preferred him to have remained in the sixth form at school, as his sister had done, and to study what they regard as 'proper A levels'. His school, however, did not offer the Performing Arts programme but wanted Jonathan to take an A level programme, including English literature and theatre studies.

Since transferring to college, Jonathan has enjoyed the freedom of being allowed to organise his own time, although he has found it difficult to meet coursework submission deadlines. He has taken an active part in drama productions and student affairs and is particularly interested in music; much of his time outside college is spent rehearsing with a local band and doing occasional 'gigs'.

He is now starting to think about 'next steps' and has asked his tutor about possible options. She has suggested that Jonathan consider applying for a degree programme in music technology at a London college. His sister, now a medical student, thinks the idea 'ridiculous' and suggests that Jonathan should think about something more 'realistic'. Jonathan's parents have already indicated that they would not be willing to pay fees for such a course, nor to support him in London. They are unhappy about the influence that the college tutors appear to have had on their son's decision to pursue a career in the performing arts.

Scott

Scott is on a full-time Level II programme in Leisure and Recreation. He left school last year with 4 GCSEs, grades D–E. He had no idea what he wanted to do and there was very little on offer at his school for those who had failed to achieve good GCSE grades. His mother insisted that he find some further course of study because she did not want him 'hanging around the house'. Scott is eligible for an Educational Maintenance Allowance (EMA) because he is in full-time education and because his mother's income is low. Scott is very interested in football and thought that the course might be a reasonable way of spending the time. The course also provides an opportunity to gain a coaching certificate.

The course has proved to be a disappointment, mainly because it is not what he expected it would be. He enjoys the practical work, particularly playing football and spending time in the gymnasium. He dislikes the theoretical aspects of the course and finds the assignments very difficult. He cannot keep up with the volume of work and is constantly late in handing in assignments. He feels that he is falling further and further behind and is unable to manage his time to do anything about it.

He has two part-time jobs; one of them is in a sports retail outlet, the other in a local restaurant, usually washing-up and preparing vegetables. They take up all his time at weekends. Sometimes he feels so tired in the week that he does not want to attend college, but he knows that attendance is a condition of receiving his EMA.

Recently, he missed two days from college and Scott's tutor had to point out that he would be unable to sign his attendance card. Scott was angry about the tutor's attitude since he had always felt that the tutor was an 'OK guy'. He was also concerned that his mother would find out that he had been missing from college because he knows that she is hoping that he will do well there.

Sharon

Sharon is 42 and is a student in her second year of a 'two plus two' degree programme which is run jointly by her college and the local university. The first two years of the programme are delivered by the college and involve a social science foundation course followed by a first-year undergraduate programme in one area of the social sciences. Sharon has chosen to continue her studies in economics. Before starting the course Sharon had helped her husband in his building business; she had been responsible for the clerical and administrative side of the work and had dealt with the accounts and payment of salaries.

Although Sharon left school at 16 she had always pursued some form of part-time education through attendance at evening classes. She had gained qualifications in bookkeeping, word processing and accounts, which had enabled her to help in the family business. However, when her two daughters started their secondary education, Sharon felt she would like to have the opportunity of pursuing a full-time course. She approached her local college about possible options and was surprised to find that she could enrol on the degree programme.

She approached the first year with trepidation and found the return to full-time education extremely unsettling. Although she found she could cope with the work she was always anxious about the expectations of staff and about the adequacy of her performance. She was particularly concerned about oral presentations and disliked having to give papers to other students and to lecturers who appeared to be about half her age.

She successfully completed the first year of the programme and achieved particularly high marks in the statistics examination. Now she is in the second year she feels more confident about the work and is doing well in her chosen specialisation, economics. Nevertheless, she finds the work demanding and is anxious about the transfer to the university for the third and fourth years of the course. She fears that most of the students will be the age of her daughters. The college staff have assured her that she will be able to cope but she remains unconvinced.

Gary

Gary is 16 and has been in college for six weeks on a Level 1 course in catering. It is a short course designed for young people who have not yet decided upon career destinations and who have left school with few qualifications and with poor basic skills. The catering course is essentially practical and provides the opportunity to acquire National Vocational Qualifications (NVQs) in catering and other related subjects such as food handling and hygiene. Basic numeracy and communication skills are also included in the course content.

Although keen at the beginning of term, Gary's enthusiasm began to wane after three weeks. He started to miss theory classes and by the fifth week he was turning up late for practical sessions. Staff noticed that he was not wearing correct kitchen uniform despite being repeatedly told about it. He appeared to resent any criticism from the staff.

The quality of his practical work is good when he is left on his own to complete a task. He is aggressive when asked to work with other students and takes extended breaks, which delay the completion of any joint activities. Other students have begun to resent this and have mentioned it to the lecturer in charge. The lecturer has discussed this with Gary who has given assurances about his future conduct. Gary has been told that he will not be allowed to participate in the work experience placement unless his behaviour improves.

During a practical session Gary became involved in an argument with another student who had suggested that Gary could not weigh or add up quantities correctly. Gary became abusive and threatened the student. He also used offensive language to the kitchen assistant who has lodged a formal complaint. The catering lecturer has intervened and asked Gary to discuss the matter with him fully.

Arpinder

Arpinder works for a firm of accountants and attends his local college one day a week for an accountancy course. He is 32 and decided to study for accounting qualifications because he has friends who run a successful accountancy practice. He sees the course as the first step towards achieving full professional qualifications. He realises, however, that it will take a long time. Before starting his present job he worked for a retail chain as an assistant store manager, but he did not like the long and irregular hours of work.

The company he works for is reasonably supportive of Arpinder's attendance at college and allows him time off work to attend. However, they are not prepared to pay his fees. So far he has been able to meet the cost himself.

He is very keen to progress as quickly as possible and has found the course helpful, although he has been irritated by the repeated changes in the teaching staff. During a recent busy period his firm asked him to remain at work on college days with the promise of making up the time later when he needs some exam revision time. He cannot envisage the situation improving in the foreseeable future. In addition, his father has recently been seriously ill and he has had to spend a considerable amount of time supporting his family.

He is becoming anxious about the effect this is having on his course and the possible outcome for his examination result. He feels he has invested heavily in the course in terms of financial, personal and emotional commitment. He is becoming increasingly dispirited and depressed about the possibility of not meeting the goals which he has set for himself.

Grace

For three mornings a week Grace attends a *Skills for Life* programme run by the FE college at a local community hall. She is a single parent aged 28 and has three children aged 6, 8 and 10. She had an extremely negative and disrupted school experience, having attended four different schools in a period of six years. She left school at the earliest possible opportunity without any formal qualifications. She did not expect, nor want, to have any further contact with the education system. On leaving school she took a series of low-paid, unskilled jobs – none of which lasted for very long. She has had no paid employment since the birth of her first child.

When her children started school she began to take an interest in their work and in some of the activities in which the school sought parental involvement. She was interested in helping in a practical way but when approached about the possibility of 'listening to readers' she became very anxious. She was reluctant to become involved in case her own deficiencies were exposed.

When her husband left, Grace decided to try and find some part-time employment but soon realised that it was virtually impossible to find any work unless she improved her reading and writing skills. She also wanted to improve her basic numeracy skills. She found that there were a series of classes being held in her local community hall, just ten minutes' walk from home. The FE college had been contracted to deliver them at a series of neighbourhood sites, as part of a project sponsored by the Regional Development Agency's 'Skills Now' programme. It was hoped that by making an initial contact with FE through an outreach activity students might be encouraged to continue their studies at the college itself.

Grace was extremely nervous about returning to study. For the first few weeks she attempted to disguise the nature of the course when talking to friends and neighbours. However, after a short time she began to gain confidence and discovered a new group of friends among the class members. The atmosphere was extremely supportive and the lecturers were friendly. She began to look forward to the mornings spent improving her writing skills and started to enjoy reading. This new-found confidence tended to spill over into other areas of her life. She was approached about standing as a parent governor at her daughter's school.

Grace now wants to continue her studies with the intention of gaining some qualifications. She has discovered that the next stage of the programme will be held in the college and not in the local hall. She is reluctant to travel the 5 miles (8 kilometres) to the college but she is even more reluctant to become a student there. The prospect of entering a formal education institution is threatening; she is concerned about her ability to cope with the work.

George

At 35, George has been unemployed for the past 18 months. Prior to that, he was employed as a storeman at a manufacturing company. The company was forced to close, resulting in some 350 job losses. Some of the skilled workers eventually managed to find alternative employment but the large number of unskilled workers, like George, found it virtually impossible to find work.

George and several of his old workmates now attend college as part of a government-funded programme designed to help the long-term unemployed. This scheme is open to those who have been unemployed for more than six months. Funding for the programme is provided by the government through the Local Learning and Skills Council (LLSC). The LLSC is responsible for managing the programmes locally and may contract FE colleges to provide the off-the-job training element. All programmes must lead to the acquisition of NVQs. Trainees are paid a weekly rate, the receipt of which is dependent upon attendance at the programme. Colleges receive payment for the trainees, part of which is related to successful outcomes.

George is attending a painting and decorating training programme. He is hoping that even if he does not secure employment in a company, he may be able to become self-employed. In addition to the practical elements of the programme, sessions on how to complete job applications, interview techniques and presentation skills are provided by college staff. Having already suffered 18 months of unemployment, George is unsure about the value of some parts of the programme in helping him to secure a job.

Tom

Tom is a Year 11 pupil at a large, inner-city comprehensive school. He attends the local FE college one day a week as part of the Increased Flexibility Programme (IFP) (see Chapter 3) which the college runs in partnership with a number of local secondary schools. In addition to his day at college, Tom spends another day on a placement at a local agricultural showground. The remaining time he spends at school following core curriculum subjects including English, maths and ICT. On his college days he is working towards a Level 1 NVQ in horticulture.

Tom enjoys the day at the college, but prefers the time he spends at the showground doing practical landscaping work. He dislikes the time he spends in school, but has come to terms with the fact that he will have to attend if he is to be allowed to continue with the college and work experience. He has a poor school attendance record, but he has not missed one day at college or on his work placement. He is concerned about the behaviour of some of the students who are in his college group, especially the ones from a 'rival' school; there have been two incidents in the car park at break times and a 'flashpoint' during a workshop.

He hopes to be able to continue with this type of work when he leaves school. He is aware that there are opportunities in this area; his uncle already has a flourishing business. He describes himself as being 'well set up' as a result of his college and work experience. His school form tutor says that he is a 'changed person' since joining the IFP. The high point in his year was when his photograph appeared in the local newspaper showing him at work during the county agricultural show.

Vicky

Vicky is 22 and has moderate learning difficulties (MLD); she attends her local FE college on a full-time basis and has done so since she left her special school at 19.

She is in a group of 10 young people with similar learning needs, although the nature of these needs is diverse and some group members have specific physical needs as well. The programme is wide and varied and includes a range of different modules geared to the students' individual needs and preferences. There is a strong core of basic skills work as well as modules on: 'managing myself'; 'money management'; 'keeping safe and healthy'. So far Vicky has taken modules on: 'small animal care'; 'horticulture'; and 'art and design'. In addition, she has gained a grade D in art and design GCSE, the first formal qualification she has ever achieved and of which she is extremely proud.

She enjoys her time at college and has met new friends with whom she has developed strong relationships. She is also very fond of her tutor, Mrs Baines, and particularly enjoys the special events which Mrs Baines organises for the group. Recently, these have included a bowling evening, a meal at the local pizza restaurant and a fancy dress Valentine's disco.

Vicky's parents are extremely pleased with the way in which Vicky has developed during her time at college. They notice in particular her increased independence and her willingness to join in conversations. Previously, she had been very withdrawn. She is now able to travel independently to and from college on public transport. Their only concern is about Vicky's future and what will happen when she is no longer eligible to attend college.

Hussein

Hussein has recently arrived from the Middle East and has joined an intensive English language course at his local college before beginning a degree in engineering at a nearby university. He realises that he will have to work extremely hard in order to pass the English language competence test set by the university. This is a condition of entry on to the degree programme. He is concerned because there are 20 students on the English programme, from many different parts of the world and with a very wide range of English language competence. He is concerned that the weaker students will hold him back.

About half the students work as au pairs with English families and seem, as far as Hussein is concerned, to be using the classes as an opportunity to socialise. They do not hand in required pieces of homework and are reluctant to join in with some of the 'speaking' exercises. He feels that he is working hard and trying his best and finds the behaviour of the young au pairs a distraction and an irritation. He wonders if he should transfer to a small private language school where he knows the fees are higher but where, perhaps, he will receive more individual attention.

Najma

Najma is 19 and on the Advanced Apprenticeship in hairdressing. She spends four days a week working as a hair stylist in a big city salon and one day at college working towards an S/NVQ Level 3 and Key Skills. Najma started doing Highers in her Scottish school, but left after one year to try and find a job. She had always been interested in hairdressing and applied for the apprenticeship with a salon in her home town. Unfortunately, she didn't get on with the salon owner and so left after six months. She then applied for her current apprenticeship. Her current salon is much more upmarket than the previous one and Najma enjoys the hectic pace and competitive atmosphere. Her work is judged closely by her supervisor and by her tutors at college, and they have identified her as a potential competitor for the regional trials of the 'Skills Challenge Competitions' organised by SkillsUK.

Najma is a very confident and articulate young woman who finds it hard to keep her opinions to herself. At college, she can cause problems for her tutors when she criticises the work of other students. Recently, she was particularly critical of a fellow apprentice during an open day for the public. This resulted in the customer complaining to the tutor as she was worried that her hair was being done by an incompetent student. The tutor had to deal with three people: the tearful customer, the tearful apprentice, and Najma.

Conclusions

All of these students will have developed their own perspective on learning and will communicate that perspective through their behaviour in the classroom, workshop, tutorial, seminar group and so on. Their prior experience of education will have shaped their attitudes to learning, to teachers and to their fellow students. These issues are explored in detail in Chapters 5 and 6, where we return to these vignettes and consider which teaching and assessment strategies might be most appropriate for helping students such as these to learn most effectively.

It will be clear from some of the vignettes that some form of inter-agency collaboration will be necessary to ensure that the students' needs are catered for and that the different 'stakeholders' who have an interest in the students' progress are kept informed and, where necessary, involved. In the case of Najma, for example, the college tutors and the salon supervisor need to review how they can each help Najma adjust her behaviour, while in the case of Tom, the college, employer and school need to find ways to share their ideas in order to support him.

Chapter 3

Diverse curricula and qualifications

What will I teach?

Introduction

Numerous curricular traditions (academic and vocational, liberal and radical) and forms are to be found in colleges, providing a range of learning opportunities for their diverse student body. The curriculum principles guiding the organisation of teaching and learning in different areas of the college will reflect the parameters within which they have to work. Some teachers will have more freedom to experiment with the curriculum than others, but many will be constrained by the requirements of regulatory bodies. Rogers (2002: 207) provides a helpful model for thinking about what the concept embraces. He proposes that a curriculum comprises five elements:

1   *Philosophical framework*: This reflects the assumptions that lie behind the way the curriculum has been designed. Hence, 'Woodwork may be seen as a series of techniques or as part of a concern for good design and good living . . . Natural history may be taught as a leisure pursuit or as part of socially concerned issues . . . In particular, it (the framework) will reflect our assumptions as to whether the education we are engaged in is designed to reproduce or transform existing social systems, whether it is aimed to lead to conformity or to liberation' (ibid.: 207).

2   *Context*: This reflects the way learning is organised in terms of the quality of the 'setting' (for example, lighting and heating, levels of noise) and the 'climate', that is the nature of the social relationship between teacher and learner, and learner and learner.

3   *Content*: This relates to the subject matter to be covered (sometimes laid down in a syllabus), the sequence in which it is handled, and the 'conditions' attached to the learning (for example, what is required of the learner, the pace of the learning, and the resources required).

4   *Events*: This relates to the planned activities through which learning is facilitated (for example, lectures, discussions, group work, use of technology) and the unplanned events (for example, disruptions or changes of direction stimulated by new insights).

5   *Processes of evaluation*: This relates to the ways in which learner achievement and experience are evaluated (for example, from formal tests through to learner feedback on how satisfied they are).

The idea of a curriculum is often seen, simplistically, as a framing device for the topics and ideas that a teacher might cover throughout a course of study. Lawrence Stenhouse, a much celebrated English educationalist, argued, however, that a curriculum should not be seen in 'product' terms, but as a dynamic space in which teachers constantly experimented with new ideas for supporting the learning of their students (see Elliott, 1983). Young (1998), however, criticises both the 'curriculum as fact' and 'curriculum as practice' models. He argues that the first is underpinned by the 'view of knowledge as external to knowers, both teachers and students, and embodied in syllabi and text books' (ibid.: 25). The model of 'curriculum as practice' appears to reverse the assumptions of the 'curriculum as fact' model, but, says Young, it 'gives teachers a spurious sense of their power, autonomy and independence from the wider contexts of which their work is part' (ibid.: 28). The problem for many teachers in colleges is that the space, time and freedom for experimentation appear to have been squeezed out as the pressure to achieve qualification targets has come to dominate their daily life. Bloomer (1997, p. 188) has argued that:

> In policy, planning and, to some extent, practitioner circles it (the curriculum) has come to mean little more than a prescription of 'content' coupled with a series of checks for its successful implementation. 'Objectives', 'outcomes' and 'quality assurance' now cover all, while 'delivery' is the metaphor to describe the process.

This might seem a pessimistic view, but qualifications now frame much of what happens within colleges. The quest then becomes one of trying to find ways to exert some agency as a teacher and think through the ways in which the demands of a qualification can be translated into teaching and learning strategies that will stimulate both student and teacher. Carr (1993: 7) reminds us that:

> The way in which the curriculum is made and remade – the process of curriculum change – is essentially a process of contestation and struggle between individuals and social groups whose different views about the curriculum reflect their different views about the good society and how it may be created.

Due to government pressure for a more 'personalised' approach, many of the colleges we visit talk about the need to develop more 'individualised learning programmes' for students:

The central characteristic of such a new system will be personalization –
so that the system fits to the individual rather than the individual having
to fit to the system. This is not a vague liberal notion about letting people
have what they want. It is about having a system which will genuinely
give high standards for all . . . And the corollary of this is that the system
must be both freer and more diverse – with more flexibility to help meet
individual needs; and more choices between courses and types of provider,
so that there really are different and personalised opportunities available.

(DfES, 2004a, foreword)

Such programmes imply that students should be able to access learning
programmes as and when they wish and in whatever location, including
perhaps from the comfort of their own homes via electronic means. However,
the physical achievement of such flexibility is still a long way off. The
appropriateness of such a curriculum design is hotly contested. It should be
remembered that many students value the opportunity of learning with others
and of working cooperatively, and that learning within a community can
challenge the prejudices and limited horizons of learners that can easily
remain unchallenged when learning becomes an entirely individual affair.

The concept also embraces the notion of the 'hidden curriculum', which
refers to the way in which all teachers, usually subconsciously, act to socialise
their students into the rules and behaviours expected of a particular educational
setting. In the same way, employees learn the 'hidden curriculum' of the
workplace. Indeed, in any setting where people come together, even in the
home, there are norms of behaviour that lie invisible, but exert a profound
influence. In her research on courses for nursery nurses in colleges, Colley
(2003), building on Hochschild's (1983) concept of 'emotional labour', has
shown how, during their work placements, the student nurses have to learn a
substantial hidden curriculum of working in a nursery, that is, how to manage
their feelings when confronted with the day-to-day realities of looking after
small children:

In a group tutorial discussion soon after the start of the course, following
the students' first few days in placement, there were many expressions
of delight at being with children. But the session also revealed events
they experienced as far from pleasant: taking little boys to the toilet;
finding oneself covered in children's 'puke' and 'wee'; and being hit by
children.

(Colley, 2003: 15)

What is 'taught' and 'learned' might, therefore, diverge, depending on where
students apply their learning.

Curriculum and context

Just as the range of students in FE colleges is too wide to enable it to be described in tidy categorisations, to talk about an FE curriculum as if it were a homogeneous entity would be totally misleading. FE's curricular traditions derive from a range of complex origins and prepare students for different destinations. Squires (1987) has suggested that, 'It is at this point that the "radical monopoly", to use Illich's phrase, of the education system breaks down, and a plethora of institutions and interests become involved' (Squires, 1987: 96). Although written twenty years ago, the observation is perhaps even more apposite to day, as Figure 3.1 illustrates. The balance of the influences depicted in Figure 3.1 will shift in response to changes in government policy, the numbers and types of students enrolling, the variations in funding mechanisms and so on.

The range of courses on offer will also be dependent upon the size of the institution and upon its location. Traditionally, colleges have served their local communities and have been dependent upon local companies sending their employees on day-release programmes, usually at a craft apprentice or

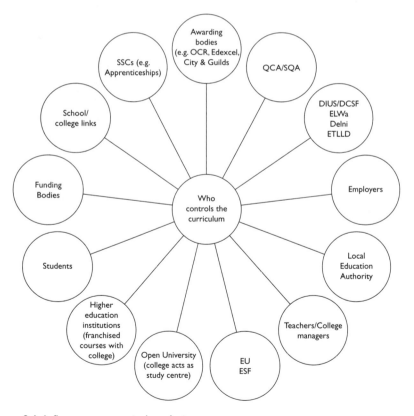

Figure 3.1 Influences on curriculum design

technician level. Notable examples were the colleges in some parts of South Yorkshire and Nottinghamshire, which were almost entirely dependent on the local mining industry for their students. Pit closures have subsequently meant that these colleges have had to diversify, to seek and exploit new markets. Similarly, many large engineering departments have contracted or closed down. Against this background, new courses catering for the burgeoning demands of the information technology industries and for the service industries have been developed. All of this will affect the curriculum offerings of a college.

In drawing up strategic plans for their institutions, college managers are supposed to pay attention to the needs of the local labour market and to reflect these in their provision. Funding is often tied to the ways in which courses meet the needs of the local community. However, this is sometimes a difficult task since local labour markets can be volatile and predicting future training requirements is not an exact science. There is also a further consideration in that the demand from students may not match the supply of jobs within the local, regional or even national labour markets. Pressures for increased student numbers and, hence, increased funding, may persuade colleges to offer those courses which are popular irrespective of job opportunities. Meeting the needs of learners and, at the same time, the needs of employers is the challenge thrown down to colleges in the recent White Paper (DfES, 2006b: 7). However, the extent to which these are coterminous is not fully explored: '. . . we want to make a decisive shift towards a system that is driven by the needs of service users. We will introduce measures that put learners and employers in the driving seat in determining what is funded and how services are delivered'.

Reflection

The diversity of curriculum provision is revealed in these titles from the classified pages of the educational press. What type of curriculum do you think is offered in these faculties/departments or divisions?

Faculty of the Built Environment
Department of Hospitality and Tourism
Department of Health and Social Care
School of Science
Division of Sport, Leisure and Tourism
Faculty of Business, Management and Humanities
Faculty of Visual Communication
Faculty of General Education and Student Services

You might also want to consider how these different aspects of a college's provision relate to each other.

Programmes of study will, of course, have a curriculum that teachers follow and this might be devised by them or imposed by an awarding body. Most courses in colleges lead to nationally recognised qualifications as it is the qualifications that trigger funding. The curriculum content of these courses will differ in style according to the nature of the qualification. Competence-based qualifications are derived from occupational standards and so do not, as such, have curricula attached to them. They are designed to be assessment-led and achievable without the need to attend a programme of learning, though, of course, most individuals working towards such qualifications need to acquire new skills and knowledge and, hence, teachers have to design curriculum content in order to support their students.

The dominance of qualifications in the UK education and training system has been heavily criticised (see Unwin *et al.*, 2004 for a review). Since the 1980s, public funding has been more and more closely tied to the delivery and attainment of qualifications and qualifications form the basis of numerous government targets. As we write, fundamental changes are being made to the Qualifications and Credit Framework (QCF) via which the different parts of the UK organise nationally recognised qualifications, which, in turn, trigger public funding. In Chapter 1, we outlined the wider policy context for these reforms. For the purposes of this chapter we focus on the ways in which the proposed changes to qualifications are likely to impact upon the nature of the curriculum offering within FE colleges. At the time of writing the reform programme is ongoing and some of the recommendations will not be fully in place until 2013, including, for example, the entitlement for all 14- to 19-year-olds in England to have access to all 14 lines of learning within the proposed new diplomas. Even the name of these qualifications has changed during their gestation, and may change again before the first 5 lines begin piloting in September 2007. This serves to point up the scope and pace of change within the sector and a book of this nature can only present a snapshot of the world as it is now; you will need to keep abreast of changes by constant reference to relevant websites, including: www.qca.org.uk (for England); www.wales.org.uk (for Wales); www.ccea.org.uk (for Northern Ireland); and www.sqa.org.uk (for Scotland).

Levels and frameworks

Many countries now have a national qualification framework (NQF), which arranges nationally recognised qualifications in a level-based system so that people can see how different qualifications equate to each other. Young (2003: 3) has conducted a review of frameworks round the world, which he says are driven by powerful political and economic forces. He states that: 'Not surprisingly the idea of an NQF is also invariably linked to that of a learning society which is contrasted with societies of the past in which learning, at least recognised and accredited learning, was largely restricted to initial education and training'. Young has found that frameworks tend to share the following goals:

- to be transparent to all users in terms of what they signify and what learners have to achieve;
- to minimise barriers to progression, both vertical and horizontal;
- to maximise access, flexibility and portability between different sectors of education and work and different sites of learning.

While these goals are certainly laudable, frameworks can exert a malign influence over education and training systems in that they require qualifications to follow an outcomes-based model so that everything can be shaped to fit the framework. As shown later in this chapter, the outcomes-based approach has proved to be very controversial in recent years.

Figure 3.2 (see p. 54) illustrates the way in which qualifications in England are classified. This classification is regulated by the Qualifications and Curriculum Authority (QCA). Scotland has its own Scottish Credit and Qualifications Framework (see Raffe, 2003 for a critique). In Wales the regulatory function is carried out on behalf of the Welsh Assembly by DELLS (Vocational Qualification and Lifelong Learning Division) www.wales.org.uk, and in Northern Ireland by CCEA (Council for the Curriculum, Examinations and Assessment) www.ccea.org.uk.

Attempting to locate all qualifications within a common overarching framework, and to assign equivalences to them, is a major challenge (see Young, 2008). Since qualifications differ in their type, composition and purpose, it is difficult to make the necessary comparisons in order to assign levels. Qualification frameworks need to be adapted as new ideas about the meaning of 'levels' and the relationship between different curricular areas emerge. By 2010 in England, for example, the QCA and LSC have promised to put in place a new Foundation Learning Tier. This is intended to tidy up the myriad of qualifications available below Level 2 and identify clearer 'Progression Pathways' through the existing framework.

We begin a discussion of the relationship between curriculum and qualifications with the age-old UK debate about the 'academic/vocational divide'.

Bridging the academic/vocational divide

The most recent and thorough review of the 14–19 curriculum in England was conducted by the Working Group on 14–19 Reform: the Tomlinson Review (DfES, 2004b), with part of the recommendations being carried forward by government in the 14–19 White Paper (DfES, 2005b), and the 14–19 Implementation Plan (DfES, 2006a). For a detailed investigation of the

Framework level	Level indicators	Example of qualifications
Entry	Entry level qualifications recognise basic knowledge and skills and the ability to apply learning in everyday situations under direct guidance or supervision.	Qualifications are offered at entry 1, entry 2 and entry 3, in a range of subjects
Level 1	Level 1 qualifications recognise basic knowledge and skills and the ability to learning with guidance or apply supervision.	NVQ 1; Certificate in Plastering; GCSEs Grades D–G; Certificate in Motor Vehicle Studies
Level 2	Level 2 qualifications recognise the ability to gain a good knowledge and understanding of a subject area of work or study, and to perform varied tasks with some guidance or supervision.	NVQ 2; GCSEs Grades A*–C; Certificate in Coaching Football; Diploma for Beauty Specialists
Level 3	Level 3 qualifications recognise the ability to gain, and where relevant apply a range of knowledge, skills and understanding.	Certificate for Teaching Assistants; NVQ 3; A levels; Advanced Extension Awards; Certificate in Small Animal Care
Level 4	Level 4 qualifications recognise specialist learning and involve detailed analysis of a high level of information and knowledge in an area of work or study.	Diploma in Sport & Recreation; Certificate in Site Management; Certificate in Early Years Practice
Level 5	Level 5 qualifications recognise the ability to increase the depth of knowledge and understanding of an area of work or study to enable the formulation of solutions and responses to complex problems and situations.	Diploma in Construction; Certificate in Performing Arts
Level 6	Level 6 qualifications recognise a specialist high level knowledge of an area of work or study to enable the use of an individual's own ideas and research in response to complex problems and situations.	Certificate or Diploma in Management
Level 7	Level 7 qualifications recognise highly developed and complex levels of knowledge which enable the development of in-depth and original responses to complicated and unpredictable problems and situations.	Diploma in Translation; Fellowship in Music Literacy
Level 8	Level 8 qualifications recognise leading experts or practitioners in a particular field.	Specialist awards

Figure 3.2 Qualification level indicators

Source: www.qca.org.uk/493.html

'Pathfinder' projects in England, which brought together schools and colleges to develop and share best practice for 14–19 provision, see Higham and Yeomans (2005). Abbott and Hudleston (2004: 243) argue that:

> Central to these reforms is the need to build a system which meets the needs of a diverse range of learners, which permits a wide choice of courses and qualifications, which allows for flexibility across and between learning pathways, for example, schools, colleges and workplaces.

The 16–19 phase of education in England, Wales and Northern Ireland has been particularly resistant to change, and the divide between vocational and academic routes has yet to be bridged, although many attempts have been made to do so. Young (1993: 220) previously categorised the English and Welsh 16–19 curriculum as representing 'divisive specialisation' with:

- sharp academic/vocational division
- insulated subjects
- absence of any concept of the curriculum as a whole.

The Tomlinson Working Group (DfES, 2004b) proposed a unified diploma system for all 14- to 19-year-olds to replace all other qualifications. The proposals attracted a considerable groundswell of support from across the political parties, the worlds of education (public and private) and business, trades unions and the media. There was enormous disappointment, therefore, when Tony Blair announced that the government would not support the replacement of GCSEs and A levels, but would pursue a version of the diploma for vocational education. There had been criticism of Tomlinson's proposals. Some argued that the fundamental principle of trying to 'unify' the academic and the vocational actually serves to further devalue vocational education. Others argued that the proposals were overly complex and did not pay enough attention to how young people in apprenticeships would be covered (see Huddleston et al., 2005). The key breakthrough, however, was that Tomlinson drew nationwide attention to the divisive and inadequate nature of the current arrangements (for more detailed discussion, see www.nuffield14-19review.org.uk).

In contrast to England, Scotland, which has always had its own separate education system, has been moving towards a more unified 16–19 curriculum since the mid-1980s and reached an important stage with the publication of Higher Still in 1994 (see Howieson et al., 2002). In Scotland, a single ladder of academic and vocational modules, aimed at both older and younger learners, has been put in place. Since the establishment of the Welsh Assembly, Wales has signalled its desire to break away from England and develop a unitised framework of qualifications which, like the Scottish approach, allows for greater flexibility in mixing academic and vocational provision (National Council-ELWa, ACCAC and HEFCW, 2003). Wales has combined elements of the Tomlinson diploma and the International Baccalaureate to create the Welsh Baccalaureate. This has been piloted since 2003 and became available nationally at intermediate and advanced levels from September 2007. The new qualification includes existing A levels and GCSEs, as well as vocational qualifications, but they form 'options' to be taken alongside a 'core' programme consisting of four components: Key Skills; Wales, Europe and the World; Work-related Education; and Personal and Social Education.

In November 2005, ministers in England agreed to the development of a QCF, as part of a wider Vocational Qualification Reform Programme, to 'develop a jointly regulated credit and qualifications framework for England, Wales and Northern Ireland' (www.QCA.org.uk/15708.html). In April 2006, the regulators in the different parts of the UK (QCA, DELLS, CCEA) commissioned work on 'tests and trials' of such a framework with the following objectives:

- to develop and test an operational model of the framework with stakeholders;
- to evaluate whether a unit-based system underpinned by credit can support a range of qualifications and learning programmes across sectors, learning and training contexts and awarding bodies;
- to evaluate whether a fully functioning credit system can support and improve learner progression and achievement;
- to evaluate whether potential benefits (including flexibility, inclusiveness, simplicity and reduced bureaucracy) can be delivered through the framework;
- to evaluate through the tests and trials in England whether the development of the framework can contribute to the LSC's strategic priorities and targets for publicly funded qualifications. (QCA, ibid.)

There is a distinct sense of déjà vu in much of this since, in 1996, just prior to winning the 1997 General Election, the Labour Party in England published *Aiming Higher*, which called for the broadening of A level programmes, improvements to vocational programmes, and the merger of all 16–19 qualifications within a single credit-based framework (see Hodgson and Spours, 1999). This drew on the 1996 Dearing Review which examined the complex system of regulation governing award-bearing courses for 16- to 19-year-olds in England, Wales and Northern Ireland. Dearing's concern, probably shared by thousands of teachers and managers in the post-compulsory sector, was for greater coherence in the system. One outcome of the Dearing report was the reduction in the number of awarding bodies, mainly as a result of the merger of boards previously responsible for the award of vocational and academic qualifications. For example, BTEC merged with the University of London Examinations and Assessment Council (ULEAC) to form Edexcel.

Once in government, Labour watered down its earlier proposals and published *Qualifying for Success* (DfEE, 1997). This caused Hodgson and Spours (1999: 124) to conclude that 'New Labour's evolutionary approach to qualifications reform is practical but piecemeal and somewhat backward looking' and 'essentially reactive to the Conservative legacy', reflecting 'a historical preoccupation with academic learning'. You might wish to reflect upon the extent to which the current reform proposals share these characteristics, or whether they represent fundamental change.

In September 2000, steps were taken along the road of reform in England with the introduction of vocational A levels (AVCEs), which replaced GNVQ Advanced, and the modularisation of A levels into groups of three and six units. This reform was intended to pave the way for greater flexibility post-16, thus affording students the opportunity of mixing vocational and academic qualifications. The AVCE was revised and respecified in 2005 as an applied GCE, a qualification more akin to its A level cousin.

These qualifications are now based on groups of three, six and twelve units, with the Advanced Subsidiary (AS) level comprised of three units, the full Advanced (A) level six units, the applied AS three units, and the applied A level six units, or twelve units if the double award is taken. (Note that A and AS levels are currently being revised and will be reduced in their number of assessment units from six to four). Assessment within the applied A level is now graded in the same way as A level. The reforms, commonly referred to as *Curriculum 2000*, also introduced the opportunity for key skills (communication, application of number and information technology) to be available to all students, not just those pursuing a vocational programme. Key skills were also made a compulsory element for the achievement of the government-supported apprenticeship programme. At this point, it might be helpful to include some analysis of the development of key skills.

The idea that young people should develop generic skills that take priority over subject specific knowledge or practical skills has been debated by educationalists, employers and policymakers for at least 40 years in the UK (see Green, 1997; Canning, 2007). These so-called skills have been variously labelled 'generic', 'core', 'interpersonal', 'transferable' and 'life skills'. In 1979, the then Further Education Unit (FEU) published a landmark report, *A Basis for Choice*, which called for a 'core skills' curriculum, an idea that was forcibly promoted by the Confederation of British Industry (CBI) in its 1989 report, *Towards a Skills Revolution*. The basic idea is that there is a definable set of core or key skills, in, for example, communication and problem solving, that are essential for employability, for transferring learning from one context to another, and for learning to learn. Over the years, various lists and categorisations of these skills have been produced. Most notoriously, the Manpower Services Commission (MSC) produced a list of 103 core skills to be acquired by trainees on the Youth Training Scheme in the 1980s. The current key skills specifications include:

*   Communication
*   Application of Number
*   Information Technology
*   Improving own Learning and Performance
*   Problem Solving
*   Working with Others.

According to the former Learning and Skills Development Agency (LSDA) and the DfES, these skills are 'the generic and transferable skills that everyone needs to succeed in education and training, in work, and in life general' (LSDA, 2001). Green (1997), however, argues that this fixation with key skills 'represents an impoverished form of general education' that has always been missing from the UK's approach to vocational education (see also Canning, 2007). There are complex philosophical and educational debates about whether such skills can be neatly categorised and whether they can be separated from the actual context of the subject that is being studied or, indeed, the workplace. The policymakers are certainly confused: one minute they advocate that key skills should be seen as embedded in subjects and contexts and so should be developed in an integrated fashion; the next minute they are saying it is possible to isolate key skills in order to set tests to assess them (see Unwin and Wellington, 2001, for a detailed discussion).

The debate around key skills continues to rumble on, with the CBI suggesting that some employees not only lack the basic skills of literacy and numeracy, but also the necessary 'soft skills' to succeed in the workplace. This is a recurring theme within the Leitch Review (2006): 'By 2020 . . . 4 million people will still lack functional literacy skills, and over 6 million will lack functional numeracy skills' (Leitch: 13). The response has seen the inclusion of what are now defined as functional skills – English, maths and ICT – within the proposed 14–19 reforms. All students, on whatever learning pathway, will be expected to work towards, and, it is hoped, gain a Level 2 qualification in functional skills, and the achievement of a grade C, or above, in English, maths and ICT will require the functional skills component to have been achieved.

In their research, Abbott and Huddleston (2004: 244) have found that greater coherence across the curriculum for 16- to 19-year-olds is still not happening:

> Although Curriculum 2000 was intended to broaden the range of academic and vocational qualifications which could be accessed by young people post-16, in reality this has not happened to any significant extent. Young people have tended to take additional qualifications within the same subject group and to continue to pursue a vocational or academic pathway, rather than a mixed diet.

Reflection

Consider this statement:

The academic-vocational divide is not just about whether people learn welding or economics. It is about esteem and status. This means that colleges of further education which deliver vocational provision have an especially tricky mission. Many of their students have had a highly unsatisfactory experience of education. Their enthusiasm for learning may be low. They are often ill-prepared for big choices about their future working lives or about the education they may need to achieve it. They have already experienced failure by comparison with other people of the same age.

(ESRC, 2007: 58)

- How far does this compare with your experience in college so far?
- To what extent might the proposed reforms to 14–19 education and training improve this situation?
- Are the issues highlighted here so deep-seated as to require a multi-agency, cross-sector approach beyond the remit of the FE sector?

General education

Advanced level curriculum

Most of the provision within the general education category in England, Wales and Northern Ireland includes GCE A/AS level, GCE Applied A levels, and GCSEs. The overall standard of passes is lower in colleges than schools but one should remember that FE colleges (not necessarily sixth-form colleges) accept students with lower grades at GCSE than is the case in most school sixth forms.

The subject specifications are set by QCA; awarding bodies develop these specifications into awards, oversee assessment and set and mark examinations. (In Scotland SQA has both a qualification development and regulatory role.) They are subject to QCA's quality assurance procedures to ensure that specifications are complied with and that there is standardisation across the different awarding bodies. Students are free, subject to the capacity of the college, to choose which subjects they will study at A level. Although full-time students may take a programme of several A level subjects, there are other students who may study one A level on a part-time basis by evening attendance.

Some may combine both academic and applied A levels, or may include other types of qualification within their programme. A levels were first introduced in 1951 and have, until recently, been the only entry route into higher education. As Young and Leney (1997: 53) note, 'A levels represent a highly insulated form of subject specialisation which directs learners' attention entirely to individual subjects treated separately.' During the past fifteen years or so there has been increasing criticism of the narrowness of A levels, particularly since young people were forced to make choices at 16 which would effectively limit their opportunities to pursue a broader based curriculum. For those who have an interest in these issues, there is an extensive literature on the subject, which we do not have the space to fully consider here. (See, for example, DES/WO, 1988; Finegold et al., 1990; Nash, 1992; Dearing, 1996; Hodgson and Spours, 1997; Edwards et al., 1997; Raffe et al., 1998; DfES, 2004b).

In addition, Young and Leney (ibid.) remind us that, 'knowledge is more and more being produced at the interface of subjects and disciplines, not in subjects in isolation from each other' (see also Guiles, 2006).

The current A level is divided into six units (note that it is proposed to reduce the number of units to four within the current reform programme), each of which is assessed through examination and coursework. The first three units of the A level form the Advanced Subsidiary (AS) level. This is both a qualification in its own right and the first half of the full A level. To achieve a full A level candidates must complete a further three units, known as A2. Both AS levels and A levels are qualifications in their own right; the A2 units are not a qualification. A maximum of 30 per cent coursework is permitted in most A levels, with the exception of practical subjects where a higher percentage is permitted. Examinations may be re-sat, either at the unit level (once) or for the whole qualification. The applied A level has replaced the former GNVQ (Advanced). This qualification has been substantially revised to make it more comparable with other A levels.

It could be argued that the advanced level curriculum is merely a collection of subjects, and only gains coherence at individual student level. In this model a teacher's attention is naturally focused on achieving the desired number of student passes, and at acceptable grades. There may be a danger of 'teaching to the test' rather than considering the development of the whole individual. This situation may be exacerbated by the fact that a proportion of students taking A levels in colleges may be resitting examinations in which they have previously been unsuccessful. Since entry to HE is normally dependent upon achieving specified grades at A level, there is pressure on students and teaching staff to concentrate on 'getting through'. As a teacher your lesson planning will be informed not only by the subject specifications but also by the content of past examination papers.

Every summer, when the A level results are published, there is an outcry from certain sections of society who claim the exams must be getting easier as each year the pass rate improves. The elite universities (such as Oxford, Cambridge, Durham and Bristol) also complain that it is getting harder to distinguish between the best A level candidates – what Hodgson and Spours (2003: 28) refer to as 'differentiation at the "top end"'. As a response to these criticisms it is intended, within the 14–19 reform programme, to introduce the opportunity for candidates studying at Level 3 to undertake an extended project. This will be a single piece of work requiring a high degree of planning, preparation and independent research. While it will be optional for A level students, it will be a compulsory element of the new 14–19 Diploma (see below). The project is currently undergoing a pilot phase and will be available from 2008. It will be about the size of an AS qualification in terms of teaching and learning time.

In addition it is proposed to introduce an A* grade at A level, as well as the inclusion of more open-ended examination questions that demand longer written answers. In their analysis of academic A levels, Young and Leney (1997: 52) remind us that although they 'enable students to gain unrivalled access to bodies of specialised knowledge in a small number of knowledge areas and to the concepts that go with them . . . there is a price to pay for these advantages . . . the A level curriculum is both socially and intellectually selective'. The introduction of an A* grade would seem to perpetuate these problems. (Further information about the A level reforms may be found at: www.qca.org.uk/12086 16611.html).

A final consideration within this section is the proposed extension of the International Baccalaureate (IB) to more sixth form and FE colleges within the period to 2010. The IB is currently available in about 95 institutions across the UK, many of them within the independent sector. It is a broad two-year programme of study in which students have to follow six subjects including their own language, a second language, an arts subject, and a science subject, as well as some compulsory elements, which include theory of knowledge, community service and an extended project. (For further information about the proposed extension of the IB visit: www.ibo.org).

GCSE curriculum

The second major area of general education provision within the FE sector in England, Wales and Northern Ireland is that covering courses leading to GCSE. There has been a long tradition in FE for students to enrol in order to resit GCSE examinations in which they were unsuccessful at school. These numbers are dropping as young people choose to make a fresh start by enrolling on different types of programme, very often vocational in orientation rather than retaking GCSEs. Some students, particularly adults, may be tackling GCSE subjects for the first time, perhaps combining one or two of these with other qualifications. As with the A level programmes, curriculum content will be determined by the subject criteria laid down by QCA. Examinations are externally set and marked by a range of awarding bodies. There is also the opportunity for a limited amount of coursework assessment.

For those teaching on general education programmes that are accredited by awarding bodies, the content of the curriculum is, therefore, prescribed. The flexibility comes in the way in which teachers interpret the content and in the manner in which they seek to deliver it. The question of teaching style is considered more fully in Chapter 6. You will, no doubt, wish to reflect upon the type of approach, or variety of approaches, that you might wish to adopt when teaching on general education programmes.

The starting point will be the specifications issued by the awarding body with whom your candidates are registered. It is from these that the teacher will need to plan a coherent scheme of work. This will then be broken down further into individual lesson plans. You may already have noticed that in this curricular tradition there is an emphasis on input, or knowledge to be imparted, to achieve a particular outcome; that is, success in the examination. However, as teachers you should always be mindful of your students' wider developmental needs as learners. These may include: help with study skills; additional or specific learning support; personal and interpersonal skills development. As Dimbleby and Cooke (2000: 78) argue, 'A curriculum model based on developing the broad talents of each individual leads to a range of learning models.' Chapter 4 will help you to think about students' different learning preferences.

Applied GCSEs and increased flexibility at Key Stage 4

From September 2002, new GCSEs in vocational subjects, or applied GCSEs as they later became known (note the continuing concern over the 'v' word) became available at Key Stage 4 and post-16 (see Blunkett, 2001). These are intended to provide an introduction to a broad vocational area and to facilitate progression to further education, training or employment. They incorporate many of the features of their predecessor qualification, the GNVQ Part One. For example, content should be well contextualised within the vocational area, opportunity should be provided for links to the 'world of work', including extended work experience, and coursework drawing upon real business practice forms part of the assessment design.

Nine subjects are currently offered and each applied GCSE is the same size as two 'traditional' GCSEs. The titles emphasise the applied nature of the award; for example, Applied Art and Design, Applied Business, Engineering, Health and Social Care, Applied ICT, Manufacturing, Applied Science, Construction and the Built Environment. The award consists of three common, compulsory units in each subject. The subject criteria have been developed in consultation with the relevant Sector Skills Councils (note the link forward to current design features of the proposed 14–19 diplomas), subject associations and other interested parties. Assessment combines both internal and external elements – an externally set and marked test and internal assessment of the candidate's portfolio.

The awards are intended to allow schools and colleges to provide a more flexible offering to students by creating opportunities for the integration of work placements, practical activities and visits, amongst other things, into the programmes. It has also provided opportunities for schools and colleges to work together on the delivery of such programmes, for example through the use of college facilities such as workshops, and with vocationally qualified staff.

The introduction of the Increased Flexibility Programme (IFP), also in 2002, has made possible the creation of more partnerships between schools and colleges, since pupils may access vocationally tailored provision at a local college, or local training provider. The IFP aims to:

- raise the attainment in national qualifications of participating pupils;
- increase skills and knowledge;
- improve social learning and development;
- increase retention in education and training after 16. (DfES, 2002)

The IFP allows students to access a curriculum more suited to their needs and preferred learning styles, students for whom the traditional National Curriculum offering has been demotivating and who are in danger of being lost to the education and training system at 16, if not before (see Golden *et al.*, 2005; Harkin, 2006).

This sometimes creates challenges for FE staff, who may have had no training, or experience, of teaching younger students. However, as noted in Chapter 1, many college staff have become accustomed to teaching younger pupils since the introduction of the 1996 Education Act, Section 363, made provision for the 'Disapplication of the National Curriculum at Key Stage 4 to permit a wider focus on work-related learning'. This legislation created opportunities for pupils to be 'disapplied' from parts of the National Curriculum in order to 'give schools more scope to use work-related learning opportunities to motivate pupils and encourage them to learn, and to offer courses that are not compatible with existing statutory requirements' (QCA, 1998: 1). We met one of these students, Tom, in Chapter 2.

One large London college has been running a very successful programme for pupils from five neighbouring schools, including a Pupil Referral Unit. The specially designed programme, entitled Learning for Work, involves small group vocational work, personal skills development, a work placement, IT, and an enterprise module in which students have to research, develop and sell a product, or service, to fellow students and friends. The evaluation of the programme points to the motivational aspects of the course and to high levels of student satisfaction (Huddleston, 2000).

This type of integrated provision requires securely founded and adequately resourced partnerships of providers, who have a commitment to learners' entitlement to high quality, applied learning delivered by those with recent and relevant sector experience and within realistic learning environments.

General vocational education

We now turn to the curriculum tradition of general vocational education. The FE sector has always been the main provider of general vocational education in the UK. During the 1980s there were some developments within schools in both pre-vocational and vocational education through initiatives such as the Certificate of Pre-Vocational Education (CPVE) and the Technical and Vocational Education Initiative (TVEI) (see Pring, 1997 for a discussion). However, since the introduction of GNVQs (now replaced by other qualifications) in 1993, the involvement of schools in this area of work has increased considerably. In many parts of England and Wales, schools and colleges are in direct competition for students; the new partnership arrangements underpinning the 14–19 diploma design will be challenging for some providers since they will have to work together in order to allow all young people access to the full diploma entitlement by 2013. Unlike schools, however, colleges offer many types of vocational programme. This provision may be offered in a variety of modes: part time, full time, as a short course, face-to-face or at a distance. They are offered at a variety of levels from entry level to higher levels on the NQF. One large FE/HE college advertises its provision thus:

> The College offers a vast number of courses spanning an unrivalled breadth of subjects, both academic and vocational, covering the following areas: AS and A levels, Applied and Sports Science; Creative and Performing Arts; Information and Communication Technology; Medical, Healthcare and Vocational Science; Skills for Life; Teacher Training; Technology.

Despite schools' forays into this area of general vocational qualifications, there is nothing like the breadth of provision available that we would rightly expect to find within FE colleges.

Vocational qualifications (not NVQs)

There are still programmes leading to National and Higher National Certificates and Diplomas and other types of vocational awards that are well respected by employers, popular with students, and which are not NVQs. Examples of such awards include the BTEC suite of certificates and diplomas and those offered by OCR and City and Guilds. Some specialist awarding bodies may offer a small number of highly specific qualifications, for example those offered within the land-based sector for gamekeeping and farriery, a large number of these vocational qualifications still remain outside the NQF. Professional bodies also award vocational qualifications, as do some multinational companies such as Microsoft.

General vocational qualifications also form the technical certificates required for some apprenticeship programmes. Concern about the breadth of training on (what was then called) the Modern Apprenticeship, were raised in 1999 by the National Skills Task Force (NSTF), which recommended that all apprentices should complete a Related Vocational Qualification (RVQ). The RVQ would 'attest to their (apprentices) technical knowledge and understanding as well as an NVQ which attests to their competence' (NSTF, 1999: 41). The NSTF also highlighted the fact that only 20 per cent of apprentices were on programmes that contained mandatory periods of off-the-job training (ibid.: 33). In response, the then Department for Education and Employment (DfEE) asked the QCA to develop a range of vocationally-related qualifications, to be called 'Technical Certificates'.

These Certificates would:

- deliver the underpinning knowledge and understanding relevant to the NVQ included in the particular Modern Apprenticeship framework;
- be delivered through a taught programme of off-the-job learning;
- permit a structured approach to the teaching and assessment of the underpinning knowledge and understanding of an NVQ (or a related suite of NVQs).

(QCA, 2001)

Between 2002 and 2006, all advanced apprenticeship programmes were required to incorporate a technical certificate, but since then SSCs have been allowed to remove the qualification from their apprenticeship frameworks if they can show that underpinning knowledge can be adequately tested through the assessment procedures used for the NVQ. The demand for this has come from sectors such as hairdressing and hospitality which have argued that the technical certificate simply replicates the content of the NVQ. Given that technical certificates were intended to ensure that all advanced apprentices in all sectors had access to substantive vocational education as well as competence-based training, the freedom to remove them would appear to be a retrograde step, one which has the employers' interests in mind, rather than those of the apprentices (see Fuller and Unwin, 2003, 2004).

We now provide illustrations from the BTEC approach to vocational qualifications to show how knowledge and skills are integrated. We have chosen the BTEC First Certificate in Business and the Edexcel BTEC First Diploma in Business. These are Level 2 qualifications and represent 180 guided learning hours for the certificate, and 360 guided learning hours for the Diploma.

The BTEC Firsts in Business have been designed to:

- allow learners to acquire technical and employability skills, knowledge and understanding which are transferable and will enable individuals to meet challenging circumstances;
- enable learners to gain nationally recognised vocational qualifications to enter employment or progress to other vocational qualifications;
- assist learners already employed in the business sector to develop their underpinning knowledge and skills;
- enable course teams to develop their own innovative coursework that will enthuse and motivate learners;
- allow course teams to develop the knowledge, understanding and skills of learners to meet the needs of the business sector.

(Adapted from Edexcel, July 2006)

To gain a First Certificate, students have to successfully complete three units, one of which is compulsory (Exploring Business Purposes), the other two selected from a list of nine optional units.

You will probably be perplexed as to how this might be transformed into a scheme of work, or into individual classes, especially if your own experience has been on academic programmes. The subject specifications provided by the awarding bodies are your starting points. These have recently been redesigned to be more user friendly and student focused. Each specification comprises a number of sections:

Unit abstract: This provides some contextual information about the topic to be covered, outlines the knowledge and skills to be developed, and makes links to other units within the qualification.

Learning outcomes: This section describes what a learner should be able to 'know, understand or be able to do' upon completion of the unit.

Unit content: This may look to you more like a 'syllabus'; it identifies 'the depth and breadth of knowledge, skills and understanding needed to design and deliver a programme of learning sufficient to achieve each of the learning outcomes' (Source: Edexcel, 2006).

Grading grid: This states exactly what evidence students have to produce in order to meet the grading criteria for the unit, for example 'to achieve the first pass criterion learners need to describe a minimum of four business organisations and be able to describe their purposes, size, ownership and scale. Each should be of a different type and the selection should also cover different sizes and scale' (Source: Edexcel, ibid.). The guidance goes on to state precisely what the portfolio should include and indicates the criteria for a pass, merit or distinction grade. In every case the achievement of the higher grades of merit and distinction require the learner to apply more qualitative evidence, for example to achieve a pass grade, learners are asked 'to describe four different types of business'; to achieve a merit, learners are expected 'to compare and contrast' or 'explain', whereas to achieve a distinction grade learners are expected to demonstrate skills of evaluation.

Essential guidance for tutors: This section is particularly addressed to tutors and provides further advice on approaches to delivery, assessment, links to other units within the qualification, to other qualifications, and to National Occupational Standards, essential resources and indicative reading for learners.

Key skills: Opportunities for key skills development are signposted within the unit specifications. For example, when candidates are presenting findings on business performance they may be able to compare data from their selected case study businesses and compare them with national data, thus fulfilling some of the criteria for the numeracy key skill. Similarly, they will be able to present data in the form of charts and tables and so complete some of the IT key skill criteria. The inclusion of key skills, through an integrated approach, is part of the curricular design, although in practice this integration has been difficult to achieve. The achievement of key skills is not a requirement of BTEC qualifications, although it is encouraged. You need to ensure that you keep abreast of the content of all the specifications for which you have a teaching responsibility, including key skills, if applicable.

Reflection

You might wish to consider the ways in which you could incorporate opportunities for key skills development in some of the following vocational assignments. Remember, the key skills are: communication, application of number and information technology. The so-called wider key skills are: improving own learning and performance, working with others and problem solving.

1   Prepare a plan of the layout of the workshop indicating options for optimising use of space. Remember to consider the health and safety implications of your choices (Engineering).

2   Provide a monthly breakdown of the numbers of customers using the college restaurant, the most popular choices from the menu, the average spend per customer, the percentage of waste (Hotel and Catering).

3   Together with other members of your assignment group, prepare a presentation for the steering committee on the feasibility of offering access to the college's sports facilities to local residents on a paying basis (Leisure and Recreation).

You will already have recognised that teaching and learning on BTEC and similar vocational certificate and diploma programmes are different from those encountered on traditional academic programmes. In the majority of certificate and diploma programmes, the emphasis is on developing the skills of the learner, to enable him or her to become more self-reliant. The responsibility has to shift from the teacher to the learner but these are skills that have to be cultivated. It may be difficult for teachers who have been accustomed to 'leading from the front' to change to a more student-centred approach. Equally, it may be difficult for students to come to terms with a more flexible approach.

Here are some responses to group work from different students in the same BTEC First in Business programme; they were working together on Unit 2, 'Developing Customer Relations'. The tutor had decided to use customer service role play in order to allow learners the opportunity to practise their customer service skills. ('Delivery and assessment of the practical aspects in workplace or realistic conditions are ideal. However, where such opportunities are unavailable, simulated alternatives are acceptable. Care must be taken that learners understand what type of business in being simulated and tutors for this unit should consult with colleagues delivering other units to provide useful vocational links', Edexcel, 2006.)

> 'I really enjoyed this, it was a laugh. Baz was really going over the top, acting up and everything. Still it's better than taking notes. There should be more classes like this.'

> 'Bill (the tutor) should give us more idea what to do, I felt stupid, I don't like working in groups because I don't get on with other people and I've had some trouble with that. It's worse when you have to do this acting stuff.'

> 'I thought it was OK because Bill explained what we had to do and we had some time to prepare first, also he said how we could use this in our coursework assignment, which is always good because we are always stressing about getting the assignments in on time.'

The new diplomas

From September 2008, the 14–19 Diploma, will be available to young people in schools and colleges. This marks a major change in the curriculum on offer to this age group and on the way in which it will be delivered. Diplomas will be composite qualifications available at three levels and incorporating three elements: principal learning; additional specialist learning; generic learning (functional skills, and personal and thinking skills); and there will be the opportunity for an extended project, or similar, at all levels. The model is represented in Figure 3.3.

The content of the diplomas is being developed by Diploma Development Partnerships, which are led by the relevant SSCs and include representatives

The Model

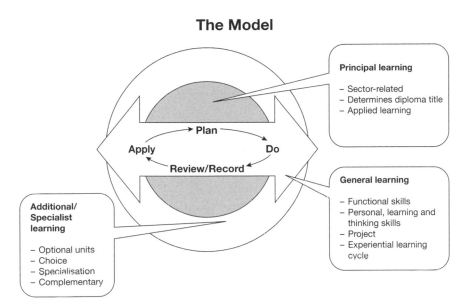

Figure 3.3 Proposed diploma model

from employers, education and schools. The principal learning includes the core diploma subject, for example, Creative and Media. This gives the diploma its title and is supposed to be aligned closely with industry standards and requirements. Content should be properly contextualised and related to current sector practice, including access to workplaces and practitioners. All diplomas will include an element of work experience.

The generic element of the diploma will include functional skills, English, ICT and maths as well as the opportunity for independent learning through an extended project, or similar piece of work appropriate to the level of the diploma. The additional specialist learning is intended to complement the principal learning and might include, for example, a GCSE in a related subject at Levels 1 and 2, or an A level at Level 3. Someone studying for a diploma in Society, Health and Development might wish to include a GCSE in science. A student taking a Level 3 diploma in Creative and Media might wish to include an A level in art and design. The model is designed for flexibility and to enable learners to combine a learning programme that suits their needs and aspirations.

Crucial to the successful delivery of these diplomas will be the partnerships between schools, colleges, training providers and employers. It will be impossible for any one institution to deliver diplomas on its own. In some areas it will be impossible for all fourteen lines of learning at all three levels to be available without recourse to some innovative delivery, including the use of Virtual Learning Environments (VLEs).

At the time of writing, partnerships have submitted their proposals to the DfES in order to be considered for the first tranche of delivery; this has been termed the Diploma Gateway process.

The first five diplomas will be available for teaching from 2008 and will include:

- ICT
- Engineering
- Creative and media
- Construction
- Society, health and development.

In 2009 a further five will become available:

- Land-based and environmental
- Manufacturing
- Hair and beauty
- Business administration and finance
- Hospitality and catering.

In 2010, the final four will come on stream:

- Travel and tourism
- Retail
- Sport and leisure
- Public services.

By 2013 it is envisaged that every 14- to 19-year-old in England should have an entitlement to study one of the fourteen diploma lines at all three levels.

A great deal is riding on these new qualifications; it is a high-risk strategy not least because it will require a wide range of providers to work together in new and different ways. The diplomas must be seen to have credibility with young people, their parents, employers and higher education. As a result of the curriculum and qualifications reform programme outlined above, it is likely that the number of young people attending college, not just between the ages of 16 and 19, but also between 14 and 19, is likely to increase over the next ten years.

NVQ/SVQs and job-specific training

FE has a long tradition of providing job-specific training for both young people and adults covering a wide range of occupational sectors. The provision of vocational training was the *raison d'être* of many early technical colleges and much of this provision was on a day-release basis. Employers generally funded this training and were sometimes represented on college advisory boards. In the main, however, employers would have to place employees on courses that were available at colleges and had very little influence over what would be provided or when or how this would be achieved. In this sense, provision was provider-led; that is, colleges offered a range of courses structured around a traditional 36-week college year and it was anticipated that demand would follow supply.

In addition to day-release provision, colleges have always provided evening classes for those wishing to pursue job-related qualifications in their own time. Many of those achieving vocational qualifications in the past have done so by attending evening classes for anything up to five years or more. This pattern has now changed and is likely to change even more given the provision within the FE White Paper (DfES, 2006b) for a more 'demand-led' system.

This section focuses specifically on the impact of NVQ/SVQs on college provision since this has introduced a significant change in the way in which teaching and learning takes place. It is important to recognise that an NVQ/SVQ is not a course of study and it is not necessary to undertake a specific training course before competences are demonstrated. NVQ/SVQs confirm that the holder possesses the competences required to carry out a specific job.

Of course, not all these qualifications are awarded through FE colleges. Assessment of candidates for the award of an NVQ/SVQ must be done through a recognised centre. Such a centre can be a workplace, a college, a training provider or a voluntary organisation. Assessment through a college does not imply that the training took place at the college but that assessment was carried out through the college. This often involves college staff, who are qualified assessors, assessing candidates in their workplaces. For example, one college located within a popular tourist town offers local guesthouses the opportunity of NVQ/SVQ assessment for their staff within the workplace. It is clear, however, that FE still remains the major provider of vocationally specific training both for NVQ/SVQs and for traditional vocational awards.

There is a considerable literature on the introduction of competence-based qualifications in the UK, much of it highly critical (see, *inter alia*, Hyland, 1994; Hodkinson and Issitt, 1995; Wolf, 1995; Raggatt and Williams, 1999; Unwin *et al.*, 2004). At the heart of the criticism is the concern that by separating qualifications from learning, the competence-based model takes us back to the Taylorist approach to work-based training in which workers were only allowed to acquire the minimum skills and knowledge required to do an immediate job.

NVQ/SVQs are unit-based qualifications. The number of units required for each qualification is set out within the specifications and will vary according to the occupation and level. A unit is the smallest part of an NVQ/SVQ for which a candidate may be awarded a certificate. In order to gain a full

NVQ/SVQ candidates must complete all the units necessary for the award. As with other awards, NVQ/SVQs are available at different levels across the NQF (see Figure 3.2).

Each unit clearly specifies what 'evidence' the candidate will need to provide in order to meet the 'performance objectives' for that unit and also the 'essential knowledge' that he or she needs to understand. In general, the successful completion of a unit requires the candidate to undertake knowledge and practical tests.

Here are some examples taken from a specification for the unit 'Contribute to Workplace Good Housekeeping' (City and Guilds, General Units G1/V1).

Evidence (some examples)

Produce evidence of cleaning the part of the work area for which you are responsible on 3 separate occasions; produce evidence of undertaking basic, routine checks of all the following types of work tools and equipment on 3 separate occasions:

- hand
- electrical
- mechanical
- pneumatic
- hydraulic.

Performance objectives (some examples)

Wear suitable personal protective equipment throughout all housekeeping and equipment maintenance activities; select and use cleaning equipment which is:

- of the right type
- suitable for the task.

Essential knowledge (some examples)

- Workplace policies and schedules for housekeeping activities and equipment maintenance;
- How to work safely when cleaning and maintaining work tools and equipment.

The assessor, who may be a college lecturer or, equally, a work-based trainer, has to confirm evidence that the candidate can carry out such tasks either in a real or simulated workshop. In the example above the specification states that: 'Evidence from simulated activities is not acceptable for this unit.' The reason is, of course, obvious.

Candidates may draw upon evidence, for example witness statements provided by workplace supervisors. Other forms of evidence may also be permissible for inclusion in a candidate's portfolio, for example, artefacts, design drawings, photographs, depending upon the nature of the award being sought. In all cases assessors must confirm that 'assessment was conducted under the specified conditions and context, and is valid, authentic, reliable, current and sufficient'.

Although NVQ/SVQs were designed as essentially work-based qualifications, many of which would be taken by adults already in employment, a large proportion of uptake has been by young people in initial training. This is not surprising since they have long been the mandatory requirements for government-supported training programmes.

Assessment methods for NVQ/SVQs include workplace observation of performance, skills tests, practical projects, assignments, written and oral questioning. Because of the need for candidates to demonstrate competence in the workplace, colleges have had to find suitable work placements for full-time students and unemployed students working towards NVQ/SVQ accreditation. This has not always been easy for colleges, particularly since there are many competing demands on employers to provide work placements. Some colleges have been able to provide realistic learning environments, for example in college restaurants, motor vehicle workshops, or hairdressing salons. For other colleges it has been much more difficult to provide a simulated work environment. The former FEFC (2001: 19) indicated that in engineering this may be more difficult, since 'the quality of accommodation and equipment across the sector is very mixed. In some cases, the facilities are modern and the equipment good. In other cases, accommodation is less satisfactory and/or machinery and equipment are out of date. This applies to both computer-aided engineering and basic engineering.' It is interesting to note that in reviewing the delivery of the new applied GCSEs in schools in 2004, Ofsted raised similar concerns (Ofsted, 2004). Some employers are also doubtful about the validity of assessment undertaken in a simulated environment.

NVQ/SVQs are not dependent upon any particular mode, duration or location of study. This is one of several significant changes which colleges have had to face in reorganising their provision for those wishing to acquire NVQ/SVQs. Candidates may claim credit for competence previously acquired providing that they can furnish sufficient evidence to demonstrate such competence. This process is known as the accreditation of prior learning (APL). Colleges show enormous diversity in their capacities to handle APL effectively.

The development of competence-based curricula in FE colleges has highlighted the need for some significant changes of approach in course delivery. These may be summarised as follows:

- the need for more flexible and responsive provision which can accommodate individual student needs;

- the development of learning support materials and learning resource centres which students can access individually according to their own needs, with or without the help of a lecturer;
- the modularisation of curricula, although this is by no means universal, to enable students to 'pick and mix' units which they require in order to complete an NVQ/SVQ, rather than having to follow a complete programme;
- the development of partnerships with employers in order to ensure an adequate supply of work placements for students;
- the design of simulated work environments within colleges, for example, college restaurants, hairdressing salons, vehicle maintenance workshops, to allow students to demonstrate competence under the same conditions and pressures as they would in employment;
- the need to develop adequate systems of guidance, advice and counselling to enable students to access the appropriate parts of the curriculum;
- the incorporation of support structures to enable students to build portfolios of evidence and to identify learning opportunities within the workplace and within the college.

These may, of course, be seen as pre-conditions for the so-called flexible college.

Reflection

- How does the teacher juggle these possibly competing demands?
- How can the potential learners seek impartial and informed advice?
- How does modularisation (or unitisation) of the curriculum affect the teaching timetable?
- What are the implications for teachers of a modularised (or unitised) curriculum?
- If students are allowed to 'pick and mix' units, how can they build a coherent programme of study?

The fact that such questions, and many more, were raised by the introduction of competence-based approaches suggests that there are, and have been, some significant challenges to colleges in introducing new qualifications. Because NVQ/SVQs are specified in terms of outcomes rather than inputs and can be assessed in any context where competence can be appropriately demonstrated, colleges do not have the monopoly in job-specific training. Colleges are in competition with private training providers and with companies' in-house training programmes. Cost may be an important factor when employers decide where to place their training contracts. In an ongoing climate of competition, colleges are competing not only with companies and private training providers but also with each other. The DfES in England is certainly in favour of such competition:

> To promote dynamism and innovation we will encourage new high quality providers into the FE sector. New competition arrangements will make it easier for new providers to enter the system, where significant expansion of high quality provision is needed. This will enable good existing colleges to expand, federate or create a Trust, independent voluntary sector training providers to enter the sector, or wholly new institutions to be established depending on needs.
>
> (DfES, 2006b: 10)

Higher education (HE) and advanced studies

Higher education generally refers to those advanced courses usually, though not exclusively, provided by a university or by its constituent or associated institutions. Advanced in these contexts refers to courses which are deemed to be beyond A level, or equivalent, standard. Although some FE colleges have always provided a certain amount of advanced work, for example through Higher National Diploma (HND) and Higher National Certificate (HNC) programmes, the provision of degree-level courses is relatively recent. Nevertheless, some colleges have expanded their provision rapidly in this area through franchising arrangements with universities.

It is not the purpose of this book to debate the nature and form of the HE curriculum; this has been considered elsewhere and there is an established literature on the subject. The intention is to highlight the developments that have occurred within the FE sector in its relationship with HE institutions.

Squires (1987) suggests that 'the pattern of undergraduate studies in the UK depends on two things: where one studies and what one studies' (Squires, 1987: 130). He then goes on to explore some of the features of academic and professional courses and draws attention to developments in the modularisation of some undergraduate programmes. In those universities where modularisation has been whole-heartedly embraced, the course unit or module becomes the essential element of the programme. In its most extreme form students may 'pick and mix' across a very wide range of units to build a whole programme. Each unit may be assessed and accredited on completion until a full degree has been built up. There are obviously various stages along the continuum from what Squires has described as a 'holistic' to an 'aggregative' curriculum.

One of the reasons for drawing attention to these developments is to suggest that once the curriculum has been unitised in this way then the place in which it is studied becomes less important, provided there is adequate quality control. The Open University allows students to study through a variety of means and in widely dispersed locations. The unifying factor is, of course, the content of programmes, which is centrally regulated. By devolving delivery in this way, universities can reduce their costs, or rather not incur further costs, while increasing student numbers.

The delivery of some parts of undergraduate programmes in colleges has enabled students to access the HE curriculum locally. Relationships between colleges and HE institutions may vary. In some cases colleges are delivering the first two years of a degree programme, with the third and fourth years being delivered in the university. In other cases, colleges may deliver the whole of an undergraduate programme. There may be franchising arrangements in place or colleges may have their own programmes accredited by an HE institution. Sometimes the HE institution may not be local to the college. There are further examples where colleges may be running whole, or parts of, degree programmes from several different HE institutions.

Where FE colleges are delivering programmes through franchising arrangements then curriculum content will be prescribed by the HE institution. There will also be control over the staffing of programmes and other resource issues. Standards of assessment will be monitored and verified, and examinations will be set by the university. Those involved in teaching such programmes in colleges may be located within a separate department or unit specialising in HE courses. This will not always be the case, however. HE courses may fall within the remit of a Department of General Education or within a curriculum area, for example, Business and Management.

Students on HE programmes may have come through special access courses, which the college offers, and many of them will be mature entrants. As teachers you will need to consider these factors in developing your teaching strategy. If you return to Sharon, the HE student described in Chapter 2, you will see that she has particular learning needs as an HE student, some of which derive from a lack of confidence.

There is a continuing debate concerning the role of FE in HE provision. Just over ten years ago, some FE practitioners argued that colleges should concentrate on the delivery of high-quality vocational education and training and that they should 'not turn themselves into universities' (*TES*, 9 February 1996). However, the picture has now changed quite substantially in many colleges. The targets set for increased participation of adults in higher education (29 per cent in 2005, with an aspiration for 40 per cent by 2020) (Leitch, 2006) mean that growth will have to come via the FE rather than solely through the HE route. The FE White Paper (DfES, 2006b: 7) has reinforced this message:

> We will strengthen the role of colleges and training providers in providing HE programmes linked to their economic and social mission. We will develop colleges' role in regions where access to HE institutions is limited, through the lifelong network learning programme . . . We will

prioritise the development of some larger college providers of HE as centres of excellence, with a major part to play in developing work based HE programmes for employers.

As shown in Chapter 1, another development which has resulted in more HE level provision within the FE sector has been the introduction of foundation degrees (see Webb *et al.*, 2005; and Smith and Betts 2003, for critiques). It is estimated that in 2006–7 over 60,000 students were registered on these programmes (www.hefce.ac.uk/pubs/hefce/2007/07_03). Courses cover a wide range of subjects such as: aircraft engineering; classroom assistance; commercial music; fashion design technology; hospitality; retail technology and logistics; and sports science. They are intended to be flexible. Many students study while in employment and the degree includes an element of work-based learning.

Given the changes outlined above, it seems likely that FE's involvement in the delivery of Level 4, and above, provision is likely to increase. This poses a significant challenge for staff recruitment and development.

General adult educaton

Alan Tuckett, the Director of NIACE, has argued that:

> Adult learners are the core business of the further education sector, yet it is not designed around their needs. The idea of a distinctive adult curriculum is often contested, since adults have such a diversity of learning interests. Here it is taken to mean their minimum entitlement and the full range of processes supporting effective adult study. Over the next decade, with two in three jobs to be filled by adults, with larger numbers of older workers, as well as extended retirement for many, the work of the sector will need to be re-balanced better to meet adults' needs. Since adults mainly learn part-time, often episodically, occasionally on day release or in other intensive spells, and for a diversity of purposes, the system needs to increase the responsiveness of its offer, and its capacity to recognise achievement gained in a range of ways. A key task will be the development of a unit-based qualifications system based on credit, to recognise valid and meaningful achievement in learning, wherever it is gained.
>
> (Tuckett, 2005: 1)

The term 'adult' as applied to education is not easy to define. For some it has connotations of anything beyond the phase of compulsory schooling, whereas for others it may be regarded as post-initial education, that is the period beyond initial HE. Some institutions may use age 25 to distinguish between ordinary and mature students, whereas for funding purposes 19 is frequently regarded as the difference between youth and adult status.

The scope of adult education has always been, and is, extremely wide. There are some institutions which exist primarily to teach adults, for example, the Workers' Educational Association (WEA), the Open University, and adult education services – where they still exist – provided by local authorities. (For a more detailed discussion of the history of adult education provision see Fieldhouse and Associates, 1996.) Adult education may also be engaged in through a whole range of informal mechanisms, including, for example, church groups and voluntary organisations. In its widest sense, adult education may be described as any form of education or training in which adults engage. The current interest in the fostering and development of lifelong learning has focused some attention on the ways in which, and the means by which, adults engage in continuing education and personal and professional development. It is worth noting that many universities across the UK have begun to rename their adult education and continuing education departments as Institutes of Lifelong Learning.

The concept of lifelong learning came to public attention in 1994 when it formed a major part of Jacques Delors' European Commission (EC) paper on competitiveness and economic growth (CEC, 1994) and the EC declared 1996 the European Year of Lifelong Learning. Since then, governments around the world have urged their citizens to become lifelong learners. Field (2000: viii–ix), in a detailed critique of lifelong learning, bemoans the way in which 'lifelong learning has been used by policymakers as little more than a modish repackaging of rather conventional policies for post-16 education and training, with little that is new or innovative'. He continues,

> This tendency to wrap up existing practice in a more colourful phrase can also be seen in the rush by providers to claim their adherence to lifelong learning: and even professorial titles have all been subjected to this rebranding. The educational result is a kind of linguistic hyperinflation, in which the term is constantly devalued.
>
> (ibid.)

Field goes on to argue that although politicians have largely promoted lifelong learning as being essential for economic prosperity, the 'silent explosion in informal and self-directed learning' has 'only partly been driven by economic changes' and has equally as much to do with 'transformations in peoples lives and identities' (ibid.). (See also Coffield, 1999 and Johnston, 1999 for critiques of lifelong learning.)

One way in which the Labour government has responded to the lifelong learning agenda is through the creation of Learndirect, which is the operating name of the University for Industry (UfI). In 1998, the then DfEE published its prospectus for UfI, which it saw as a UK-wide network of learning centres, many of which would be based in colleges, public libraries, schools and other existing sites of learning (DfEE, 1998). A pilot version of UfI was established in Tyne and Wear in the North-east of England where 35 learning centres were linked to a central database which could be accessed through a call centre and a web site. The initiative attracted criticism for:

- using the name 'university'
- using the term 'industry' which suggested its function was purely economic
- setting up yet another quango which would take money away from existing providers.

An example of the media reaction to the UfI name is the following extract from an editorial column in the *Times Higher Education Supplement* in April 1998:

> The first obvious thing about it is that it is no university. It is designed to trawl the highways and byways, using all the modern means of public persuasion, to draw in those who have learned little and like it less. Only very much second and later is it to help people who are already skilled but seek retraining . . . Tackling educational failure and skill shortages is admirable, but calling the project a university risks debasing the currency which the government has said it wishes to defend.
>
> (*THES*, 1998, p. 11)

The tone of the THES's comments does, of course, say a great deal about the academic vocational divide in the UK and social class. In response to criticisms about the name, the government relaunched UfI as Learndirect. An example of a Learndirect centre is Optimum, based in a residential suburb of Derby and linked to Derby Tertiary College. Optimum is open seven days a week, including four evenings, and has full disabled access including facilities for the visually and hearing impaired.

Other notable government responses to lifelong learning have been the introduction of Individual Learning Accounts (ILAs) and the Union Learning Fund. Like Learndirect, ILAs and the Union Learning Fund represent a human capital approach to education and training by placing responsibility on the individual to improve their skills and knowledge. This approach has been criticised for failing to address the deep structural, social and cultural problems which prevent people from participating in formalised education and training (see Coffield, 1999). They also reflect a view held by UK governments since the late 1980s, that individuals will be encouraged to engage in more learning if they can operate as 'customers' in an education and training marketplace. An earlier example of a policy which attempted this was the failed Training Credits initiative aimed at 16- to 19-year-olds (see Unwin, 1993, and Hodkinson *et al.*, 1996, for critiques). In November, 2001, the BBC Radio 4 programme, File on 4, broadcast a damning exposé of financial mismanagement at the heart of the ILA infrastructure. It was found that some providers had taken advantage of the system, causing the DfES to immediately suspend ILAs, while the police were brought in to investigate allegations of fraudulent practice. This debacle highlights the dangers inherent in presenting learning as just another commodity. Sadly, many of the learners whom ILAs were supposed to help may be even less persuaded to join the lifelong learning bandwagon than ever.

The Union Learning Fund has a much more positive history than ILAs. Established in 1998 by then the DfEE, the fund has enabled trade unions to train learning representatives who provide advice and guidance to potential learners in the workplace, and to develop a range of collaborative projects to stimulate participation in education and training. The Union of Textile Workers, for example, has used funds to develop an on-site learning resource centre in a Staffordshire manufacturing company, working in partnership with a local FE college, the Open College Network, and other related agencies. Trade Unions have, of course, a long history of providing educational opportunities for their members.

As shown in Chapter 1, adult education provision in colleges now encompasses the Skills for Life strategy providing help with basic skills and ESOL, while, at the same time, there has been a retraction in the number of places available for adults who want to learn for pleasure. It will be clear from this diverse picture that it is quite impossible to talk about a single adult education curriculum. It is perhaps more useful to think about the ways in which adults learn and the strategies that we as teachers might develop in order to help them learn more effectively. These themes are returned to in Chapters 5 and 6.

Reflection

If you return to the students in Chapter 2, you will see that several of them are following a mixed curricular model. This means that their experiences as learners may be quite different in different parts of the programme. This is not just because they may be taught by different staff but because the content and, more importantly, the pedagogy of the separate elements may be different. For example, Sharon is an HE student, but she is also a mature student. Gary is following a general vocational education programme with some job-specific elements. You might like to consider the programmes being followed by the other students. To what extent are they having a mixed curricular experience?

Conclusion

This chapter has attempted to outline the range and diversity of the curriculum post-16. As a teacher you will be constantly re-examining your position in relation to these differing curricular models. It is not only you as a teacher – your students too may be exposed to a range of curricular models.

Part II

Teaching and learning

Chapter 4

The process of learning

Introduction

We begin this chapter with three comments on teaching and learning:

> When adults teach and learn in one another's company, they find themselves engaging in a challenging, passionate, and creative activity. The acts of teaching and learning – the creation and alteration of our beliefs, values, actions, relationships, and social forms that result from this – are ways in which we realise our humanity.
>
> (Brookfield, 1986: 1)

> The constructs a learner brings to the learning environment are interwoven with personal meaning and value, are frequently implicit and deeply embedded. Any acquisition of new knowledge will entail adjustments to this system and if personal horizons of understanding are to be extended, new learning must be assimilated with what is already known.
>
> (Harkin, Turner and Dawn, 2001: 37)

> ... teaching and learning are primarily social and cultural rather than individual and technical activities; they should therefore be studied in authentic settings; this in turn means addressing their complexity, through a cultural perspective on the interrelationships between individual dispositions and agency, and institutional and structural contexts.
>
> (Colley et al., 2003: 3)

In order to meet the challenge of teaching in the FE sector, it is essential to have some knowledge of the different theories that help us to understand how people learn. We began Chapter 1 with the statement that 'teaching and learning are situated activities' and, hence, any discussion of teaching and learning must always pay attention to the nature of the context in which it takes place and the wider context of which it forms a part. At the same time, teachers much take account of the contexts within which students live and work, their personal biographies, and their dispositions towards learning. As with any space in which people gather together, colleges are sites of conflict, power and control. Teachers wield considerable power over their students, but are themselves subjected to powerful controlling mechanisms that reflect the ethos and values of the college in which they work. Students too can exert power, particularly if they are paying substantial fees for their courses and some may choose to create problems for particular teachers if they regard themselves as being unfairly treated.

Before we continue, we need to say something about terminology. The terms 'teaching' and 'learning' are used in everyday parlance, but the terms 'learning' and 'learner' have come to have much more prominence over the past few years due to a recognition that a great deal of learning takes place outside formal education and training settings and that individuals continue to learn throughout life. The historical narrative that has led us from the notion that education was the preserve of the privileged classes learning in a small number of exclusive institutions to the concept of learning as a socially situated, ever-present process in which everyone participates, is perceived to be one of empowerment and progression (see Unwin, 2008, forthcoming). While we would agree that a much more inclusive concept of learning is to be welcomed, we have to be careful that we remain alert to the potential pitfalls. A key concern is that if the term 'learning' is substituted for the word 'education', then people will focus much more on process and give less attention to the nature of what is being learned. Secondly, while, of course, individuals do a great deal of learning without the aid of a teacher (in the formal sense of that role), teachers are crucially important in helping and pushing learners to go beyond their immediate comfort zones. Throughout this book we have tended to use the word 'student' rather than 'learner' to signify that most of what we are concerned with here is the relationship between teachers and their students. You will have your own views on these issues and might reflect on the terms you and your colleagues use.

Another term that requires attention is 'pedagogy'. This term is often used interchangeably with teaching and comes from the Ancient Greek word *'paidagogas'*, which relates to the 'leading' (*agogas*) and 'instruction' of children by slaves (*pais*). The term has come to encompass the complexities of the teaching/learning relationship. Miriam Zukas (2006: 71), who with Janice Malcolm has examined pedagogical approaches in relation to lifelong learning, argues that pedagogy is much more than the restricted notion that teaching consists of a bag of techniques and tricks:

> Instead of conceptualizing pedagogy as teachers' actions inside class-rooms to bring about learning, such that teaching is a decontextualised transfer of knowledge, skills and practice to the acquisitive learner, we have tried to escape this teaching/learning polarization by conceiving of pedagogy as encompassing 'a critical understanding of the social, policy

and institutional context, as well as a critical approach to content and process of the educational/training transaction'.

(Zukas and Malcolm, 2002: 215)

The quotation refers to 'a critical approach to content and process'. A major figure in the promotion of the concept of 'critical pedagogy' was the Brazilian educator, Paolo Freire (1974), who identified three stages of learning: task-related; learning about personal relationships; and 'praxis'. This latter term relates to Freire's belief that learning should develop individuals' capacity to examine their surroundings critically and, hence, lead to some form of action. Others have argued for pedagogical approaches and 'democratic practices' that take account of student diversity in terms of social class, gender, ethnicity, sexual orientation, and age (see, *inter alia*, Clarke, 2002; Sachs, 2001; Mcleod *et al.*, 1993; Shain and Gleeson, 1999; Giroux, 1991). Bathmaker and Avis's (2005: 16) research into the experiences of trainee FE teachers led them to argue for a more realistic and pragmatic approach – one that sees critical pedagogy as an aspiration which recognises the 'complexity, contradictions and messiness of classroom practices'.

The following comment from Mary Hamilton (2006: 136), who writes from the perspective of the way adults acquire and use literacy, brings some of these ideas together and poses a challenge to all teachers. She argues that we need:

pedagogies that keep in touch with change, that are responsive, exploratory, that ask questions, that are prepared to constantly challenge the institutional walls we build around learning, not just inviting others in but going out, barefoot into the everyday world.

This discussion of the complexities that lie behind the creation and use of pedagogical approaches poses considerable challenges to attempts by governments and others to reduce teaching to a simplified list of 'skills' or techniques (see Edwards, 2001). As we saw in Chapter 4, the government's standards-based approach to FE teacher training was initially seen by many in the sector as inadequate, though the latest version suggests that a much more considered attempt has been made to move beyond mere technique. For example, in Domain A (Professional values and practice), standard AK 4.1 calls for teachers to 'know and understand' the 'Principles, frameworks and theories which underpin good practice in learning and teaching' (LLUK, 2007: 8). Gleeson (2005: 242), drawing on evidence from the ESRC's Learning Cultures in Further Education project (see James and Biesta, 2007), stresses that individual teachers should be treated as professionals and, hence, encouraged to pursue their own ways of working with students.

We return to these standards in the conclusion and in Chapter 5.

The study and development of pedagogy has a troubled history in the UK, whereas in many other European countries it is given much greater importance.

The leading historian of education Brian Simon (1999) traces this back to the view in English public schools in the nineteenth century that teachers were there to socialise their upper and middle-class pupils. The teachers came from the same backgrounds as the pupils and this, accompanied by a degree from Oxford or Cambridge, was sufficient qualification for the role. In terms of FE, as shown in Chapter 1, it is only relatively recently that government has required all teachers in colleges to have a teaching qualification. The approach to teacher training for FE in the UK also differs from that of some other European countries where closer attention is paid to developing pedagogical approaches that are appropriate for specific disciplines, including vocational and practical subjects. Regardless of whether you are training to teach catering or hairdressing in the UK as opposed to, say, mathematics or English literature, you will study on the same generic course. Clearly, all teachers, regardless of their field of expertise, need to share a common core of pedagogical expertise, but there has been concern for some time that FE teacher training does not pay enough attention to what might be termed 'practical learning'.

In his study of community colleges in the United States, Grubb *et al.* (1999: 98) also found a neglect of what he refers to as 'occupational teaching', other than cursory references to 'hands-on learning and project-based instruction'. He argues that such teaching is 'rich and complex' with many competencies to master, including: 'manual and visual abilities, problem solving, and interpersonal skills as well as conventional linguistic and mathematical abilities' (ibid.: 99). In the best examples, Grubb *et al.* (ibid.) found that vocational (or occupational) teachers used a much more holistic approach than their academic colleagues, drawing on students' own experience, varying the types of task and making connections between what was being learned and the workplace.

The characteristics of learning

As discussed in Chapter 2, you could be teaching students whose ages range from as young as 14 to those in advanced old age, all of whom will have spent some years being taught in other educational institutions and learning in informal settings, and possibly in their places of work. You will, therefore, be confronted with people who have a great deal of experience as learners, and that experience will be of a particularly personal nature. For some of your students, their learning experiences may have been entirely pleasurable, whereas for others learning may be equated with anxiety and even pain. You will meet students who lack confidence as learners and many who find it difficult to know how to learn for themselves without being totally dependent on a teacher. The nature of a person's prior learning experience has a profound effect on their approach and attitude to further learning activity. As such, teachers do not start with a clean sheet. It may seem unnecessary to point out that people, whether they are teenagers or adults, learn in different ways, but it is a truism whose implications can be lost in the hectic whirl of the average teaching day. Just as your students will approach their learning in different ways, you too will have developed your own strategies for acquiring knowledge and understanding and for learning new tasks. That very personal approach to learning will influence your approach to, and style of, teaching.

Reflection

Give some thought to the following questions and try to answer them as honestly as possible. You could also try them out on a friend, partner or member of your family.

1   What was the last thing you learned?
2   Do you attend a regular class of any kind, for example, keep-fit, camera club, local history? If you do, why do you attend and how did you get started?
3   Do you enjoy learning? Do you, for example, enjoy learning from books, listening to lectures, watching experts, finding out answers for yourself?
4   Do you consider yourself to be a good learner? How would you define a good learner?
5   Given your answer to question 4, were you a good learner at school? Have you improved as a learner since leaving school?
6   Is there anything which prevents you from learning?

In answering the questions above, you may have revealed aspects of your persona as an adult learner that even you find surprising. The last question, for example, may have brought forward a certain personal barrier to learning that you have not articulated before.

Your answers may also reveal something about your own personal definition of what learning means. You might, for example, agree with the 'behaviourists' who say that, in order to claim learning has taken place, a person's behaviour has to change (see Skinner, 1968). The 'behaviourist' school of thought was pre-eminent in the 1950s and 1960s, particularly in the USA through the work of B.F. Skinner, and had a great influence on workplace training and the programmed learning approach adopted in correspondence courses. Indeed, the competence-based approach (discussed in Chapters 3 and 6) has been criticised as being a return to the techniques of behaviourism. What the 'behaviourists' overlooked (a result of which they are now seen to be the 'bad guys' of learning theory) is the contribution and agency of the learner.

Kolb, whose work has been influential in adult education and workplace training, defines learning as 'the process whereby knowledge is created through the transformation of experience' (Kolb, 1984: 41). His 'learning cycle' claims that learners progress through four stages – observation and reflection; generalisation and abstract conceptualisation; active experimentation; and concrete experience – each of which can be entered first, on their learning journey. Although praised for its contribution to the development of learning theory, Kolb's model has also been criticised for being too simplistic. For example, Jarvis (1987) has pointed out:

> consider the situation where a person is reading a complex mathematical tome and is involved in abstract conceptualisation from the outset: the next stage of the learning process might be reflection rather than active experimentation and so the arrows would need to point in both directions. In addition, Schön (1983, pp. 49–69) discusses the idea of reflection-in action in which they occur almost simultaneously. Hence there may be stages of Kolb's cycle that are not sequential.
>
> (Jarvis, 1987: 18)

Despite the flaws in his model, however, Kolb's key contribution is his emphasis on the central importance to learning of experience. There is a general consensus among adult learning theorists that the experiences that adults gain during their lives play an important part in any learning activity on which they embark. Those experiences can have both a positive and negative effect. They can help adults contextualise and conceptualise new information, but experience can also hinder learning by reminding adults of past failures. The recognition that adults learn in different ways and that each adult comes to learning with a unique set of experiences has contributed to the development of the theory of 'experiential learning', echoes of which are to be found in the work of Piaget and the American educationalist John Dewey (see Piaget, 1970 and Dewey, 1938). In its simplest form, experiential learning recognises that adults approach any learning activity with some preconceived idea about what it is they are about to try and learn. This is because of the wide range of experience they already have, so they do not approach learning with a totally blank mind. A great deal of teaching, in all sectors of education, undervalues this prior experience in learners, and tends to follow what Freire called the 'banking' concept of education:

> Education thus becomes an act of depositing, in which the students are the depositories and the teacher is the depositer. Instead of communicating, the teacher issues the communiques and makes deposits which the students patiently receive, memorise, and repeat.
>
> (Freire, 1974: 58)

Although the role of the teacher in FE may be constrained by the prescriptive nature of much of the curriculum, and, particularly, by the emphasis on the assessment of predetermined outcomes, a recognition that learning is a highly personalised activity should guide the teaching and learning process. Indeed, it could be argued that many of the developments in the FE world, such as the modularisation of courses, competence-based qualifications, open and flexible learning, and the redefinition of the student as a 'consumer' of learning, necessitate teaching styles that are largely learner-centred and experiential in emphasis. The danger in treating students as consumers, however, is that the 'product' (for example, a module or a qualification) they are 'buying' becomes more important than the learning process. Whether they are learning on their own or in groups, students should not be seen as, or even allowed to be, simply passive participants.

For some FE teachers, the promotion and advocacy of learner-centred and flexible approaches to teaching and learning by management are to be viewed with suspicion and even cynicism, as Wilmot and McLean found when they evaluated one college's attempts to introduce flexible learning:

> The thread that runs through teachers' discussion about flexible learning is that it is being promoted for non-educational reasons. Several teachers feel that flexible learning is an educational justification for an economic measure. An important observation among teachers is that encouraging students to become self-motivated is not a cheap option. The economic pressure for larger class sizes and shorter class contact time militates against workshop style delivery – and not for it. Likewise economic pressures leading to less contact time with students may reduce opportunity for supervised discovery methods of learning, which take more time – as one teacher observed: 'Nothing can be done more quickly than telling students all the answers' . . . They (teachers) are not opposed to flexible methods which enhance the process of guiding the students to more independence, but there are two sources of tension between teachers and managers. First, teachers are anxious that management's priority of cost-effectiveness will mean that flexible learning is interpreted in ways that are not educationally desirable. Secondly, teachers point out that management do not directly observe student responses to flexible learning styles and, at times, evince unwillingness to accept that some independent learning strategies do not result in positive outcomes for students.
>
> (Wilmot and McLean, 1994: 103)

A question of age: the concept of adulthood

You may be surprised by the references to adult learners and adult learning when we began this chapter by acknowledging the fact that you could be teaching people as young as 14. If you were teaching in a school, you might regard all students up to the age of 18 as children and would probably, therefore, turn to theories of how children learn for some insight before preparing to teach. People mature differently and there are some 12-year-olds who demonstrate greater sophistication as learners than many twice or even three times as old. Colleges of FE have always seen themselves as being different to schools in a number of ways, but a key difference is in their attitude to students. The vast majority of students in colleges have left the compulsory stage of education and entered the non-compulsory world in which they will be required to take responsibility for their own learning. Although, in reality, significant numbers of students in the 16–19 age bracket may have been persuaded to attend college by their parents, from the college's point of view they have chosen to attend as opposed to being obliged to attend by the state. The following quotations from college prospectuses illustrate this:

> 'We treat our students as adults who want to take responsibility for their own lives and who will thrive in the supportive and lively atmosphere of the college.'
>
> (Sixth form college)

> 'The college prides itself on creating an adult atmosphere in which all students are treated with respect and seen as individuals with individual needs and aspirations. In return, we ask our students to behave responsibly and make the most of their opportunities at college.'
>
> (College of art and technology)

That colleges actively promote themselves as being 'adult oriented' reflects their appreciation of the fact that young people in the 16–19 age bracket, who could continue their post-16 education in schools, are attracted to FE colleges precisely because they want to get away from the 'child-oriented' ethos of their secondary education. As they enter the second half of their teenage years, these young people will be developing a sense of self which, according to Rory Kidd (an influential writer on adult learning), 'is essential to all learning' (Kidd, 1973: 127). Attending college offers young people the chance to develop this sense of self within a context that allows social interaction with people of all ages. It is not surprising, then, that colleges devote considerable resources to ensuring that the social and student support facilities they provide are of a high enough standard to encourage social interaction in addition to that which takes place in the formal learning situation. For the more mature students in a college, development of a sense of self may also be a central feature of their college experience, particularly if they are returning to learning and studying for the first time in a number of years. In their research with American women mature students in HE, Belenky et al. (1986) asked these women to try and describe how they saw themselves. One woman said, 'I don't know . . . No one has told me yet what they thought of me' (p. 31).

Reflection

It might be useful at this point to revisit the vignettes in Chapter 2 and consider the ways in which the development of a sense of self applies to those students. Consider these questions:

1   How might Jonathan's parents affect his personal development?
2   How might Sharon overcome her self-consciousness about her age?
3   How could Grace be helped to transfer with confidence to the college?
4   Will Tom's experiences at college affect his attitudes towards school?

In Chinese culture, there is a tradition which says that people cannot be classed as adults until they are married. In the UK, the legal system has a curiously confused approach to adulthood. For example, a 16-year-old can marry but cannot vote, drive a car or be served with alcohol in a public place. Employers, too, often display somewhat illogical attitudes to age in their recruitment strategies. For example, some employers advertise for experienced and skilled people yet only consider applicants under the age of 35, whereas others categorise all 16- to 19-year-olds as lacking enough maturity. Given the spread of student age in an FE college, you could find you are teaching people a great deal older than yourself one day, followed by a day when your students are very close to your own age or the same age as your children.

Younger learners

As explained in Chapter 1, colleges in England are now having to make provision for students as young as 14. There are dangers in separating out 'young learners' for special attention. As Griffin (1993: 23) explains, 'Youth/ adolescence remains a powerful cultural and ideological category through which adult society constructs a specific age stage as simultaneously strange and familiar.' Adults criticise young people for behaving badly while, at the same time, reminding themselves that they probably behaved in the same way when they were teenagers. In the 1950s and 1960s, radical forces in society, including the civil rights movement in America, the student riots in Paris, the huge growth in youth consumerism, and the close links between music and drug-taking led to young people being defined as a social problem (see Furlong and Cartmel, 1997, for a detailed discussion). Economic prosperity gave young people the financial means to indulge their interests and greater leisure time than had been enjoyed by their parents. Although the economic crisis of the late 1970s and early 1980s put a stop to the relatively smooth transition from school to work that teenagers had been enjoying in the previous two decades, the importance of identifying oneself as part of a youth culture had been firmly established. We see this continuing today with the importance young people place on having the right make of mobile phone and designer clothes, and the means to go clubbing, even if that means getting into serious financial debt. Furlong and Cartmel (1997: 61) explain that, 'In late modernity, the visual styles adopted by young people through the consumption of clothing are regarded as having become increasingly central to the establishment of identity and to peer relations.' They stress, however, that although this consumerism is evident across all social classes, not everyone has the financial means to keep up with the latest fashions, resulting in a pattern of both financial and cultural exclusion.

The way in which many teenage students in full-time education service their consumer needs is by working on a part-time basis, sometimes as much as 20 hours per week. We know from research that many 16- to 19-year-olds work part-time, and many have some work experience from the age of 14, so that 'earning and learning' has become the common experience for young people (Hodgson and Spours, 2001: 386). The massive growth of the service sector in the UK has benefited from a willing army of young, part-time workers whose identity shifts, often on a daily basis, between student, employee and consumer. Service sector employers can offer flexible hours, the possibility of working long shifts to earn extra money, and employment close to home. And employers will often demand little in the way of prior experience or qualifications (see Lipsig-Mumme, 1997).

For teenagers concerned to earn just enough money to cover their social life and mobile phone bills, such jobs are very attractive. The implications of this shift in meaning of the term 'full-time student' are considerable. Teachers in schools and colleges alike are finding that they cannot assume that young people will devote their time outside the classroom to homework or that they will be alert enough to pay attention in class. Some teachers are trying to solve these problems by making use of their students' work experience in, for example, the development of key skills, or as the basis for assignment work. What is clear is that where once colleges relied on young people using their 'free' periods to continue their studies in a self-directed manner, they now have to acknowledge that this time is more likely to be spent on the till in the local supermarket.

The nature and scope of young people's life chances are largely dependent on their family background, current level of educational attainment, gender, ethnicity and geographical location. As the work of Furlong and Cartmel (1997) and Hodkinson et al. (1996) has shown, young people's lives do not generally follow the neat linear pattern envisaged by policymakers. Their 'horizons for action', to use Hodkinson et al.'s term, may expand or constrict, sometimes through their choice and sometimes because of circumstances beyond their control. And as Evans (1998: 20) points out, 'Young adults may be caught in disjunctions and contradictions of policies which do not recognise the interplay of the private and public domains and are based on invalid assumptions about common characteristics and needs of age ranges.' For the FE teacher, it is worth remembering that, as Furlong and Cartmel (1997: 41) explain, youth is a 'period of semi-dependency which forms a bridge between the total dependence of childhood and the independence of adulthood'. It is a time of great experimentation and indulgence, but it can also be a time of great anxiety.

Teenagers can find themselves homeless as a result of family breakdown, they may be coming to terms with having suffered sexual and/or physical abuse, they may be single parents, and they may be responsible for the care of a parent or sibling. As Harkin *et al.* (2001: 59) point out, 'We know that educational achievement is likely to be as much the product of environmental factors as of any innate tendency to a particular learning style or type of intelligence.' The instabilities of modern life can catapult teenagers into a more adult role than they would wish, or are capable of performing.

As highlighted in Chapter 3, developments in ICLT mean that many young people are used to using the Internet as a means to acquire information, and are skilled in word processing. Such assumptions can, however, be misleading for teachers who may find that a significant proportion of their young students have only really used computers to play games. In addition, the reliance on the Internet that some young people have developed for gathering information may have had a restricting influence on their ability to think critically or to study subjects in depth. Although the use of ICLT has to be handled with care, these new technologies also offer considerable potential for aiding learner autonomy, for delivering ongoing feedback and, through the use of email and web-based chat rooms, for more creative types of group interaction. Young people will expect ICLT to play a considerable part in their learning experience at college.

In their research into young people's experiences in FE, Bloomer and Hodkinson (1997: 61) developed the concept of the 'learning career' which they define as 'the development of a student's dispositions to learning over time'. These 'dispositions' are affected by experience both within and outside college, but Bloomer and Hodkinson (ibid.) found that the vast majority of the young people they studied were surprised at just how much their dispositions changed during their time in FE. Although, for some young people, the extent and type of transformation they experience as learners will be influenced by their previous life history, in the main, the pattern of one's learning career was not wholly predictable. Some of the many factors which Bloomer and Hodkinson (ibid.) found contributed to changing dispositions to learning were:

- examination results
- new teachers
- fellow students in a class
- course content

- course assessment
- learning activities
- college resources
- course availability
- course status
- financial circumstances
- job opportunities
- access to advice.

Bloomer and Hodkinson (ibid.: 79) conclude that, 'For those entering FE from school, it is a period of maturation, of unfolding and developing personal identity, of transition, transformation and change' (see also Hodkinson and Bloomer, 2000).

Teenagers and young adults can find that being a student does not sit well with their life outside college. There are a number of difficult issues with which young people may have to grapple:

- personal identity and life goals
- sexual orientation
- the generation gap with their parents
- their status in society
- personal finances
- balancing part-time work with their studies
- relationship with siblings
- relationship with peer group
- coping with living apart from their family.

In addition to any personal problems they may have, young people are aware of the fragile nature of the labour market and recognise that they may have to be prepared to change career several times during their working lives. Indeed, the problems faced by young people have been of concern throughout the European Union for some time, as this CEDEFOP report highlighted:

> The youth phase has become more extended in duration; established and normative sequences of transitions are breaking up into much more variable and individually less predictable patterns; many young people's material circumstances have deteriorated in absolute or relative terms; lifestyles and values are also shifting and becoming more pluralised. At the same time, of course, macro-social and economic change in Europe is producing new structures of opportunity and demand in the labour market; and systematic social inequalities have by no means declined, but have rather intensified and become more complex.
>
> (CEDEFOP, 1994: 6)

It would be ridiculous to give the impression that all young people are suffering from stress or experiencing significant hardship, but many of them do encounter problems that will have an impact on their ability and motivation to learn.

Research carried out in Cheshire, by one of the authors of this book, sought the views of 16–19 year old FE students as to where and when they encountered barriers to learning (see Unwin, 1995). They identified seven areas of concern:

1   teaching and learning styles
2   curriculum issues
3   progression between courses and institutions
4   peer group relationships
5   financial worries
6   level of family support
7   labour market pull.

The young people who were interviewed were studying full time for either A levels or vocational qualifications. They came from different social backgrounds; some lived in rural areas, others in urban settings, and they were all part way through a two-year course. As they talked about their experiences at college, they reflected on their schooldays and compared being a student then to now. The following quotations have been selected to show how the learning of young people is affected by the actions of others and also by their own perceptions of their personal ability and situation.

Learning styles (notably study skills and transition from one style of teaching/learning to another):

> At school you were made to work and you had the teacher telling you what to do . . . college is different: I like it but I have to do it on my own now . . . it's hard.

> I wasn't used to all this taking notes, they seem to want to cram as much in as possible. I don't think I'm enjoying it as much as I thought but perhaps it's because I'm worried about how I'm going to get through all this stuff.

> We seem to get a load of assignments to do all at once, six or seven just before Christmas but none for ages. Why can't they be more consistent? It would help if we had the books we need, the library is useless. My friend helps, she's good at using her notes and she can write the assignments – I wish they would show you early on how to do what they want. I feel as though I'm a little kid again, as if I haven't been to school before; it feels stupid but I want to get through.

It depends on the lessons, some are really good. Organisation, they need to be more organised so that we can plan our time better.

My mate left because he couldn't get his stuff in on time. There's another lad who will leave too, he's had enough. They should spend some time at the start making sure you know what you're doing.

Curriculum and timetable (nature of chosen course may not meet expectations, prove to be too difficult, be too far removed from their previous experience, too much freedom):

I've made the wrong choice – my fault. I didn't really know what I wanted to do and now I'm stuck with it.

I chose the course [A level] because it followed on from my best subjects at GCSE but it's nothing like the same. I'm amazed at this; they should have told us it was nothing like the GCSE.

I wanted a job really but my parents said stay at school. The courses go together, I suppose, but I'm not interested as I don't want to go to university.

Being at college is much better than school but we do waste time – like when we have, say, three hours in the middle of the day free we go into town and so there's not much point going back for an hour at 4 pm. School made you turn up; here it's a lot easier to miss lessons.

Progression (level of difficulty may be far higher than the recognised feeder course prepared them for):

The BTEC First was dead easy and we did lots of projects together. Now [the National] it's all taking notes and learning tons of subjects. You're not as involved as a student as last year.

It must get the teachers down that we find the course too hard but we were told we could come on it because we'd passed last year. I might leave. I'm a bit fed up with not doing well, gets you down.

Peer group (relating to a new group of people can cause problems, yet the need for group support is vital):

In my group we're all glad we're not in the other group – they mess about and seem weird.

We all help each other. The residential at the start of the year was brilliant. I didn't know anyone when I came here as my friends had gone to another college, but I've got a great set of friends now. I wouldn't like to be left out.

Our group gets on my nerves . . . the teachers don't like the group but nothing gets done.

Some people in the group can't do the work so the teacher has to spend ages with them . . . why do they let these people on the courses?

Financial (issues here range from actual poverty to peer pressure related to dress and possessions):

The costs of this course [BTEC art and design] are incredible, I've just spent another £12 on paint and next week we've got to have some thick card that costs a fortune. I reckon I spend about £5 a week on materials and sometimes it's a lot more.

You can't survive without a job.

My course expects you to go abroad on a trip and we had a residential weekend to pay for.

Family support (domestic difficulties cause pressure at home; some students leave home to live independently):

There's nowhere to work at home.

My dad is out of work . . . he's really down so I just moan at college . . . I've got to moan somewhere.

I've got a room now but I won't be able to afford it so I'll have to leave and get a job. The college helped, gave me some money, but it's no use.

Labour market pull (temporary jobs, albeit low paid, are available in all areas):

There's a German supermarket opening in Crewe soon . . . jobs at £6.00 an hour. Lots of my friends are going to go down there and see what it's like.

This agency lets you ring up when you've got some free time and gives you part-time jobs, so when I've got a day off college or I've not got any assignments due in I ring up. It's better than having a regular job like my mates . . . I can fit my college work in better. We all know we should finish our course but if there was a job some of us would go for it . . . I know this lad who's earning £150 a week.

The financial difficulties experienced by young people deserve comment. The majority of those interviewed explained that they required money for equipment related to their courses, for food and clothes. There was some evidence of peer pressure as regards fashion and appearance but, in general, young people were struggling to find enough money to meet their everyday expenses.

Mature adults can face many of the problems identified by the younger students above, particularly if those problems are introduced by their teachers and the college in which they are studying, or if they are created by external pressures. In addition, mature students are more likely to face health problems and have the general burden of the responsibility for managing households.

For many mature women, their barriers to learning are wrapped up in the very fact of being female (see the reference to feminist critical pedagogies at the start of this chapter). Their lives tend to be more disrupted than men's as they take time out of education and careers to raise children or to support partners. The following comment from a 30-year-old mother of three captures the battle in which some women have to gain lost ground:

> I'm just getting to the point where everybody else starts. Do you understand what that means? Most people, when they leave home or graduate from high school, already have an idea of what they are worth. An idea that they go out and conquer the world. I'm just getting to where everybody else is at.
>
> (Belenky *et al.*, 1986: 53)

In order to support women who are returning to learn and who may feel threatened or ill at ease in the company of male students and tutors, some colleges run women-only courses. Maggie Coats, who advocates such courses, found from her own research (Coats, 1994: 118) that there are both advantages and disadvantages for the women who attend:

Advantages

- allows women to gain confidence from shared experiences and group support in a non-threatening environment;
- encourages women to locate their own personal experiences in a wider social context and thus understand those experiences;
- provides a secure base from which to go out into wider society and to which women can return for further support and encouragement.

Disadvantages

- The experience of women-only provision can only be transitional and women will lose the support of the group when they progress to further education, training or employment.

- The relevant practical support needed may not be available in other provision.

Although many would argue against separating men and women for educational or training purposes, the issues which concern the advocates of women-only courses apply to the central issue of the impact of gender on learning.

Reflection

Consider to what extent your own gender might influence the way in which you will teach and relate to your students. For example, if you are a young man, how will you relate to mature women or to young teenage girls? If you are a young woman, how will you cope with teaching a class full of 18-year-old male apprentices or a room full of aspiring managers from the private sector? How will your students see you?

How do people learn?

Stephen Brookfield, whose quotation opened this chapter, has said:

> To specify generic principles of learning is an activity full of intellectual pitfalls. Even if we leave aside the variables of physiology, personality, and cultural background, we still have to consider the implications of those developmental theories that hold that adults function in very different ways when responding to the societal and personal imperatives required of them in young adulthood, midlife, and old age. This suggests that the generic concept of adulthood is so broad and oversimplified as to be of limited use as a research construct.
>
> (Brookfield, 1986: 26)

Brookfield goes on to recognise, however, that a number of people have contributed since the late 1950s to the creation of a theory of adult learning, which has proved to be important to both learners and teachers:

- Gibb (1960) – adult learning must be problem and experience-centred, provide feedback, and have learner-set goals.
- Miller (1964) advocated cognitive models of learning above behaviourist models.

- Kidd (1973) placed importance on lifespan, role changes, egalitarian relationship between teacher and student, self-directedness of adults, meaning of time and the prospect of death.
- Knox (1977) – adults learn continually and informally, achievements modified by individual characteristics, learning is affected by physical, social and personal characteristics, and by content and pace. Adults underestimate their ability and allow school experience to dominate, prior experience can both hinder and advance capacity to learn.
- Brundage and Mackeracher (1980) identified 36 learning principles including: adults learn throughout their lifetimes, they construct meaning through experience, they learn best in situations which value the status of the learner and when they are in good health and stress-free, they need clear goals to learn new skills, they enjoy a combination of individual and group activity.
- Smith (1982) adults have four key characteristics: multiple roles and responsibilities, many accumulated life experiences, experience of a number of development phases (physical, psychological and social), and anxiety and ambivalence about their learning activity.

The theorists cited by Brookfield all recognise the significance of internal and external pressures that impact on any adult's capacity for learning. One study of adult learning, carried out in Canada by Allen Tough and reported in 1971, was particularly influential in seeking to identify the ways in which adults differed in their learning from children. Tough observed the ways in which adults plan and organise their own learning and how they set about acquiring knowledge and understanding. His key finding was that adults are 'self-directed' in their learning for which 'more than half of the person's total motivation is to gain and retain certain fairly clear knowledge and skill or to produce some lasting change in himself' (Tough, 1971: 6). Tough's findings built on earlier work in the USA by Johnstone and Rivera who found that a huge number of adults were engaged in learning outside the formal adult education system, which they termed 'independent self-study' (Johnstone and Rivera, 1965). This and later studies of adult participation in learning showed how the amount of adult learning could be wildly underestimated if the only measure was the numbers attending formal classes in institutions. By recognising the determination of adults to further their learning and that this motivation made them much more self-directed than children, the need for the development of distinctive models of adult learning theory was advanced.

One of the most distinctive theories has been put forward by Malcolm Knowles (1978) who developed the concept of 'andragogy' (from the Greek *aner* (stem *andra*) meaning 'man'), which stresses that children and adults approach learning in different ways and that this should be taken into consideration by those who help adults learn. Knowles noted the following differences between adults and children:

1 Children see themselves as dependent – adults see themselves as independent.
2 Adults bring experience to learning and value that experience.
3 Adults are ready to learn for specific reasons as their development is linked to the evolution of their social role – children's development is physiological and mental.
4 Children see much of their learning as being for the future – adults learn as a response to the here and now.

Although much of this work has a common-sense ring to it, there is a danger that the individual learner becomes lost in a sea of generalisations. The vignettes in Chapter 2 show how dangerous it is to generalise. Take, for example, the case of Clive whose behaviour as a learner seems to have more in common with the characteristics of children as identified by Knowles above, rather than with those of self-directed adult learners. There is a sense, too, with Grace that she may still be at a dependent stage as a learner owing to a lack of confidence, despite her age and experience.

Reflection

Given below is a list of instructions based on the Japanese art of Origami for making a salt cellar. (When made up, some of you may recognise the object as one which was, and may still be, popular at school for playing a game of 'choices'.) In order to learn how to make this object, you could do one of the following:

1 Go through the instructions step by step as you would an instructional manual.
2 Ask a partner to assist you – one reading, one folding the paper.
3 Ask a partner to make the object first and then demonstrate to you as in a typical class in which, for example, the teacher demonstrates how to ice a cake or set up a chemistry experiment.

Using one of the above methods, have a go at making the object and record your experiences. When reflecting on your performance, try to consider the following questions:

1 Do you learn best by yourself or do you like/need the support of someone else?
2 Do you follow instructions to the letter or do you improvise?
3 Would you have worked better from a picture?
4 Do you prefer to be shown how to do something?

If you have the time and/or the opportunity, ask a fellow adult and a child (under the age of 13) to attempt the same exercise and compare their learning experience with your own.

Paper folding instructions:

1   Take as an A4 sheet of paper.
2   Place paper portrait way up.
3   Fold bottom right-hand corner at 45° until it meets left-hand edge.
4   Take scissors and cut off rectangular unfolded section of paper, and discard.
5   Unfold square paper.
6   Make another diagonal fold, so that there are now two diagonal folds that cross in the centre of the paper.
7   Unfold.
8   Take the left edge of paper and fold over to meet right edge.
9   Unfold.
10   Take bottom edge of paper and fold over to meet top edge.
11   Unfold.
12   You should now have a square piece of paper with two diagonal folds and two square folds that cross in the centre of the paper.
13   Fold all four corners, one at a time to meet the centre point.
14   Turn work over.
15   Fold all four corners, one at a time, to meet the centre point.
16   Turn work over.
17   Push diagonal folds together and open out the pockets in each of the corners to produce a 'salt cellar'.

When you analysed your approach to, and experience of, the paper folding exercise, you may have found yourself engaged in Kolb's learning cycle. You might also recognise some of your experience in the following eight-stage model of learning which has been advocated by Gagne, an educational psychologist who developed and extended some of the early work on behaviourism. We have summarised and adapted Gagne's model and suggest that the term 'learning' be seen as encompassing knowledge, skills and understanding:

Stage one: Motivation (Student's motives and expectations identified and brought in line with teaching objectives)
Stage two: Apprehending (Teacher gains student's attention by various means)

Stage three: Acquisition (Knowledge, skills and understanding acquired by the student in a form in which they are ready to be lodged in the memory)

Stage four: Retention (Student is helped to memorise and assimilate new learning)

Stage five: Recall (Student encouraged to retrieve learning ready for application)

Stage six: Generalisation (Student transfers learning to range of situations)

Stage seven: Performance (Student tries out newly acquired learning)

Stage eight: Feedback (Student is helped to judge performance and reflect)

As with all models, this one has a simplicity which can be misleading – teaching and learning can often be a messy business and individuals do not, necessarily, want to have their learning confined within a chronological framework. Clearly, the stages shown above can be fused and their order might be rearranged or disrupted in order to reflect particular circumstances. It is, however, a useful model for teachers to keep at the back of their minds when they are planning teaching sessions and it can be used during sessions as an evaluation tool if a teacher feels the right amount of progress is not being made. We return to this model in Chapter 5 when we examine teaching strategies.

You will have seen that Stage one in Gagne's model is 'motivation', a word which will figure highly in most teachers' everyday discourse, whether they are thinking about their own levels of motivation or that of their students. Just like the weather, motivation can change from one hour to the next and it is a difficult concept to unpack. Rogers (2002: 95) explains that motivation can be said to be dependent on either 'intrinsic' or 'extrinsic' factors:

Extrinsic factors consist of those incentives or pressures, such as attendance requirements, punishments and rewards, or examinations to which many learners in formal settings are subjected or the influence of other persons or organisations. These, if internalized, create an intention to engage in the learning programme. Intrinsic factors consist of those inner pressures and/or rational decisions which create a desire for learning changes.

It is clear that even this differentiation is problematic. Rogers (ibid.: 95) acknowledges that within intrinsic motivation there is a hierarchy of motives. He gives this example: 'a desire to please some other person or loyalty to a group, which may keep a person within a learning programme even when bored.'

A key theorist of motivation was Maslow (1968) who devised what he called a 'hierarchy of needs', pictured as shown in Figure 4.1. In this rising model of motivation, Maslow asserts that adults and children move up the layers as their need in each one is satisfied. Despite its limitations, this model has proved useful to teachers in pointing to the need to remember that their students are

Figure 4.1 Maslow's hierarchy of needs

individuals with emotional, intellectual and physical needs. Harkin *et al.* (2001: 62) have adapted Maslow's model by filling in some useful detail: they convert 'Food' into guidelines for making the learning environment pleasant, including adequate refreshment breaks; 'Shelter and safety' refer to non-threatening classrooms, ground rules and induction programmes; 'Love and belonging' covers openness of communication, recognition of different learning styles and valuing learners' life histories; 'Esteem' relates to setting achievable tasks, giving positive feedback and support for learner autonomy; and 'Self-actualisation' is concerned with supporting progression and transfer of learning.

Another theorist whose work offers useful insights for understanding how people learn is Bloom, who distinguished between learning that takes place in the cognitive domain and that in the affective domain (see Bloom, 1965). For Bloom, cognitive learning runs in parallel with affective learning so that at the same time as a learner develops knowledge, his or her behaviour as a learner is also developing. The affective side to learning can be seen as a way to introduce some kind of value system to the learning process so that as one acquires knowledge, one also learns to appreciate the role that knowledge plays which, in turn, encourages the learner to be committed to the process.

Situated and expansive learning

A particularly powerful view of the way in which people learn is that provided by Jean Lave and Etienne Wenger (1991) who introduced the concept of 'communities of practice', which stresses that learning is as much a collective as an individual activity. This is a social theory of learning, which sees learning as 'an aspect of participation in socially situated practices' (Lave, 1995: 2). What is important here is that knowledge and skills are seen as not belonging solely to an individual, but things which are to be shared and developed collectively. In addition, it is the historical, social, political, economic and cultural dimensions of any community of practice and the nature of the interactions between members that determine how much learning occurs. Fuller and Unwin (2003b, 2004), for example, have argued that the quality of learning on apprenticeship programmes is very dependent on the way in which a company's existing community of practice sees apprentices as primarily learners or productive workers. They have built on Lave and Wenger's ideas and drawn from the work of the Finnish academic, Yrjo Engestrom (2002) to develop the concept of expansive and restrictive learning environments. Fuller and Unwin have examined the way in which different workplaces can be plotted on an 'expansive–restrictive' continuum according to the nature of the learning opportunities created within them. In the workplaces towards the expansive end of the continuum, employees have greater opportunity to share their skills and knowledge, to cross work boundaries and have access to off-the-job training.

The concept of a community of practice, which has tended to be used primarily by researchers exploring workplace learning, can be applied to a college, a classroom or group of students working together on a project. It can provide a useful device for teachers to examine the social context in which they expect their students to learn. In addition, by examining their own community of practice, whether as members of a department, a course team or at the level of the whole college, teachers can also reflect on how those communities facilitate or impede their professional development and sense of worth (see also Fuller et al., 2005). Central to Lave and Wenger's theory is that learning is partly about 'becoming' – that is, individuals engaged in the social relations that constitute a community of practice learn what is involved (beyond surface knowledge and skills) in moving towards becoming an expert, in whatever type of work, be it plumbing, hairdressing, engineering, bakery, nursing or law:

> The person is defined by as well as defines these relations. Learning thus implies becoming a different person with respect to the possibilities enabled by these systems of relations. To ignore this aspect of learning is to overlook the fact that learning involves the construction of identities . . . identity, knowing and social membership entail one another.
>
> (Lave and Wenger, 1991: 53)

A key part of the college element of work-based or work-related programmes is to provide the codified knowledge and the opportunity to practise skills within a less pressurised environment than the workplace. This all contributes to the process of 'becoming', though students will often complain that they cannot see the immediate connection between what they learn off the job and what they learn on the job (see Silver and Forrest, 2007). The challenge for the FE teacher is to create activities that help students make connections, and, importantly, create space for them to reflect on the aspects of the workplace learning that they find problematic. This might include issues related to interpersonal relationships and dealing with superiors.

Practising skills and applying knowledge in simulated or real work situations enables people to build up a reservoir of tacit expertise. We are all aware that when we perform tasks we utilise some skills and knowledge that we would find difficult to describe. Michael Polanyi (1967) developed the concept of tacit knowledge in the late 1950s and early 1960s as part of an enquiry into the nature and justification of scientific knowledge and more broadly the character of human knowledge. He drew a distinction between tacit (practical) knowledge and explicit (codified) knowledge but acknowledged that the boundary between the two was not at all clear, arguing that all knowledge was a combination of the codified and the tacit and that the two worked together to enable human beings to act. Neisser argued that there is a direct link between action-centred skills and tacit knowledge:

> The skilled carpenter knows just how a given variety of wood must be handled, or what type of joint will best serve his purpose at a particular edge. To say that he 'knows' these things is not to claim that he could put his knowledge into words. That is never entirely possible . . . The practitioner's knowledge of the medium is tacit. It is essential to skilled practice: the carpenter uses what he knows with every stroke of his tool.
> (Neisser, 1983: 3)

In terms of teaching and learning, the tacit dimension has always been understood by vocational teachers and workplace trainers, but some are less willing than others to create the appropriate opportunities for their students to develop their tacit expertise through practice. This can, of course, be difficult due to health and safety regulations, time constraints, and the cost of raw materials. Awareness of the tacit dimension is also important in terms of considering students' prior experience. Adult students in particular will come to college with expertise gained through work, but may not have any formal accreditation to prove what they can do, and they may not be able to articulate their skills and knowledge due to lack of confidence or, quite simply, because this expertise is tacit in nature (see Evans *et al.*, 2006). Providing opportunities for students to demonstrate their skills and knowledge can unlock hidden talents and build confidence.

Boreham (2002) has argued that the UK should look to the German concept of '*arbeitsprozesswissen*', which roughly translates as 'work-process knowledge', as a way to bring the concepts of tacit and codified knowledge closer together. Work-process knowledge embraces:

an employee's knowledge of the work process in the enterprise as a whole, including the labour process, the production process and the way in which the various departments and functions are inter-related.

(Boreham 2002: 232)

This concept is helping to improve the German 'dual system' whereby apprentices split their week between off-the-job learning in a college or workshop setting and on-the-job training in a workplace. By gaining a much more rounded understanding of how the theory they learn off the job relates to the practical tasks they perform on the job, apprentices are better able to utilise the different types of knowledge and skills they acquire. This process also demands a much closer relationship between vocational teachers and employers to ensure that the former is up to date with regard to changes in workplace procedures.

Lave and Wenger's work has connections to socio-cultural activity theory which builds on the work of the Russian psychologist Lev Vygotsky (see Cole, 1985; Engestrom, 2001). As Guile and Young (1999: 113) explain, Vygotsky was concerned with 'the progress that students make with their studies as they relate their "everyday" concepts — the understanding that emerges spontaneously from interaction with other people and in different situations — to the "scientific" concepts that they experience through textbooks and the formal curriculum'. Vygotsky developed the concept of the 'zone of proximal development' which he defined as: 'the distance between the actual development level as determined by independent problem solving and the level of potential development as determined through problem solving under adult guidance or in collaboration with more able peers' (Vygotsky, 1978: 85).

Where Vygotsky was concerned with child development, researchers such as Lave and Wenger and Engestrom have extended his ideas to adults and to learning outside formal classrooms, including the workplace. Guile and Young (1999) have argued that social-cultural activity theory could provide a way of linking work-based and school/college-based learning.

Barriers to learning

There are an infinite number of barriers which prevent people from learning, some of which are external in nature, perhaps caused by domestic or financial difficulties, and some of which are internal, arising from psychological or physiological problems. In addition, teachers can, of course, create barriers for their students. These barriers might be created as a result of the following:

- a teacher's personal behaviour towards a student;
- the choice of teaching technique;
- lack of attention to the teaching environment, for example too much noise, room too hot or too cold, not enough light, and so on.

Reflection

Consider the ways in which you have been prevented from learning during your life and, in contrast, try to identify anything which has been a positive support to your learning. Make your notes in two lists:

>   List one: Barriers to learning
>   List two: Support for learning

In the lists you made, you may have identified your family or domestic relationships as a feature in one or perhaps both lists. Clearly, domestic life has a major impact on the way in which children and teenagers learn, but it can be forgotten that young and mature adults can be equally affected by their domestic environment. In his study of married, male, full-time university students in Canada, Lauzon makes the following comment:

> The decision to become a student and the subsequent changes in the student's personal identity will necessitate changes in family members and patterns of family interaction. One way of conceptualising these changes is to examine the student from a familial systematic perspective. This perspective views the family as the main unit of study; all family members are subsystems of the main family system. Any change experienced at the subsystem level will necessitate change at the system level. In the case of a family where one member experiences changes in social roles, responsibilities, beliefs and/or values, other members will be required to make changes in order to accommodate the change at the level of the system (Satir, 1983). Hence not only must the individual adapt but the family must also adapt. The decision of the adult to become a full-time student forces all family members to make some behavioural and emotional adjustment. The bulk of the adjustment, however, would appear to occur in the husband/wife relationship rather than the father/child relationship . . . Despite the obstacles and demands placed in front of, and on, the adult student, they continue to pursue their dreams. As one respondent put it: 'It's the dream that keeps me going. Knowing that something better is just over the horizon.' But sometimes the dream turns to a nightmare and the world of the adult student falls apart. A few months after this study was completed the researcher had the opportunity to talk to one of the respondents. He reported that he was currently engaged in a vicious divorce and custody battle and attributed the breakdown of his marriage to his being a student. Sometimes the dream just isn't enough; education for the adult can be costly.
>
> (Lauzon, 1989: 43–4)

Only a minority of adult learners end up in the regrettable position of the one quoted above, but Lauzon is right to draw attention to the stress and tensions that having a student in the family can create. Although his research was based on male, full-time university students, Lauzon's conclusions about the impact on family life and the adult learner would seem applicable to female as well as male students and to a wide range of learning situations.

One of the authors of this book was responsible in the past for running a series of residential training courses for in-company trainers and supervisors. Many of the participants on these courses had not attended a course of study for several years and often not since they had left school. One of the most interesting aspects was to observe the changed behaviour of some of the women who attended the courses. These particular women had not stayed away from their partners and children before and came away worrying about how their families would cope without them. One woman related in detail how she had filled the freezer with meals and separately labelled packs of sandwiches for lunches and had arranged for a neighbour to be on standby to wash and iron items of clothing at a moment's notice. By the end of the third day of a one-week course, the women began to question their attitudes and by the end of the course they were threatening domestic revolution. The last thing the group facilitator wanted was to cause mayhem in families, but the power of the learning situation, and particularly the chance to draw support and ideas from peers, was considerable for those women.

In her study of why mature students leave FE and HE courses before completion, McGiveney (1996) reminds us that whereas women students tend to cite family commitments as their main reason for withdrawing from courses, men tend to cite problems with the course, finance and employment-related issues. But McGiveney also points out that it would be unwise to stereotype adult learners as potential course 'drop-outs':

> several studies have found that mature students are currently slightly more likely than younger ones to complete courses. It has been suggested that this may be because students who remain in full-time education mainly because of the erosion of job prospects for school leavers are unlikely to be totally committed to study (Payne and Storran, 1995), whereas adults with work experience and those who have made considerable sacrifices in order to participate in further or higher education will be far more highly motivated.
>
> (McGiveney, 1996: 111)

In their study in South Wales, Rees *et al.* (2000: 186) found five key indicators of whether adults were more or less likely to participate in lifelong learning:

- time (older people felt they had had fewer opportunities when younger);
- place (the culture of where people are born and brought up);

- gender (men were more likely to participate than women;
- family (social class, educational history and family religion all had an impact on participation);
- and initial schooling (positive experience plus extended schooling both encourage participation).

Usher *et al.* (2002: 79) have drawn attention to the 'negative imagery' of the concept of barriers to learning. They write, 'The learning process is characterized as one full of blockages and barriers, things that impede or hold back the self-as-learner from attaining various ends, such as efficacy, autonomy, self-realisation or emancipation.' Instead, they argue that the 'postmodern story of the self' means that 'we tell stories about our experience' and that our subjectivity is always 'shifting and uncertain'. This is a complex debate, but the importance of Usher *et al.*'s analysis is that learners' identities are not fixed and, therefore, simplistic notions of what constitutes a barrier to learning might be very misleading when trying to understand learners' needs.

While engaging in the process of learning, individuals also learn 'how to learn' and all teachers play a role in helping their students to develop what is referred to as their 'meta-learning' or 'meta-cognition' capacity (see, *inter alia*, Black *et al.*, 2003; Hargreaves, 2004). This will clearly be important in also helping students overcome any barriers they have towards learning. There is a great deal of debate in the research literature about the theory of 'meta-learning' and whether it can be 'taught'. We do not have the scope here to enter into these debates, but we would argue that if teachers can involve their students as much as possible in the planning and organisation of their learning and get them to engage in reflective exercises to review their own progress, then learning how to learn will become embedded in their overall participation in the learning process. This approach will involve teachers and students developing a natural dialogue about the joint enterprise in which they are engaged. There is a danger that if teachers attempt to 'teach' students how to learn, they will invent activities which are too abstracted from the students' interests and will struggle to help students make the connections.

The teacher–student relationship

At the beginning of this chapter, we explored some of the theories that might explain how individuals approach learning. There is a long-running column in the *Times Educational Supplement* in which well-known people from all walks of life recall the special characteristics of a teacher who, at some point in their lives, had a particular impact on them. Other newspapers and magazines often carry similar features, the common link between them being that individual teachers have the power to affect people's lives, sometimes in quite dramatic ways. The comedian and author, Ben Elton, who left school at 16 to do a drama and liberal arts course at an FE college in Warwickshire, has written about one of the college's drama teachers:

> He believed that drama was an essential part of life, that you shouldn't have to want to be an actor to enjoy it but that you should see drama as a way of learning, a way of understanding life and other people . . . He believes, passionately, that young people should be encouraged (with great vigour) not to shrug their shoulders and say 'Oh . . . it's all crap', not to be cynics but to get involved. He led by enthusiasm and I believe that the greatest gift a teacher can have is that ability to enthuse, to inspire with interest, to get people involved . . . He was a good teacher. He did the formal bit thoroughly and made it interesting . . . In setting up that course Gordon was a major, major influence on my life. He was a ball of energy. He enabled me to stay in education at the same time as sort of leaving it, and he did fundamentally affect my growing up.
>
> (*TES2*, 8 September 1995, p. 20)

To be praised by an ex-student in this way would make any teacher feel proud and, of course, most teachers, at some point in their careers, receive thanks and best wishes from their students. Most of the time, however, as in the rest of life, any gratitude that students feel tends to go unspoken and teachers have to plough on in the hope that their work is appreciated. Just as teachers can have a very positive effect on their students, they can sometimes be a negative force and there are many people who would claim that their insecurities and blocks about learning stem from a certain teacher who made them feel inadequate. The teacher–student relationship is, therefore, a complex and dynamic one and, as such, needs to be treated with care.

The following table lists a number of labels which can be applied to someone in a 'teaching' role and to someone in a 'learning' role.

Teaching role	*Learning role*
Teacher/lecturer	Student
Instructor/demonstrator/supervisor	Apprentice
Trainer	Trainee
Tutor	Learner
Facilitator	Participant
Assessor	Candidate
Mentor/coach	Pupil

Each of these labels carries with it a great deal of terminological 'baggage' and much has been written about the power of labels in determining behaviour. For example, the term 'facilitator' is used widely in management training where it is regarded as being much more learner-centred than terms such as lecturer or teacher. On the other hand, teachers in FE colleges are often still referred to as 'lecturers' despite the fact that many of them spend very little time giving 'lectures'. From the point of view of learners, how they are described could denote how they might expect to be treated, the culture and ethos of the institution, and the context in which they are learning. Terms such as 'trainee' and 'apprentice', for example, are generally used in work-based settings, though the term 'trainee' might also be used in colleges for young people on work-based programmes. Labels can also change so that a 'student' might become a 'candidate' at the point when he or she is going to be assessed; a 'lecturer' becomes a 'tutor' when seeing a student for an individual tutorial meeting.

Teaching in a college will require you to switch between the different roles suggested by each of the labels listed above. Whatever your subject area, you might, in any one session, carry out the following functions:

- spend ten minutes giving a 'lecture';
- facilitate a group discussion;
- demonstrate how to use a piece of equipment or perform a certain task;
- spend a few minutes with individual students to give them specific tutoring;
- supervise small groups of students carrying out project work.

To be able to switch from one role to another certainly requires flexibility, but it also demands that the teacher is able to recognise which role is the most appropriate in a given circumstance. (Chapter 6 provides more detail on choosing and applying teaching strategies.) Rory Kidd (1973), building on earlier work by John Dewey, has described learning as a 'transaction' to which both the learner and the teacher have to bring something of value for both parties to feel the transaction has been effective and produced the desired outcomes. In order for this to happen, teachers and learners have to get to know each other and be prepared to change and adapt. This may take time but the process can be accelerated through the willingness of the teacher to create an atmosphere that encourages the following:

- enables students to articulate their learning needs;
- enables students to identify and discuss any barriers which might prevent them from learning;
- enables students to develop the confidence to share their own ideas and actively contribute to the learning situation;
- provides students with constructive criticism and praise so that they feel supported and, in turn, learn how to support each other;
- encourages all students to achieve at their own pace, regardless of ability;
- encourages both teacher and students to work together with a sense of community and shared purpose;
- promotes respect for individuals within the learning community.

As Ben Elton found with his drama teacher, the individual approach and personality of each teacher mark them out as being distinctive, and so teachers differ as much as their students. Indeed, it would be a very dull day for a student if all teachers were the same. In terms of maintaining order within the teaching situation, whether it be with one or a group of students, teachers will certainly behave in different ways and choose different methods for ensuring that both teacher and students concentrate on their joint purpose in coming together. As teachers gain in experience, keeping control of the proceedings becomes a subconscious activity, so that neither the teacher nor the students are aware that control is being exerted. Students, too, can be encouraged to develop self-discipline, to control their behaviour in respect of the community in which they are learning, and learn how to maintain order as a group. A useful model for sharing ideas about control and order is transactional analysis (TA) which was developed by the American psychologist, Eric Berne.

Berne calls TA a 'theory of social intercourse' and used it to help people understand and improve their behaviour towards others. He wrote:

> Observation of spontaneous social activity, most productively carried out in certain kinds of psychotherapy groups, reveals that from time to time people show noticeable changes in posture, viewpoint, voice, vocabulary, and other aspects of behaviour. These behavioural changes are often accompanied by shifts in feeling. In a given individual, a certain set of behaviour patterns corresponds to one state of mind, while another set is related to a different psychic attitude, often inconsistent with the first. These changes and differences give rise to the idea of ego states.
>
> (Berne, 1970: 23)

Berne identified three ego states which, he believed, people move regularly in and out of during their daily lives:

- parental
- adult
- child.

Of the three ego states, the adult (demonstrated when a person is in control and displaying maturity) is thought to be present in everyone but often needs to be uncovered or activated. The child state can be exhibited in two forms: the adapted child, who modifies behaviour under the influence of a parent, and the natural child, who is freed from parental influence to be creative or to rebel. In this latter state, the child can be petulant and difficult to handle. The parental state also has two sides: first, it can be authoritarian ('Do as I say'); second, it can be nurturing ('Let me help you').

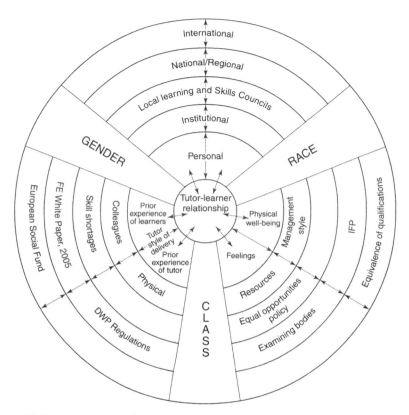

Figure 4.2 Teacher–learner relationship

Berne's hypothesis is that problems occur when these ego states are at cross-purposes. For example, if someone who is in the natural child state meets someone in an authoritarian parental state, then they will have trouble communicating. Similarly, if students in the adult state meets someone in the nurturing parental state, they will feel frustrated or even patronised. The trick, as far as being a teacher is concerned, is to recognise both your own ego state and that of your students. You can also use TA as a model for handling colleagues and running meetings.

The teacher–student relationship will, of course, like any other interpersonal relationship, be constantly tested and there may be some occasions when it breaks down completely. In the main, however, the relationship will work because most of the people involved will realise that, if it is effective, then life for everyone will be happier.

Some of the pressure on the relationship will come from external forces that the teacher or students can do little about and that can have a positive or negative effect. Figure 4.2 illustrates how those external forces, as well as the internal feelings of teachers and students, can impact on the teacher–learner relationship. The model (adapted from Unwin and Edwards, 1990) is overlaid with three bands – class, gender and race – which exert influence throughout society and from which no relationship can be exempted.

Reflection

You might wish to make your version of the model to reflect the particular circumstances in which you are working. You may, for example, expand some of the bands so that you can include more variables. One way of creating your own version is to use coloured card. The model could also be used with students as a way of encouraging them to identify the variables which affect their relationship with you as a teacher and/or as a group of learners. This works well as a group activity so long as individuals are not forced into isolated positions.

Group learning

Most of the teaching you will do in FE will be with groups of students. As in all sectors of education, pressure on resources demands that group teaching (and often in groups of considerable size) is the dominant mode. Despite the managerial reasons for favouring group-based learning, however, there are distinct benefits that students gain from learning together. We look at specific strategies for achieving effective learning in groups in Chapter 6, but, for the moment, we will briefly explore the general benefits to be gained from group-based learning.

We have paid a great deal of attention in this chapter to the needs of individual students, and you saw in the student vignettes in Chapter 2 how different those needs can be. By bringing students together, they can begin to learn how their own needs compare and contrast with others', and develop shared strategies for advancing their learning and for overcoming problems. Learning in groups can often be much more fun than learning singly, and can facilitate the continuation of learning once the formal session has ended. Students may continue to discuss ideas outside the classroom or workshop and apply themselves creatively to group tasks.

Given the emphasis in current policy on 'personalised' learning, and the increasing use of ICLT, there is a danger that learning in colleges may become too individualised. Although groups of students may be together in the same space, they might all be working completely separately on different

	Task	Socio-emotional
I N T R I N S I C	Expressing selves in subject	Greater sensitivity to others
	Judging ideas in relation to others	Judging self in relation to others
	Examining assumptions	Encouraging self-confidence
	Listening attentively	Personal development
	Tolerating ambiguity	Tolerating ambiguity
	Learning about groups	Awareness of others' strengths and weaknesses
E X T R I N S I C	Follow-up to lecture	Giving support
	Understanding text	Stimulating to further work
	Improving staff/ student relations	Evaluating student feelings about course
	Gauging student progress	Giving students identifiable groups to belong to
	Giving guidance	

Figure 4.3 Types of aims and purposes in group teaching

Source: Jaques (1992) reproduced with permission from Taylor & Francis Ltd

tasks or units of competence. For Wildemeersch, such a scenario represents a 'farewell to dialogue and a welcome to individualised technicism' (Wildemeersch, 1989: 68).

The collegiality created by group-based learning can act as an important locus of support for students who lack confidence, have problems outside college, or who gain extra motivation from the discipline of having to keep up with their peers. The teacher can capitalise on that collegiality to encourage the more able students to help others. Jaques (1992) has stated that groups operate at both a task and a socio-emotional level and within both intrinsic and extrinsic dimensions. (See Jaques' diagram, Figure 4.3.) He notes that there is a tendency to concentrate on the extrinsic dimension and explains:

Teaching is often solution-orientated rather than problem-orientated and seems to take external requirements as its starting point rather than the needs and interests of the students. Moreover, a lack of attention to the socio-emotional dimension means that many of the task aims cannot be achieved. Without a climate of trust and co-operation, students will not feel like taking the risk of making mistakes and learning from them. To achieve this, the tutor would have to balance a concern for academic standards with a capacity to understand and deal with the workings of group processes as well as an attitude of generosity and praise for new solutions to old problems.

(Jaques, 1992: 72)

There are groups and groups, of course, and not all will provide the collegiality referred to above. Rory Kidd states that there are three characteristics which have to be present in a group if effective learning is to take place:

1   a realisation by the members of the group that genuine growth stems from the creative power within the individual, and that learning, finally, is an individual matter;
2   the acceptance as a group standard that each member has the right to be different and to disagree;
3   establishment of a group atmosphere that is free from narrow judgements on the part of the teacher or group members.

(Kidd, 1973: 80)

Support services for students

One of the most important ways in which learners can be supported is to give them access to a range of support services. Such support can include advising them as to the most appropriate modules in a course, how to stagger their studies to fit in with professional demands, how to seek financial support for fees, and putting them in touch with professional counsellors if personal problems become too difficult to handle alone. A great deal of support can be provided by organisations and teachers actually listening to students and interpreting their needs correctly.

A major issue here is the extent to which individual teachers accept that they have a role to play in supporting learners above and beyond putting across the actual subject matter of a particular course of study. In particular, the teacher can have a significant impact on a student's sense of well-being, as McGiveney emphasises with this quote from an FE teacher talking about part-time students:

The reality of formal part-time study is that individual tutors can make or break a learner's experience. The tutor is central to the creation of the essential, supportive social environment of the classroom which reduces drop-out. We can talk till the cows come home about the vital importance of guidance but we are seriously in error if we do not acknowledge the pivotal guidance role of the tutor for the part-timer. For many the teacher is the guidance system.

(McGiveney, 1996: 135)

Egan's (1975) three-stage model of the skilled helper originated in his work as a counsellor, but it can be usefully adopted by teachers as a basis for supporting individual students:

Stages	Steps
Stage 1	Exploration Focus on specific concerns
Stage 2	Developing new perspectives Setting specific goals
Stage 3	Exploring possible ways to act Choosing and working out a plan of action Implementing the plan Evaluation

Colleges arrange their student support services in recognition of the fact that students' support needs stretch from, for example, help with basic skills such as literacy and numeracy, to careers information, but also include the need for access to a confidential service to deal with very private matters. Lewisham College in London encapsulates its commitment to student support in its Student Charter (see Figure 4.4, pp. 122–3).

A key deficiency with many induction programmes is that they tend to be one-off events, whereas the process of induction should carry on throughout a student's lifetime in the college. That is, at various points in his or her career in the college, a student will need to be inducted into a new stage, to meet new tutors and fellow students and so on, or to be re-inducted with parts of the college or course that are long forgotten. Figure 4.5 (see p. 124) shows how a college's guidance and support system should span all aspects of college life from student entry through to student exit.

Reflection

Imagine you are about to start a course in a college. What items would you want to see covered in an induction programme? As you make your list, consider the circumstances of the students we introduced you to in Chapter 2.

The teacher's approach to learning

As noted in Chapter 1, just as the student population in FE is extremely diverse in terms of its background and prior experience, so too is the teaching force. This variety provides a reservoir on which the sector can draw to enhance the learning experiences of its students. For example, a majority of those teaching in the sector will have had relevant vocational experience before taking up a career in teaching. Others will still be working within their vocational sectors and perhaps teaching part time. Some may have taught in secondary education before moving into the post-compulsory phase and others may have been workplace trainers.

Clearly, this will have an impact on the way in which they approach their teaching and their attitudes to learners, and will underpin their own philosophy of teaching. We now invite you to reflect upon the following series of vignettes of typical lecturers to be found in any college. As you did in Chapter 2 with the student vignettes, we suggest you think about the following questions:

1   What perceptions do you have of each of the lecturers and how his/her previous experience might impact on the students?
2   What do you see as the potential staff development needs of the individual lecturers?

Leslie

Leslie is 49 years old and is head of the hospitality and catering programme area in a medium-sized general FE college situated in an attractive town. The college has a fairly wide rural catchment area, and the local economy mostly covers the tourism, hospitality and agricultural sectors. The college offers a wide range of courses, including a substantial A level programme.
Leslie began his career in catering, moving through a succession of jobs until he became head chef in a prestigious hotel. His professional skills were regarded very highly and he won a number of national competitions. When he became tired of the long and unsocial hours associated with hotel work, he decided to move into teaching. He had already had some experience of training younger chefs, which he had enjoyed, so a move into lecturing seemed a natural progression.

He began by doing some part-time lecturing while running a small catering business from home. He successfully completed the City and Guilds FE Teachers' Certificate and decided to take on full-time teaching. As his confidence grew in his new profession he was keen to develop his career. He enrolled on a degree programme at the local university and began to like the idea of part-time study more and more.

When the impact of new funding regimes, targets, qualification reform, and an impending merger began to bite at the college, Leslie became increasingly dissatisfied

WHAT YOU CAN EXPECT FROM US:

- Help you to choose a programme of study that suits your needs
- Provide an induction to your programme of study
- Guarantee the delivery of your programme
- Make sure that classes start and end on time (and let you know quickly about unavoidable changes)
- Provide Learning Centres and services to support your studies
- Give you a clear picture of how you are to be assessed and advise you regularly on your progress
- Encourage you to help evaluate the course throughout your period of study
- Provide access to advice, information and counselling on any educational or personal matter throughout your time here
- Provide an increasingly safe, secure, pleasant and accessible environment for your studies
- Respond quickly to any problem you tell us about and support you in confidence if necessary
- Promote a caring and supportive atmosphere
- Respect and celebrate the differences of all in our community, and promote the College Equal Opportunities Policy
- Keep you informed and up to date about developments within the College which may affect you

THE COLLEGE HAS A STUDENTS' COMPLAINTS PROCEDURE TO HELP YOU IF WE FAIL TO MEET THESE COMMITMENTS

WE EXPECT YOU TO:

- Take pride in the good name of the College and abide by College rules
- Take responsibility for your learning by attending regularly and punctually, working hard at your studies and completing all your assignments on time
- Co-operate with your tutors and other College staff and make active use of learning support
- Seek help if you need it
- Help to make the College a safe place for all
- Be considerate of the rights and interests of other College users
- Take care of the College buildings and furnishings, and respect other people's property
- Treat everyone with respect, regardless of differences in culture, ability, race, gender, age, sexual orientation or social class
- Play an active part in Equal Opportunities by refusing to take part in jokes or behaviour that degrade others, challenging and reporting discriminating behaviour
- Let us know quickly if you feel we have not provided the service we have promised, or if you have any other problem

THE COLLEGE HAS A STUDENTS' DISCIPLINARY PROCEDURE WHICH WILL BE REFERRED TO IF NECESSARY

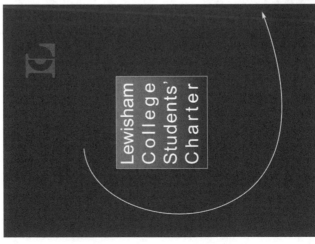

Lewisham
College
Students'
Charter

We will provide:

- a college prospectus and course information within 72 hours of receiving your request
- individual help to choose your course from a specialist member of the teaching staff, a Guidance Officer or a Careers Officer
- an interview date within five working days of receiving your application May–September
- the result of your application within five working days of your interview
- specialist advice and our Disability Statement for those with particular learning requirements
- advice about course costs and how you can pay

O U R   C O M M I T M E N T S
STUDENTS

During the first four weeks of your course we will provide:

- a Student Guide for every student
- a course handbook for all those studying 14 hours a week or more
- a signed agreement about the learning programme you will follow
- a thorough introduction to the College and your course

To help you achieve on course we will provide:

- a named tutor
- regular planning and review tutorials for those studying 14 hours a week or more

O U R   C O M M I T M E N T S
STUDENTS

- high quality teaching and learning support
- assignment and coursework which say clearly what you must do and how you will be assessed
- prompt return of your coursework with clear feedback, usually within four weeks
- Learning Centres, including access to over 150 PCs, open five days, four evenings and during the holidays
- specialist help with Key Skills, research and independent study
- a Guidance Team who can help with any personal, practical or study problem you may have, available five days, one evening and during the holidays
- opportunities to enrich your learning and take on new challenges

During your stay we will ensure:

- the College is open six days and four evenings each week during term time and throughout the day in the holidays
- a high quality learning environment which is graffiti free
- security staff and a Duty Principal available at all times
- College canteens which offer a balanced meal for £2 and a daily vegetarian option
- a programme of events, including student fairs and prize giving, throughout the academic year
- a chance to benefit from the skills of your colleagues including use of student-run restaurants and fitness centre and invitation to dance, drama and music performances
- financial and childcare support to applicants who meet published eligibility criteria
- clear ways of listening to your concerns and dealing with them promptly

O U R   C O M M I T M E N T S
STUDENTS

To help you achieve your future goals we will provide:

- career planning support
- a reference for a job, university or another course
- your exam certificates within three months of completing your course

O U R   C O M M I T M E N T S
CONTINUOUS IMPROVEMENT

We will ask for your comments and suggestions about the College through:

- a Student Forum which directly channels student views to College Governors
- student satisfaction surveys, comments systems and user surveys
- a clear, timed complaints procedure
- and we will use your feedback in ensuring that learning is high quality, relevant and promotes equality of opportunity

You can find out how we are doing by asking to see:

- information about what our students achieve and what they go on to do
- summaries of student and employer surveys
- reports of College inspections
- the College Annual Report, Self Assessment Report and Quality Improvement Action Plan - these are held in the Learning Centres

This Charter is reviewed and updated each year. Complaints about any failure to meet the commitments should be made through the College complaints procedure.

Figure 4.4 (a and b) Student charter

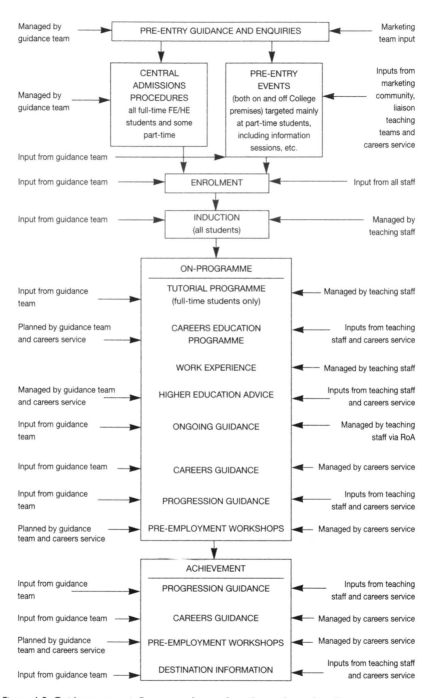

Figure 4.5 Guidance team influence on learner's pathway through college

with his teaching and more and more interested in developing his own skills as a researcher. He enrolled on a part-time Master's degree and submitted his dissertation on 'Changing Employment Patterns in the FE Sector'. The MA successfully completed, he returned to his teaching with renewed critical reflection but little in the way of career progression. The college introduced a redundancy package, but Leslie was turned down because he was needed to lead the hospitality programme area. He feels he would still like to do some personal academic work, but the pressure of increasing student numbers, departmental targets, new vocational qualifications and the administrative burden of running a large programme area preclude it.

Bill

Bill is a lecturer in business studies at a large city college. He joined the college five years ago, having previously worked as an assistant manager at a High Street bank. He started work in retail banking immediately following his completion of a degree in economics. While a junior manager with the bank he was encouraged to take part in a college's Young Enterprise scheme, acting as its business adviser. He enjoyed the experience so much that he seriously began to consider a change of career. He decided to leave the bank and enrolled on a full-time PGCE (FE) course. Having successfully completed it he took up his first teaching appointment at his current college.

He is pleased with his decision and really enjoys teaching, particularly individual tutorial work with students. There are many long-serving lecturers in his staff room and he sometimes feels their commitment to the job is not what it might be. One colleague in particular is unwilling to share any ideas or resources and is obstructive when any suggestions for change are introduced, whereas Bill always volunteers for new initiatives and is keen to be involved with external agencies and curriculum development. His students achieve well and he encourages them to do so. He feels that there is a lot more that he could do if other members of staff were similarly inclined.

A new principal has recently been appointed, following the retirement of the previous principal after eighteen years in the post. Bill can sense that there are changes afoot and decides that it is time he took a more assertive stance in the college, particularly since he has heard that there may be some restructuring within the Business Studies department.

Clare

Clare is 48 years old and works in a city college which serves not only the city but also a large surrounding rural area. She has worked in the sector for over twenty years and is a well-qualified and highly experienced teacher of English as a foreign language. She also worked abroad for a number of years as a teacher of English. She describes her role as having changed significantly over the past two years and now finds that her time is spent increasingly on basic skills tuition, in particular IT. Although not an IT specialist, she has had to adapt to the new situation since basic skills teaching is delivered alongside ESOL, a situation which she regards as less than satisfactory.

Her classes include a very wide range of learners, with very different prior learning experiences. She describes how, in classes of up to fifteen students, there are as many as ten or twelve different nationalities at any one time. Many of the students are asylum seekers and present a range of challenges to the organisation of learning. There is, she says 'no class teaching', programmes have to be highly specific and personally tailored to the needs of individual learners. This is exacerbated by the fact that learners have inconsistent patterns of attendance and sometimes disappear for lengthy periods of time, only to reappear again without notice, or often explanation. This poses problems in terms of recording and reporting achievement against college targets. Programmes are organised on a roll-on, roll-off basis, with the expectation that there will be some achievement in terms of basic skills qualifications. Students are also referred for basic skills provision from other parts of the college, a system which she feels works well.

Clare says that she still enjoys the work, but feels that this is partly because she does not really have to do it; she feels that for younger staff the situation is unsatisfactory, and unsettling. There are questions over the future funding of the work, for example, if students are required to pay fees, and with this comes job insecurity. Also, staff are required to teach in areas where they do not feel comfortable. She has been able to adapt but others find it more difficult.

Jean-Claude

Jean-Claude is 32 years old and is currently head of department in a specialist language centre based in a large city. He was born and educated in France, came to England many times during his student days and decided that he definitely wanted to teach in the country after qualifying. His first teaching post was at a large urban general FE college, where he taught French and German on a range of basic language courses, as well as some A level programmes. He was disappointed by the experience, since languages were not highly valued in the college and enrolments dwindled year on year, to the extent that his post was under threat. Several part-time members of staff lost their jobs.

He applied for his current post, little thinking that he would be successful, but recognising that he needed to take a change of direction. He is very happy with his current job and sees lots of possibilities for further development. He has already published several coursebooks. He heads a department of twenty-five staff, most of whom are part time. He finds the atmosphere lively and stimulating and he is encouraged to try new things. Most importantly for him, this college is dedicated to the area he cares most about, language learning; staff and students share his commitment. His only concern is funding. Annual fee increases always pose a threat to enrolments.

Clifford

Clifford is head of the engineering department, and director of the engineering Centre of Vocational Excellence (CoVE), at a large, successful, three-campus college formed by the merger of three former colleges. He has been at the college for twelve years and has had a series of promotions since his first appointment as a lecturer. He has taught on a wide range of engineering manufacturing programmes from Level 2 to Level 4. More recently, he has been responsible for developing extensive industrial links and designing customised programmes for a number of leading manufacturing companies. He was also involved in the development of the government-funded apprenticeship programmes in the college. Having spent fourteen years of his employed life in the automotive industry, he feels well suited to the job of CoVE director.

He has excellent working relationships with a number of local employers and has done a great deal to enhance the college's reputation for providing customised training linked to the needs of industry. The partnerships which he has been able to forge with large multi-national companies have enabled him to obtain 'industry standard' equipment for the college. Employers are happy for their staff to attend training at the college, since they know that it will be of good quality, using up-to-date equipment, and tailored to their needs. This Clifford sees as the *raison d'etre* of CoVEs and he believes that, 'that is the way we have always done things here, anyway; the CoVE just gave us more money to things that we wanted to do'.

He is optimistic about the future, and feels he has 'a great bunch of people to take things forward and a very supportive Principal'.

Hasina

Hasina is 28 years old and teaches on a range of health and social care courses at her local college. She left school at 16 with few qualifications and little idea about the type of career she might wish to pursue. She worked in a number of care settings before the manager of the day centre in which she was employed suggested that she might like to attend college in order to help her to work towards NVQ Level 2.

Although initially sceptical, she soon began to enjoy attending the college and completed NVQ Level 2 fairly quickly. Once convinced of the benefit of gaining some qualifications and the potential of promotion, she decided to continue with Level 3. At 21 she was accepted on to a foundation degree programme and managed to juggle the competing demands of full-time employment, part-time study and family commitments. Although the course put considerable stress on Hasina's family life, she admits that 'graduation day was one of the happiest days of my life'.

The college in which she currently works has earned an outstanding reputation for its outreach work and Hasina particularly enjoys this aspect of her teaching. She has done a great deal to extend the learning opportunities available to women 'returners' and to those for whom previous learning experiences have been negative. She has recently been asked by the vice-principal (curriculum) to join the college's Inclusive College Working Group. She welcomes the opportunity of enabling others to experience some of the benefits which she has gained from the 'widening participation agenda'.

Judith

Judith is principal of a medium-sized general FE college located in a small northern town, but serving a widely dispersed and deprived rural area. She has been at the college for ten years and was previously a principal in another college; before that she held a number of positions within both FE and HE. She was one of the first women to become a college principal and is nationally recognised as a leading figure in the sector.

She has made a significant contribution to the provision of outreach education within the college's catchment area – an area of high unemployment with few large scale employers. Post-16 participation rates are low and there is a general level of under-achievement, possibly as a result of low aspiration. Judith has sought every opportunity to engage 'difficult to reach' learners and has been instrumental in designing programmes with innovative approaches to access.

She is constantly facing funding crises and has had to adopt a 'fleetness of foot' in dealing with different funders, negotiating targets, securing provision and, at times, competing with predatory school sixth forms. As she approaches the end of her career, she is concerned that there appear to be few women who are prepared to take up the mantle of principal.

These vignettes illustrate the diversity of backgrounds and experiences of many of those who teach in FE. Their own experiences will inform and shape their own approaches to teaching and their attitudes to learners. FE has always had a diverse workforce in terms of background and prior experience, age profile and employment. The Foster Review highlighted this and drew attention to the challenges colleges face:

> Within the FE system, there needs to be new collective attention to . . . addressing the problems – and possibilities – of a casualised and ageing workforce and the need to improve vocational and pedagogic skills through comprehensive workforce planning.
>
> (DfES, 2005a: viii)

Conclusion

There has long been a view that effective teaching comes down to charisma or showmanship – what some might call the 'wow' factor. As this chapter has tried to show, however, charisma might work for part of the time, but ultimately, teaching is a much more complex business requiring continual reflection and the trying out of new and different ideas. Within the six domains that make up LLUK's occupational standards (see Chapter 1), Domain C (Specialist learning and teaching) is noteworthy because it draws attention to the fact that while a great deal of what happens in teaching and learning will be generic across a very broad range of discipline and topic areas, there will also be important differences. We discuss this issue in Chapter 5.

Getting to grips with the theories and concepts that have been developed over the years to help us understand the ways in which people learn and the relationship between teaching and learning can be a daunting task. Yet, as Harkin's (2005) survey of teachers in 10 colleges in the South-east of England found, theory is being used in a variety of ways. Although he found some teachers were hostile to theory and some felt guilty for what they felt was their own lack of understanding, many developed what Schon (1983, 1987) has called 'theories-in-use'. By this, Schön means that professionals integrate a range of theories (gleaned from a variety of sources including initial training, professional development, and their peers) into their continuing practice. As Harkin (2005: 170) reminds us, theory in teacher education in the UK has a contentious history, with some theories labelled in a pejorative sense as 'trendy' or 'plain crackers'. Theories also come in and out of fashion. In Chapter 5, we will see how one theory of learning, 'Learning Styles', which is used regularly in UK colleges, has recently been subjected to a highly critical examination.

Chapter 5

Teaching strategies

Flexibility and adaptability

In the opening chapters of this book, we described the complex world of FE and emphasised the need for teachers to be flexible and adaptable in order to meet the demands that their managers, students and external agencies will put on them. It is worth remembering, too, that the pressures on FE colleges to recruit as many students as possible mean that teaching staff will be faced with people who have a wide range of learning needs. Lumby (2001: 50) has argued that: 'This very comprehensiveness is both a great strength in meeting the needs of learners and a real Achilles heel in communicating what any college is about and in meeting the needs of different groups of learners.'

Given the range of reforms set out in the 2006 FE White Paper (DfES, 2006b), including a strong exhortation to better meet the 'needs of service users', the notion of 'personalisation' within teaching and learning has moved centre stage. While it may be argued that FE teachers have always been good at working with individuals with a range of different needs, from different backgrounds and across a wide age range, this will be even more important as the notion of individualised learning programmes gathers momentum in the context of the Qualification and Credit Frameworks discussed in Chapter 3.

FE teachers are sometimes referred to as 'managers' or 'planners' of learning, involved in a range of activities which stretch beyond the day-to-day business of teaching in a classroom or workshop. Young *et al.*'s (1995) description of the way in which the knowledge that FE teachers need to develop and employ has shifted over recent years is helpful:

- from subject knowledge to curriculum knowledge;
- from teacher-centred pedagogic knowledge to learner-centred pedagogic knowledge;
- from intra-professional knowledge to inter-professional knowledge;
- from classroom knowledge to organisational knowledge;
- from insular knowledge to connective knowledge.

Instead of being a teacher who is solely concerned with his or her own subject specialism, FE teachers now have to understand how their specialism 'connects' with the rest of the college's curricular provision and how generic (or core) learning can be facilitated through that specialism (see Fisher and Webb, 2006). This has been particularly problematic in terms of the delivery of key skills, where an integrated approach was axiomatic to successful delivery, and yet where the practice was often found wanting. This will become very important with the proposed inclusion of a strong generic learning component within the new 14–19 diplomas in England. In moving to a more learner-centred approach, FE teachers will have to 'manage' the process of learning as a whole and not simply be concerned with transmitting knowledge and skills. As 'managers of learning', teachers will need to seek the help and support of other professionals including non-teaching staff, and they will be members of course teams. The shift from 'insular' to 'connective' knowledge recognises the way in which FE teachers have to be aware of and build on their students' prior educational experience and their future needs.

An FE college represents a transitional stage for many students as they progress from school education through FE and on to work-based training and/or HE. Adult students may also be experiencing a sense of transition, particularly if they are retraining and building on existing expertise to change direction. Silver and Forrest interviewed college lecturers from a range of work backgrounds who drew on their own professional experience to help their students make connections between their studies in college and the demands of the workplace:

> Learners who are both work-ready and fit for the future need far more than a set of time-limited work skills and have to recognise the impact of new techniques, new materials and new technologies at work. They need to understand the unpredictability and the inevitability of change and shake off the focus on a permanent present that leaves younger learners, especially, unprepared. Excellent practical teachers open their eyes by demonstrating the radical ways that work has transformed over time, and signposting the future. They build in an expectation that skills will need constantly updating, and show that technical skills alone are not enough. Drawing on their own extensive experience, these teachers were able to tackle the behaviours commonly associated with employability but often claimed to be unteachable. Developing those generic behaviours that would secure the learners a future as well as a place at work was all part of 'becoming one of us'.
>
> (Silver and Forrest, 2007: 73)

This sense of going beyond the transmission of prescribed knowledge and skills is also reflected in Robson et al.'s (2004: 190) research with vocational teachers in FE. They argue that such teachers are concerned with the 'whole person' as opposed to seeing their students as one-dimensional individuals in a classroom or workshop:

> The fostering of criticality, creativity and pride in one's work positions the vocational teacher as concerned with the student as a 'whole person', as a potentially valuable member of a professional group and not just an employee. These teachers are not concerned simply with producing 'work fodder' nor with the narrow and commercial demands of one particular workplace. They have a broader perspective and in their expression of it, their narratives support a wider discourse of professionalism, concerned with expertise, commitment and care for others.

When they visit colleges, inspectors concentrate, in particular, on the organisation and management of the learning situation and note the strengths and weaknesses of the following:

- level of coherence of schemes of work;
- level of teachers' subject expertise;
- level of rapport between staff and students;
- clarity of aims and objectives;
- appropriateness of the pace of learning;
- range of teaching techniques in use;
- opportunities for students to participate actively;
- quality of resources, for example, technology, equipment, handouts, visual aids, etc.;
- clarity of assessment criteria;
- classroom/workshop management, for example, punctuality of staff and students, behaviour of students;
- quality of feedback on students' work;
- quality and usefulness of tasks set and appropriateness of coursework;
- quality of record keeping to inform students of their progress.

Choosing a strategy

Students attend colleges to acquire skills, knowledge and understanding related to their area of study, whether it be English literature, welding, social care or applied statistics. Separating out the skills, knowledge and understanding components within any one learning encounter is not, of course, a straightforward process, as in most encounters the three are bound together. As shown in Chapter 4, teachers also need to consider how best to ensure their students get the opportunity to develop their tacit expertise.

Given the underpinning complexity of the learning encounter in terms of content, there is also the diversity of your potential students to consider. You are clearly going to need to develop a range of strategies for helping your students to learn effectively. Once you gain some experience as a teacher, you will find that you can create your own strategies which reflect your personality and are designed to respond to your students' particular needs. Always remember that different strategies work differently for different teachers. You may be the sort of person who will never be comfortable giving a lecture or facilitating a role-play exercise, but able to get excellent results from designing group-based problem-solving exercises. Then again, you may shine as a lecturer, providing your students with stimulating talks that capture their imaginations. Gaining confidence as a teacher is important and all teachers tend to stick with the strategies with which they feel most comfortable. Your students, too, as we saw in Chapter 4, have their own preferences when it comes to teaching strategies.

There is a danger, therefore, that both teachers and students can settle into a cosy learning relationship in which neither is challenged or pushed into expanding their learning horizons. On the other hand, if the teacher disregards the preferences of the students and sticks to the teaching strategy they feel least happy about, then the learning environment is put under stress and the outcomes may be unsatisfactory for both parties. Essentially, the key message is to provide a variety of learning experiences to cater, as far as possible, for the needs of all learners. Depending on the nature of your subject area and the level at which you teach, you will need to be very aware of the literacy and/or numeracy capability of your students. Handing out written instructions and information sheets may seem to contribute to good practice, but you will need to pay careful attention to the level of literacy required to use them. In their research on the different types of literacies within FE, Ivanich and colleagues have discovered that teachers can both under and overestimate their students' abilities. For details of this important research, visit: www. lancs.ac.uk/lflfe.

Learning styles

There has been a great deal of interest over about 20 years in the much contested theory that individuals' preferred learning styles can be identified and measured, and it is now widely practised in FE colleges. Honey and Mumford's Learning Styles Questionnaire is one of the best known commercial products to have emerged from the development of a theory that has been heavily promoted by government agencies. One of the attractions of the theory is that it offers a way for teachers to gain a better understanding of the different ways their students approach learning and so provides clues as to how they might best be supported. Such a theory has also proved to be very attractive to college managers who see it as a way to improve retention and attainment. Coffield et al. (2004) undertook a major review of the learning styles field and found 71 models, of which they categorised 13 as being worthy of attention. They found widespread disagreement among learning styles theorists and a 'dearth of rigorously controlled experiments and of longitudinal studies to test the claims of the main advocates' (ibid.: 64). They conclude that:

> The main charge here is that the socio-economic and the cultural context of students' lives and of the institutions where they seek to learn tend to be omitted from the learning styles literature. Learners are not all alike . . . they live in particular socio-economic settings where age, gender, race and class all interact to influence their attitudes to learning.
>
> (Coffield *et al.*, 2004: 65)

We would argue that using a learning styles inventory can be a fun exercise to stimulate students to consider the ways in which they approach learning. Using Honey and Mumford's *The Manual of Learning Styles* (1982) will provide an instant diagnosis of where your students sit in the following categories:

1   Activist (rolls up sleeves and rushes into action)
2   Reflector (contemplates the problem and considers how to approach)
3   Theorist (consults 'experts', researches the issues before acting)
4   Pragmatist (selects the most appropriate form of action given the circumstances).

This might well trigger a discussion about the extent to which students recognise themselves and, more importantly, how they would evaluate the inventory. To base your pedagogical approaches on such a contested theory would, however, be highly inadvisable.

In choosing an appropriate teaching strategy, you have to consider four equally important issues:

1   Given a specific curriculum objective to be achieved, which teaching strategy will be most effective for transmitting the necessary skills, knowledge and understanding to your students?
2   How can you ensure that your students will fully participate in the learning process so that they learn for themselves rather than just listening to or watching you demonstrate your learning?
3   Given your knowledge of the group of students, how can you incorporate their prior learning and overcome any barriers to learning they may have?
4   How much time can you allow for this particular curriculum objective?

There are a number of strategies at your disposal and they can be arranged on a continuum (Figure 5.1) that stretches from teacher-centred methods at one end to those methods which encourage students to take more responsibility for their own learning at the other end.

The chart in Figure 5.1 is not judgemental. It is not saying that giving a lecture is wrong or that the best way to teach is to engage students in role

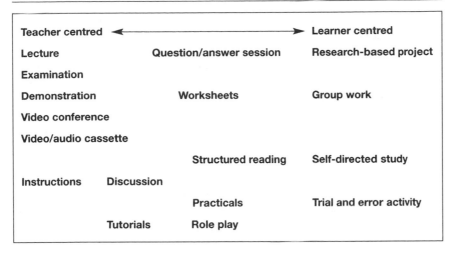

Figure 5.1 Teaching strategies continuum

plays and problem-solving exercises. It is, however, a means of illustrating how different teaching strategies will affect different learning outcomes.

Aims, objectives, goals and learning outcomes: 'what are we supposed to be learning here?'

All students come to their course with preconceived assumptions about its content and will react differently to its separate components. In addition, each student will have certain expectations about how much he or she will gain from the course. The course team has to be aware of such complexities in the student profile when constructing the learning materials and will attempt to cover as many of what it judges to be potential areas of interest. In terms of choosing the inputs or content of a learning programme, it is the teacher or course team, in most cases, who has the main responsibility. Once a learner begins to study, the teacher's control begins to diminish. What goes into a learning programme and what comes out at the other end may not, necessarily, be all that closely related, as Rogers explains:

> The planning agent (teacher-provider) initially determines the goals of the learning process. The agent has in mind certain expected outcomes, the results that will flow from the learning undertaken in changed attitudes and behaviour. However, most of the student participants come with their own intentions, which may or may not be the same as those set out by the agent; they will use the learning opportunity for their own purposes, to achieve their own outcomes. Each of these sets of purposes influences

the other. The teacher's intended outcomes to help shape the learners' expectations and the learners' intentions and hopes should affect the formulation of the teacher's intentions. Both sets of proposed outcomes may well be different yet again from the effective outcomes of the educational process. Since those being taught consist of a mixed group of learners, each of whom responds to the learning in a different way, there will always be a series of unexpected outcomes. The teacher-agent needs to keep these differences in mind when planning the learning encounter.

(Rogers, 1986: 12)

In the case of competence-based programmes, it could be argued that teaching inputs must be determined by the prescribed competences in the various elements and units of, say, the S/NVQ, but we would argue that the teaching and learning relationship is more sophisticated than even the purest competence-based approach would assume it to be. And, in most other sorts of programmes, teachers and learners still have some freedom to strive for undetermined outcomes. It is important, therefore, for teachers to be able to identify the aims and objectives of a particular teaching session, albeit with the flexibility to amend their original ideas. Furthermore, there are valuable opportunities here for teachers and students to work together to determine what each wants in the way of learning outcomes and so negotiate a micro-curriculum.

The language of learning can be so complex as to suppress understanding. Indeed, many professional educators and trainers, and particularly academics, are guilty of constructing a highly technical and often impenetrable set of terminology that shuts out teachers and students alike. It is common practice for teachers to set aims and objectives when designing learning programmes, so what is the difference between aims and objectives and learning outcomes? Furthermore, what might be the value of specifying or identifying the outcomes of learning? The following passage from a report of research into learning outcomes in higher education (HE) is useful here as its central message is equally applicable to FE:

Aims and objectives are primarily the language of course designers. They describe what the course sets out to do and can tend to preserve traditional course structures by discouraging comment and input from other voices: professions, employers, government and students. Learning outcomes, on the other hand, describe what graduates are expected to be able to do and do not relate directly either to courses or to any particular methods of teaching and learning. They can include both knowledge of the subject and the intellectual and personal qualities which are developed as a result of in depth study of a subject. The explicit and detailed nature of the learning outcomes makes it easier for those outside HE, government, employers, etc., to understand the nature of the HE curriculum and to make realistic inputs to its development. Learning outcomes also make it easier for students to understand what is expected of them and to take greater responsibility for their own learning. This can be a means of developing alternative approaches to teaching and learning resulting in greater flexibility and wider participation in HE.

(UDACE, 1991)

Here is an example of some learning outcomes set by a teacher trainer for a group of trainees on a PGCE programme:

By the end of this session you will be able to:

- understand the role of assignments within the assessment process;
- discuss the implications for the planning of assessment;
- practice developing and writing assignments;
- test out your assignments in classroom situations.

Reflection

In this reflection, we hope you will engage in some lateral thinking about learning outcomes from the point of view both of the teacher and the learner. Similar exercises to this are often used in relation to developing communication skills.

Study Figure 5.2 and follow the instructions – you will need a partner to help you. The basic outcome should be for your partner to achieve as close a representation of the original drawing as possible. When you have finished the exercise, you might find it useful to discuss with your partner the following questions:

1   To what extent was the basic outcome achieved?

2   Can you identify any other outcomes of this exercise in terms of (a) your learning and (b) your partner's learning?

3   In terms of the overall outcomes of this exercise, how important was the achievement of the basic outcome?

You could extend this exercise by reversing your roles, though you would, of course, need to use another diagram!

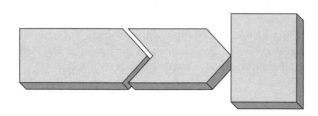

Instructions

1   Study the picture and consider how you would describe it to someone.
2   Sit back-to-back with a friend/colleague who has not seen the picture and give him or her a sheet of paper.
3   Give verbal instructions to enable your partner to draw the picture.
4   When the new picture is complete, examine it to see how closely it matches the original.

Figure 5.2 Reflection exercise

The teaching and learning involved in the exercise you have just carried out will have reflected the personalities, capabilities and learning styles of the two people involved. As the teacher, you will have had to:

*   think carefully about the nature of the instructions you supplied;
*   communicate those instructions effectively;
*   listen carefully to your partner's questions and reactions.

In judging the success of the exercise in terms of how closely your partner managed to reproduce the diagram, you will have considered to what extent each of you contributed to the exercise. Over and above the physical reproduction of the diagram, you may have discussed other outcomes: for example, your partner may have learned that he or she needs to practise following verbal instructions. By simply concentrating on the physical outcome, we can miss a great deal of associated learning which could include generic or transferable skills, as well as the tacit dimension (see Chapter 4).

The process of learning is often seen in terms of what goes in rather than what comes out. Trainee teachers spend a great deal of time constructing lesson plans detailing how they will cover a particular subject in a given period of time. Most curriculum planning takes the form of a stockpot into which ingredients are thrown until the chef decides there are enough to make a decent soup. Some thought will be given to the balance of subjects, the depth to which each should be discussed and, importantly, the presumed expectations of the potential learners. At some point, the curriculum planners will have identified certain broad aims by which their deliberations and choices are guided. These aims tend to relate to the whole curriculum or large parts of it:

> Not infrequently, such statements reflect philosophical or educational beliefs and values. Statements of aims are generally vague and tend to have little operational value (descriptively or prescriptively) in relation to the planning, development and implementation of curricula. They can, however, act as a 'reference' against which the tenability of more specific statements of intent (e.g. curricula goals and objectives) can be appraised.
>
> (Heathcote *et al.*, 1982)

Heathcote *et al.* (1982) found that three recurrent themes emerged when they analysed a range of curriculum aims taken from FE courses:

1 promotion of the individual's personal and intellectual growth;
2 meeting the needs of the individual in relation to the individual's societal and physical environment;
3 meeting the needs of society itself.

They further found that when curriculum aims were translated into more specific goals, it was to serve two closely connected but alternate functions: the first function involves the teacher acting as an agent for the curriculum planner by teaching directly to tightly defined goals; the second function sees the teacher as a much freer agent who interprets the curriculum planner's goals in the context of each specific group of learners.

The pre-eminence of either function depends, according to Heathcote *et al.*, on the following variables:

1 the amount of direction which the curriculum planner wishes to impose on the implementing teacher;
2 the extent to which the curriculum emphasises student autonomy in relation to learning outcomes;
3 the ability and previous experience of the students for whom the curriculum is intended;
4 the curriculum planner's perception of the constraints imposed and opportunities offered by the subject matter.

We would add a further and, in the light of the competence-based approach, increasingly dominant variable which concerns the teaching or learning system within which the teacher has to function. Heathcote *et al.* distinguish between the use of curriculum aims as a base from which the curriculum planner exerts control over the teacher who delivers the curriculum, as opposed to a 'staging post' where control passes to the teacher who then translates the aims into more specific objectives. They see the first approach as being objectives-based and the second as being process-based. The distinction here is that the process-based model focuses on the role of the teacher who adopts appropriate pedagogical methods in order to achieve the broad aims of the curriculum. Under the objectives-based model, the activities of the teacher are seen as merely the means to an end; that is the attainment by the students of the specified learning outcomes. In the case of distance learning materials, the materials themselves become the main 'agent' of the course team but involve a tutor or 'secondary agent' who interprets the materials for students.

Reflection

Given the above, you might like to consider the extent to which the proposals set out in the FE White Paper (DfES, 2006b) support a more learner-centred approach:

> Our reforms will renew the mission of the Further Education system, and its central role in equipping young people and adults with the skills for productive, sustainable employment in a modern economy. They will put the needs and interests of learners and employers at the heart of the system, so that their choices drive funding and performance management. (Foreword)

Are the aims espoused here compatible or contradictory? Where does this place teacher autonomy? Think also how the changes outlined in the White Paper might affect the teachers described in Chapter 4.

The objectives model of curriculum development in the training field first appeared in the USA with Franklin Bobbitt's *How to Make a Curriculum* in 1924, and was greatly refined in the 1940s by Ralph Tyler, and later in the 1950s and 1960s by R.F. Mager. The attraction of this model is that it systematically defines the skills and knowledge required to accomplish tasks and, in doing so, presents to teachers and trainers clear guidelines for selecting appropriate teaching methods and, most importantly, for designing an assessment programme. As Mager points out:

> If you don't know where you are going, it is difficult to select a suitable means for getting there. After all, machinists and surgeons don't select tools until they know what operation they are going to perform . . . Instructors simply function in a fog of their own making unless they know what they want their students to accomplish as a result of their instruction.
>
> (Mager, 1962)

What is looked for is a change in behaviour on the part of the learner, change that Bloom's *Taxonomy* (1965), widely adopted by both teachers and trainers, classifies into three domains:

Affective – attitudes and emotions
Cognitive – knowledge and information
Psychomotor – practical or physical skills

Each domain is sub-divided into a hierarchy of categories which demonstrate the different levels at which a learner may operate or be asked to operate. Bloom has been criticised, particularly for separating the cognitive from the affective, and other people have developed alternative taxonomies (see, for example, Gagne, 1988). Despite the criticisms, however, Bloom's domains and categories, when taken together, do provide a useful and fairly straightforward structure of learning. As such, they can be used as a basic template for the teacher when planning learning sessions and can also be used for the purposes of evaluating the effectiveness of a particular session.

The *affective domain* has five categories:

* receiving (taking in messages and responding to a stimulus);
* responding (taking responsibility by responding and seeking to find out);
* valuing (recognising that something is worth doing);
* organising and conceptualising (the individual develops his or her own way of arranging responses to stimuli and develops particular attitudes based on a set of values);
* characterising by value or value concept (bringing together ideas, beliefs and attitudes in a coherent whole).

The *cognitive domain* has six categories:

* knowledge (facts, categorisation of facts and knowledge in general, theories and abstractions);
* comprehension (making sense of what things mean and how they relate to each other);
* application (applying knowledge to different situations);
* analysis (breaking down knowledge into its constituent parts to gain a clearer understanding of the whole);
* synthesis (bringing together the separate constituents to create a new whole, which involves making choices);
* evaluation (reflecting on knowledge and making judgements).

The *psychomotor domain*, as developed by Harrow (1972) from Bloom's work, has six categories:

- reflex movements (in response to stimuli);
- basic fundamental movements (build upon reflex movements);
- perceptual abilities (used to interpret stimuli and behave accordingly);
- physical abilities;
- skilled movements (involve practice);
- non-discursive communication (involves creative and artistic behaviour).

Behavioural objectives have been heavily criticised by many people (see Eisner, 1985) for a number of reasons and, as discussed earlier, too much emphasis on a predetermined outcome can result in a dangerously narrow approach to learning. All teachers, however, do need to have a sense of what it is they want their students to achieve by the end of a particular session and over a certain period of time. Those 'objectives' might be largely predetermined and written in the form of 'outcomes' (as in the case of S/NVQs) or they may be framed more loosely but in such a way as to help the teacher give a structure to the learning. On some programmes, it is possible, and often desirable, for the teacher and students to negotiate a set of objectives and for the negotiation itself to be regarded as a central part of the learning process.

So far, we have been discussing 'objectives' for teaching and learning and there has been some reference to 'outcomes'. Teachers also talk about 'aims' and 'goals'. Although there is little point in getting too pedantic about terminology, it might be helpful to separate these terms and use them to differentiate between the distinct elements of a teaching/learning situation. The following example is taken from Unit 2 (Recruitment in the Workplace) of the GCE in Applied Business. This is a mandatory AS level unit and is assessed internally. This unit is broken down into a series of topics ('What you need to learn' in specification-speak), all of which have to be covered, and for which students need to provide assessment evidence. One of the topics is titled: 'The Recruitment Process'. The specification states that students need to understand the following:

- preparing person specifications and job descriptions;
- carefully planning how and when to advertise;
- identifying the strengths and weaknesses of job applications, curriculum vitae and letters of application;
- shortlisting candidates;
- how recruitment interviews are planned, carried out and evaluated;
- the legal and ethical responsibilities relating to equal opportunities.

(OCR, 2005, p. 20)

The teacher knows in advance, therefore, what is expected in terms of learning outcomes, but in order to ensure that students achieve those outcomes, the teacher has to construct a teaching plan. This is where aims and objectives come in. We asked a trainee FE teacher to devise a plan for teaching this section of the unit. She began by setting down an overall aim, followed by a set of objectives:

Aim:
To understand the process involved and the skills required when applying for a job.

Objectives:
- to understand the recruitment procedures when applying for a job;
- to respond to a job advertisement;
- to complete an application form in a clear, accurate and professional manner;
- to produce a covering letter to accompany the application form;
- to complete an employer aptitude test;
- to attend an interview with a personnel officer.

We can see from this that the aim encompasses the topic as a whole, whereas the objectives indicate the separate components which the student needs to master in order to fulfil the aim. In addition to demonstrating his or her ability in the subject area – that is, business – the student may also be able to demonstrate his or her ability in a number of key skills. For example, this particular assignment offers many opportunities for developing communication skills as well as IT skills. The teacher may want to extend the prescribed learning outcomes in order to reflect the needs of the students, or to develop the 'wider key skills' of 'problem solving', or 'improving own learning and performance'. Additional outcomes might include, for example:

- developing the students' confidence outside the classroom;
- developing the students' independent research skills;
- improving the level of written work among the students in general.

In defining these additional outcomes, the teacher would place them within the context of the course as a whole. An outcome related to the students' research skills would, therefore, be associated with more than one aspect of the assignment. Other outcomes might appear as a result of the teacher (or students) identifying a particular weakness in a previous session, which requires attention.

In designing her teaching plan, the teacher is required to make judgements not just about the subject matter, but about a variety of other factors likely to have an impact upon learning. Examples here could include gender, ethnicity, students with 'special educational needs', prior learning experiences, the resources available; the list is not exhaustive. What this suggests is that teaching strategies have to be differentiated in order to take account of different learning needs and circumstances. Planning for differentiation usually presents a challenge for the majority of beginning teachers, and, it has to be said, for more experienced teachers as well.

A common method for approaching this is by identifying what essential knowledge, skills and concepts all students *must* learn; what additional material the majority of students *should* be expected to cope with; and what some more advanced learners *could* achieve. At an individual class level, differentiation might also be accommodated by providing differentiated materials/resources (for example, large font handouts). Tasks may also be differentiated according to the level of challenge presented. Some students may be allowed extra time in which to complete tasks, others may be given additional support, from the lecturer or from a learning support assistant. Expected outcomes might also be differentiated. For example, some students might produce a written report, others might choose to present their findings as a poster display.

If we return to our trainee teacher's plan we can see that she has set 'goals' for different sections of the plan. For example, objectives 1 to 3 will be covered in three weeks; or one of the objectives will involve a group discussion or activity. It is in the planning where the teacher can be creative, despite the prescriptive nature of the specification. Our trainee teacher decided to divide the content into seven sections and to employ a range of teaching strategies (TS) as follows.

Section 1: General overview
In this section, students are asked to discuss their attitudes to unemployment and the different ways in which people can apply for jobs.

TS: 'Thought shower' as a group to get initial views, ideas can be captured on the whiteboard or on a flipchart; ask students to consider a set of case studies of people seeking work; ask students to choose two job vacancies from the local newspaper and obtain the necessary application forms (use telephone, letters and visit to job centre).

Section 2: The recruitment process
Students learn about how a typical company sets out to recruit staff.

TS: Teacher uses information from an actual company (in this case, Royal Mail) to explain the recruitment process. Teaching aids include PowerPoint and company materials. Alternatively, a company representative might agree to talk to the group. Students are also encouraged to talk about their own part-time jobs and how they were obtained.

Section 3: Letters and job specifications
Students learn how to construct a letter of application and interpret job advertisements.

TS: Students have been asked to bring in copies of job advertisements from local newspapers and to select three jobs they could realistically apply for; the students work in pairs to assess the quality of a sample of specimen letters of application; the teacher goes through the key requirements in writing a letter of application; the students work on their own to produce a letter of application for one of the jobs they selected earlier.

Section 4: Application forms and curriculum vitae

Students learn how to complete an application form and construct a CV.

TS: Students work in groups to assess the quality of specimen completed application forms; group discussion about what the applicant needs to do when completing a form; teacher reinforces the requirements by presenting a list on PowerPoint. The process is repeated for CVs. Students use computers to generate CVs, thereby covering some IT skills.

Section 5: Equal opportunities and contracts of employment

Students learn about the legal obligations employers have to adhere to when recruiting staff.

TS: Role play between teacher and student to demonstrate how certain questions could contravene equal opportunities legislation; group discussion of why equal opportunity matters in recruitment; students work in small groups to analyse a sample of contracts of employment; teacher reinforces legal knowledge with handouts.

Section 6: Preparing for interviews

Students learn how to prepare for an interview and how to conduct themselves in an interview.

TS: Teacher shows a video of good and bad interviews and students take notes; group discussion of video; teacher reinforces points related to how to prepare for an interview and how to behave as an interviewee.

Section 7: Being interviewed

Students take part in mock interviews, acting as both interviewees and interviewers.

TS: Mock interviews held using video cameras and external interviewers brought in; students watch the videos and analyse their strengths and weaknesses; teacher draws together all aspects of the element.

In devising her teaching plan, the trainee teacher was determined to provide her students with a lively and varied learning opportunity; hence she has deliberately chosen a range of teaching and learning strategies.

Assignments

The use of assignments as vehicles for encouraging participative, student-centred learning has been a central feature of college life for many years. Assignments can enable students to see their programme of study as a coherent whole in which all the parts are related to each other and through which they are encouraged to apply their knowledge, understanding and skills. In this way, assignments are an important means for enabling students to engage in learning by doing and for emphasising the integrated nature of their courses. The student-centred nature of assignments and their facility for including both individual and group tasks means that they highlight the process of learning as well as being agents for delivering outcomes of learning. When assignment work is assessed (either by teachers, or through student–peer assessments, or both), valuable lessons can be learned by reviewing the process through which the learning took place (see Chapter 6). The common features of assignments are that

- they include an element of independent student activity to be carried out individually or in groups (usually referred to in the assignment guidance as 'tasks');
- they are based on a realistic scenario;
- they can be of varying length;
- they encourage students to apply knowledge, understanding and skills to meaningful tasks in a realistic situation;
- they allow key skills to be integrated into the learning process and assessed as part of the overall learning outcomes.

Assignments can be created by individual teachers or by course teams who wish to create greater coherence between the modules, units, etc., that comprise the distinctive parts of a programme of study. Designing assignments can be divided into three areas:

1   Task – what a student does, often resulting in a product or outcome.
2   Activities – the process used in order to achieve the task.
3   Assessment – the benchmarks or criteria for the product and the process.

For example, if an assignment was built around the design and use of question-naires, the three areas listed above would translate as follows:

1   Task – devise and use a questionnaire.
2   Activities – select sources and obtain information about questionnaire design; plan the questionnaire; pilot it; amend as necessary; use the amended questionnaire; collect data; evaluate and present data.
3   Assessment criteria – range of methods used in obtaining information; fitness of resulting questionnaire for purpose – language, tone, degree of complexity, depth of analysis; clarity of presentation; adequacy of evaluation.

There is enormous scope when identifying scenarios for assignments for teachers to be creative and to utilise the expertise and ideas of a range of people. When designing an assignment, the following stages should be followed:

1   Choose the unit, topic, you wish to cover.
2   Formulate a scenario, exercise, or brief for the students to work within. (Be realistic about the amount of time available for students to cover the work involved.)
3   Correlate possible tasks with evidence criteria that will have to be fulfilled for the purposes of assessment.
4   If applicable, identify the key skills that will be assessed through the assignment.
5   Decide if this will be a graded assignment, and if so, how marks/grades will be allocated.
6   Write the assignment as a series of tasks with guidance for students.
7   Write assessment guidance (including grading criteria if applicable), indicating the nature of the evidence to be obtained.
8   Design any necessary documentation for assessment purposes, for example grids, question sheets, logs, etc.

By evaluating the implementation of an assignment, the teacher (and/or course team) can refine the different elements in order to improve it and ensure its continued applicability and viability. Once a set of effective assignments has been created, the pressure on the teacher to produce teaching materials is reduced and more time can be spent supervising the actual learning process. One serious note of caution is imperative when talking about assignment work. There is a misguided belief by some that assignments are a way of keeping students occupied and of letting the teacher off the hook. Assignments should never be used as an excuse for simply sending students away 'to get on with assignments/coursework'. In order for students to submit satisfactory coursework and to complete assignments they must receive adequate and appropriate teaching input, they must be supported through their independent research, they must be given timely and focused formative feedback, their progress should be logged and action plans drawn up for next steps. Assignments and coursework should never be regarded as an easy option; in order to support students appropriately and to ensure that learning takes place they require just as much planning as any other learning experience.

Being creative

As discussed in Chapter 4, teachers have to be aware of the different ways in which their students approach learning and try to create a learning environment in which those different approaches can be accommodated. But creativity in teaching involves risk.

The following question and answer section examines the implications for teachers inherent in outcomes-based, student-centred programmes.

What teaching will I need to devise and deliver?

The teaching will have to be designed to contribute to the assignments, in other words, to provide the underpinning knowledge which students require in order to complete the assignments. This will not always be provided by the teacher, but the teacher may act as a facilitator in pointing the students in the direction of suitable learning resources. You need to check the specifications carefully to see how much teacher support is permitted. In order to achieve higher grades students are expected to demonstrate independence in their learning. They need to be able to show evidence of synthesis and evaluation. Teachers need to ask themselves: what do students need to know in order to fulfil the assessment criteria for this unit? A supplementary question will then be as follows:

Where or from whom can this knowledge be accessed?

The important point here is that there is a wide range of resources and sources from which knowledge can be accessed and the teacher should exploit the inter-disciplinary nature of the college environment as well as drawing on resources available through the college's external networks. There is also a wealth of information available on the internet, although its sheer volume can make the job of selecting appropriate material daunting. A word of caution is required – students should not simply be directed to websites before their content has been assessed for suitability in terms of its appropriateness and relevance to the topic being studied. Surfing websites can be a huge timewaster and students do not always have the necessary research skills to select effectively. These are skills which need to be developed through appropriate induction processes.

How and where will the learning take place?

The answer to this question could be as wide as individual teaching staff wish to make it. If it is accepted that the opportunities for learning are constrained neither by the time nor the place at which it occurs, nor by the age of the candidate, then the opportunities presented by a wide range of diverse contexts and experiences are limitless. However, if teachers subscribe to the view that learning can only take place in classrooms where the teacher stands at the front and talks, then it will be extremely difficult to deliver vocational programmes effectively.

Examples of work-based learning activities include:

- work experience placements on employers' premises;
- work shadowing;
- projects undertaken in companies specifically for those companies (for example product testing);
- simulations;
- organising and running events in the college, for example open days, careers fairs, catering and general reception duties.

The importance of vocationally relevant and realistic learning environments, as described within the model for the new diplomas in England, and as already expected within many existing vocational programmes, requires close co-operation with, and support from, employers and the local community. Some variation in provision across different colleges and different programme areas exists and there are clearly capacity issues if employers are expected to take an even more active involvement in the sector in the future as recommended in, for example, the Foster Review (DfES, 2005a) and the FE White Paper (DfES, 2006b). Such concerns are also expressed in evidence given to the House of Commons Education and Skills Select Committee's inquiry into the development of the diplomas. It was noted that, 'the best interests of individual employers were not necessarily the same as the best interests of learners or the wider economy' (Education and Skills Select Committee, 2007: 23).

But, in the best-developed examples, assignments have been designed in conjunction with employers. Well-planned work placements allow students to collect assessment evidence from their experience. In some cases assessments can be undertaken by workplace supervisors and later verified by college staff. There are obvious implications for quality control when parts of the programme are, in effect, being devolved to employers. Issues about the standardisation of assessment are still being resolved. Some colleges have been able to develop effective partnerships with companies by arranging for staff teaching on vocational programmes to have work placements in business and industry.

What sort of students will be involved?

While many students following full-time vocational programmes in colleges will be 16–19 years old, by no means all of them will fit this age profile.

Part-time students will cover a much wider age range, and since the QCA in England now talks about the curriculum 16–90, it is worth remembering that we cannot neatly put our students into clearly defined age groups. It should also be remembered that many of these students also have part-time, and full-time, jobs and these can provide rich sources of vocational experience and information on which they can draw. Too often we fail to recognise this wealth of experience. In addition to age differences there will be differences in terms of gender, ethnicity, prior learning experiences, cultural and social norms. Think for example of the issues Clare is facing in developing teaching strategies for her groups of students (see Chapter 4).

How will assessment be organised and carried out?

Assessment is continuous throughout the programme and may be based on a series of assignments, or other forms of coursework, including practical workshop, or studio activities that are completed during the programme plus, in some cases a series of externally set and marked tests, even formal examinations. There has been a great deal of discussion recently about the balance of coursework and external assessment within qualifications, and there have been demands for a reduction in the amount of coursework permitted within GCSEs, and within A levels too (DfES, 2005b). However, as discussed in Chapter 6, 'fitness for purpose' should be the guiding principle in assessment design and practical activities, coursework, learning logs, investigations all play important roles within the teaching and learning process.

Evidence for assessment is often collected in a student's portfolio. The student has to satisfy the assessment criteria for each unit of the course and has to provide sufficient evidence that this has been achieved. We discuss portfolio building more fully in Chapter 6.

Choosing a strategy

It is clear that teaching strategies are chosen for reasons which go beyond being a mechanism for ensuring that the students achieve the subject-specific outcomes. Certainly, achievement of those outcomes is vitally important but the teacher also has to ensure that students develop their abilities as learners and build relationships with each other which contribute to an effective learning environment. We can portray this as a model for effective learning (see Figure 5.3).

Once you are clear about the outcomes to be achieved in a session, and have taken account of any constraining factors, you can select one or more teaching strategies. As noted earlier, those strategies will obviously reflect your preferences as a teacher but you may want to try out different approaches, albeit on a small scale at first until you begin to gain confidence in using them.

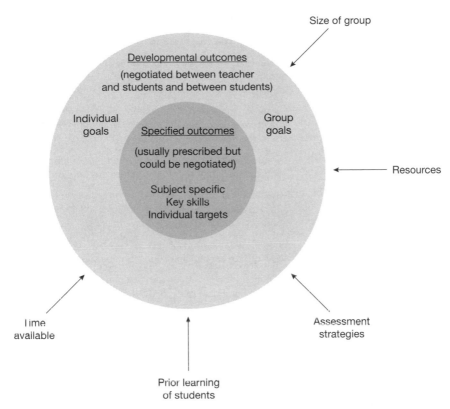

Figure 5.3 Model for effective learning

The following checklist can be used to evaluate the extent to which your proposed plan for a particular session (or 'lesson') has taken into account the different needs that have to be met. You might like to use this checklist when devising your lesson plans (Figure 5.4, p. 152).

In the following section, we identify the characteristics of a range of teaching strategies and suggest tasks which students can be asked to perform in order to ensure that they participate as fully as possible in the learning situation.

Managing learning: handling 'difficult' students

In the opening chapters of this book, we stressed the diversity of college life and, in particular, the need for FE teachers to appreciate that their students will reflect a range of abilities, needs and levels of motivation. Unlike schools, where all the students are legally required to attend, colleges expect their

Ask yourself	Quick check (some ideas)
What am I going to teach?	Topic, e.g. customer service.
Who are the learners?	Group (e.g. Level 2 catering and hospitality), size of group, age, gender, ability range, prior learning, equality and diversity issues.
Where will the teaching take place?	Classroom, laboratory, workshop, sports centre (are there any constraints in terms of location: health and safety issues?)
When will the class be timetabled?	Length of session (too long, too short, will this present a challenge? How should I structure the time?)
What are the intended learning outcomes?	What is it that I expect learners to be able to know and understand by the end of the session? Think about all, most and some (differentiation).
How?	What strategies am I going to use – whole group, small group, one-to-one support, peer support?
What range of activities will I provide?	Demonstration, speaking and listening, making notes, role play, practical work, performance, completing worksheets.
What is the balance of activities?	Teacher-led, student-led, mutually configured, supported by others (learner support staff, technicians).
How will the learning be assessed?	What strategies will I deploy, during the session, at the end of the session, in the coming weeks to confirm learning - Q and A, written test, observation of practice?
What resources will be required?	What do I need to make it happen – equipment, artefacts, PowerPoint presentation, handouts, DVDs?
What are my personal targets?	Build my confidence in working with this group; improve my classroom management skills; make a potentially 'dull' topic more interesting.
How will I evaluate this session?	In terms of students: learning, behaviour, interest, involvement, attainment.
	In terms of my teaching: giving information, questioning, providing feedback, time management, assessment, working with support staff.
What targets/action points do I want to set for next time?	Improve time management; provide more realistic and relevant examples drawn from the vocational context for students to consider; design better differentiated material.

Figure 5.4 Checklist for lesson plans

students to attend as a result of acting as responsible adults, rather than from the threat of legal sanction. Some learners, it is true, may be attending courses selected by their employers and, in the case of government-sponsored trainees or apprentices, some students may have their wages reduced for missing classes, but, even in these cases, a college would hope that the students concerned could develop enough maturity to understand the need to fulfil their obligations as course members.

The introduction of Education Maintenance Allowances (EMAs) in the UK available to young people aged 16–19 whose parental income falls below certain levels, to support them through full-time participation in education and training, has thrown this issue into sharp relief. Since tutors are required to sign weekly attendance and performance reports in order for the students' allowances to be paid, the student/teacher relationship has, in some cases, been realigned. One of the authors was recently observing a class where a young man, whose behaviour was particularly problematic, was heard saying to the lecturer: 'You can't throw me out because I'm on the allowance.' If the calls for all young people to be in some form of education or training up to the age of 18, which were gaining momentum in 2007, come to fruition, the numbers of students in colleges who feel they are being forced to attend against their will could increase. Indeed, government ministers have even been suggesting that young people who fail to comply with the any new law might be fined or even imprisoned (DfES, 2007).

All colleges, of course, have to comply with the funding criteria laid down by the relevant funding body, part of which puts particular emphasis on maintaining acceptable levels of student retention. This can lead to disputes between teachers and managers in cases where the former wish to remove particularly disruptive students from courses and the latter decide that the need for student retention overrides any difficulties in the classroom. All teachers need to feel that they have the support of their managers when faced with difficult students and should be apprised of their college's disciplinary procedures and policy on exclusions. Indeed, induction programmes for new staff to a college should include a session on this important area and should ensure that teachers have a clear picture of the support structures which exist to help them, should the need arise.

The presence of increasing numbers of 14- to 16-year-olds in FE colleges, as part of the Increased Flexibility Programme (IFP), discussed in Chapter 3, has brought a different cohort of young people into colleges with very different learning needs. Here is an example of a college's experiences with such a group:

Sunnymede College

Sunnymead College is a medium-sized general FE college situated in a market town serving a dispersed rural area. The town is a focus for tourism and there are many leisure and tourism facilities in the area; the college has therefore become a centre for hospitality, catering, leisure and tourism and business. It became involved in the IFP and is part of a partnership involving five nearby schools. The IFP is coordinated by an LEA Adviser. The college had been involved in school link programmes prior to the introduction of IFP; this has been instrumental in developing its rationale for school link work. A college lecturer is responsible for coordinating the programme in college and liaising with schools.

Pupils attend college one day a week and are working towards an NVQ Level I in catering. They gain experience of working in the college restaurant and bistro, serving real customers and producing food of a saleable quality. Pupils work to industry standards and there are high expectations in terms of dress, attendance, punctuality, working practice, time management and professionalism. The lecturer in charge of catering reports that:

> They [the schools] used to send us anybody before: people they did not want in the classroom. It was a nightmare. The behaviour was dreadful, we simply cannot have that sort of thing in a kitchen, with hot fat and knives, there's too many opportunities for flashpoints. Now it is much better. We interview students before they come, we pick the ones we really want and who have an interest in catering. We liaise very closely with schools and we involve the parents. Most of these young people want to carry on to a Level II qualification and attend college full-time after they have finished at school.

> Source: Abbott and Huddleston (2004)

It is important for all teachers to realise that some of their students may have problems which require the intervention of specialists and that, as teachers, they are not equipped to deal with such problems beyond the initial stage of encouraging and supporting an individual student to seek help. Deciding where the line falls between those students who need specialist help and those who can be supported within the everyday teaching and learning situation is, however, not a straightforward process. Sue Rees, writing about the 'growing tide' of students with emotional and behavioural difficulties in Norfolk colleges, distinguishes between those students who can be said to be 'sad' and those who are thought of as 'bad':

> The former ('sad') sub-group consists of students who are emotionally disturbed in some way. They may be lonely, isolated and have difficulties making relationships, but do not necessarily come to lecturers' attention because they do not cause obvious problems of discipline, etc., during the educational process. The latter ('bad') group may be termed as 'disturbing' rather than 'disturbed'. Their emotional state manifests itself in

behavioural problems and they are frequently aggressive and disruptive within the learning environment.

(Rees, 1995: 93)

The more experience one gains as a teacher, the more adept one becomes at managing the learning process and spotting potential flashpoints. As discussed in Chapter 4, if teachers demonstrate that they have empathy with their students, they are much more likely to create conditions that are conducive to cooperation with, and between, their students and in which all parties trust and respect each other. We also noted, however, that the pressures on students in terms of the lives they lead outside college can cause them to display behavioural patterns which appear disruptive in the classroom or workshop. But that pressure may also come from within the college if, for example, a student is struggling to keep up with their written work or if they are being bullied. And, of course, disruptive behaviour may be the students' way of telling a teacher that the sessions are boring, poorly organised or pitched at an inappropriate level. Changes in behaviour can usually be seen as signals of stress or anxiety and the teacher must be able to recognise those signals and act appropriately before the situation gets out of hand.

A key factor in the effective management of any learning situation is for the teacher to involve the students in the whole process. This involves the teacher in an exercise in sharing with students as follows:

1   Discuss with students your expectations (as a teacher) of them and identify their expectations (as students) of you. For example, try to establish a code of practice regarding lateness, the handing in of work, eating/drinking in class, dress codes, etc.
2   Explain to students the nature of what is to be covered in a particular session and how this relates to the rest of their course.
3   Explain clearly (and review at intervals) the assessment procedure you will operate – this includes both the informal (criteria you use to monitor student progress) and the formal (externally imposed criteria for summative assessment) criteria you will employ.
4   Discuss with students the constraints under which you and they must work – for example, presentation of work to satisfy external examiners, coverage of certain elements of a curriculum, the lack of sufficient computers or textbooks, etc.
5   Review your working arrangements as a group, giving students the chance to discuss whether they should be given more time to hand in work or to receive more support with a particular part of the course – this may require you to recognise any inadequacies in your initial preparation for a course or to accept that you have made mistakes.

By sharing the necessary ingredients of the learning process with students, they are given the opportunity to act responsibly and with the same degree of professionalism as the teacher. At the same time, the teacher has to be prepared to show the same degree of respect to the students and to try not to retreat into a position of isolated superiority when challenged. Working with students does not necessitate a blurring of roles to the point where teacher and student become indistinguishable. Both teacher and students have to recognise the demands of each other's roles and that the teacher, like any manager, has to take responsibility for ensuring that the collective goals of the group are achieved.

Rogers (2002) makes some very helpful suggestions for dealing with behaviour management issues, which are widely applicable across a range of teaching/group situations. He emphasises the importance of routines, clarity, reinforcing desired behaviour, and dealing unobtrusively with problems when they occur. He suggests the following principles as general good practice:

- treating all with respect in the class (peers as well as teachers/support staff);
- establishing appropriate protocols of communication in class (listening to others, speaking in an appropriate manner);
- establishing learning behaviour (how to seek support from a teacher/ others, how to support others in their learning);
- movement about the class (respecting other's space);
- dealing with problems (settling misunderstandings/arguments/potential flashpoints).

In her Norfolk study, Rees (1995) concludes that strategic planning is required to help teaching and support staff tackle the problem of 'disturbing', 'emotionally disturbed' and 'disruptive' students and suggests that staff development, particularly in 'group management', is a key feature:

> staff will require techniques for dealing with confrontation: for example non-verbal communication methods for use with aggressive students. Personal and social skills are also important, and if these are imparted effectively to staff it is likely that they will find their way successfully into the curriculum. Support groups are desirable, to provide staff with a focus and to maximise communication. By such means it will be possible to generate a positive ethos, to shape staff expectations of behaviour and to manage the general level of discipline in a constructive, staff-oriented way.
>
> (Rees, 1995: 96)

Team teaching

One of the most stimulating and rewarding ways to teach is to work with a colleague or team of colleagues. Forms of team teaching range from two people taking it in turns to address the class, to larger groups of teachers adopting a variety of roles, including facilitating small-group discussion, working on a one-to-one basis with students and coordinating project-based activities. Such teaching can be used to counter prejudice along gender and racial lines, and to overcome the difficulties in mixed-ability classes. It can also help stimulate greater responsibility on the part of students who have to learn to cooperate with teachers who display different pedagogical approaches and styles.

A particularly useful role for team teaching is during induction periods when 'ice-breaking' activities can help cement a sense of group identity and community among students and teachers. In their classic text, the *Gamesters' Handbook*, Brandes and Phillips (1985) describe a number of activities, games and strategies which can be used to promote personal development and social cohesion.

Here are a few ideas that we have used as 'icebreaker' activities:

Find a mate

On entering the room each student is given half of a definition on a strip of paper, for example *balance of* . . . another student will have the other half of the definition on a similar strip of paper, for example *payments*. Students move around the room until they find their match. When they have done so, they will take their partner to sit down and decide exactly what the definition means.

What's my line?

Tutor prepares large cards with a job title on each one (these should be taken from job roles within the vocational area the student is studying). Each student has one pinned on to his/her back so that they can only be seen by others in the group. Students move around the room and attempt to discover what their 'line' is by asking questions of other students. Responses must be restricted to 'yes' or 'no'. Once the 'line' has been discovered students sit down. When all have finished each student describes what the role entails.

Tell me a story

Students are asked to form groups of fours; tutor hands out paper bags containing 5 everyday items (one bag per group); groups are asked to construct a short story involving the 5 items. After 10 minutes, group stories are recounted to the whole class.

True or false?

Tutor prepares a set of laminated cards displaying true or false (these can be used many times). Each student is given a set of cards and is asked to respond to statements which the tutor makes, for example: 'Photosynthesis is the process by which plants use energy from sunlight to build up complex substances from carbon dioxide and water.'

From distance to e-learning

Distance learning has been available in the UK and throughout the world for much of the twentieth century, beginning with correspondence courses in which there was no contact between tutor and student other than by post. The establishment of the British Open University (OU) in 1969 led to a number of similar institutions being set up around the world. The OU was notable for allowing people to study for undergraduate degrees without any entrance requirements and for combining distance learning via multi-media materials with attendance at residential summer schools. Many FE colleges are designated as study centres for OU students who attend a limited number of face-to-face tutorial sessions in their local areas and some colleges provide courses on study skills (sometimes called 'return to learn') for adults who are considering enrolling with the OU. The term distance learning has joined a lengthy list of other terms, some of which are used interchangeably. These terms include: flexible learning; flexistudy; resource-based learning; and independent study. Although the expansion of distance learning has been largely aimed at adult learners, some of the techniques involved in the preparation of study materials have been used in schools and the learner-centred approach which drives many (though not all) distance learning programmes has influenced classroom-based and work-based teaching and learning. Now, through the rapid development of information and communication/learning technologies (ICLT) and the availability of faster access to the internet, e-learning is making its mark.

E-learning can cover a spectrum of activities from the use of technology to support learning as part of a 'blended' approach, to learning that is delivered entirely online. These flexible learning approaches are promoted in terms of their ability to provide access to learning to large numbers of people who need the flexibility of being able to study when and where they choose. The European Commission (EC), in particular, and some national governments, have extolled the virtues of flexible learning for some time. Some critics argue, however, that these newer forms of learning have grown in stature and availability as a result of the reduction in spending on staff development, training and adult education in general.

Edwards (1993) takes these arguments a stage further and suggests that the growth of open learning (which he uses as a generic term) reflects the wider societal change that is witnessing organisations shifting from Fordist (mass production lines, labour intensive) to post-Fordist (part-time working, flexible work patterns) structures. He is particularly concerned with the way in which open learning, as used in some industries, can separate employees from each other thus reducing the opportunity for critical discussion of shared concerns. Many teachers, in common with managers and other professionals, now gain their professional development through flexible learning courses which include Masters degrees and even taught Doctorates. Although Edwards's fears deserve constant attention, flexible approaches to course provision and learning are proving to be very popular, particularly with people whose professional and domestic lives allow them little time to study in conventional ways. Well-structured flexible learning programmes include opportunities, often through residential weekends, for students to come together to share ideas and enjoy the experience of being 'real' students.

Hargreaves (2004: 48) stresses the motivational power of the new technologies:

> They do this in a variety of ways. They make the work easier. Redrafting an essay is much easier to do with computer-based text than with written text, where the whole piece has to be rewritten, slowly and painfully. The Internet or the use of some commercial software can make the task of finding relevant material to support or illustrate an argument much more efficient than searching through books. They also often make the work more interesting. They give speedy access to material that is often of inherent interest: in the exploration of new sources one stumbles across the unusual and fascinating.

He describes how technology can be used to design online formative assessment tools that deliver feedback much more quickly than through more traditional means, and the important role technology can play in getting learners to take more responsibility for their own learning. In Chapter 6, we examine the dark side to ICLT – the rise of plagiarism.

If you are involved in teaching on courses which have an open, distance or electronic format, you may have the opportunity to prepare learning materials in the form of written, self-study texts, audio cassettes, instructional videos, video-conferencing and interactive computer programmes. You might also be involved in placing teaching material within what are called 'Virtual Learning Environments' using interactive platforms such as 'Blackboard'. The use of VLEs has grown dramatically in colleges (see Becta, 2006), partly as result of the 'personalisation' agenda. The extent to which you can become proficient in these media will be determined by the amount of training available and the level of resources devoted to this mode of teaching. The development of e-learning is bound to have a profound effect on the types of media available in colleges and, although one should not get too carried away by the hype surrounding such developments, it is clear that both teachers and students will need to keep abreast of the electronic revolution.

Mayes (2002) argues that ICLT and e-learning, more generally, cannot just be absorbed by teachers and students; rather, these developments require us to ask some fundamental questions about the pedagogical skills needed to utilise them properly (see also Kenway, 2001 and Laurillard, 1993). He says that we need to think about 'how technology can support the learning cycle, the goal-action-feedback loop that provides a basic model for all learning'

(Mayes, 2002: 164–5). In their research in colleges in the Netherlands and Scotland, Rommes *et al.* (2005) found that women-only classes were particularly effective in encouraging female students to develop their use of ICT for three particular reasons: positive role model effects; mutual encouragement and support among trainees; and the safety to speak openly.

Students, of course, need support in mastering the skills required to use the new learning technologies effectively. Thus, most colleges now have Learning Resources Centres. These are usually 'drop-in' centres where students can use the technology available in order to complete assignments or where they can access additional units to support other learning. They may also be able to access such material remotely. This trend may increasingly lead to more individualised learning programmes with students being able to 'pick and mix' different units and elements of courses in order to meet their own needs. This is certainly the vision set out in the proposals for a Qualifications and Credit Framework (QCF). Although this individualism may open up the whole college curriculum provision to a much wider clientele than previously, there are implications for student guidance and counselling. Students need help in accessing the parts of the curriculum that meet their needs. They also need guidance in constructing a coherent and integrated programme of learning from the wide range of offerings available. In this situation the FE teacher becomes a facilitator of learning rather than a provider. The implications for workforce development should not be underestimated.

The promotion of e-learning and the use of new technologies in general has its critics. Some are concerned about the emphasis on the individualised nature of this type of learning. For example, Field (2000: 55) points out that, 'From the perspective of an older type of adult education – dedicated to enlightenment, social improvement and the support of social movements – this individualism represents an abandonment of social purpose.' Guile and Hayton (1999: 123) raise concerns about a prevalent and very misguided belief that 'the individualised, technological approach to delivery is a cheap option'. In addition, they note that research in the UK and the US 'is increasingly demonstrating that ILT is not, by itself, a vehicle for assisting people to become acquainted with new ideas or for enabling them to think in theoretically informed ways', but rather, 'that the effective use of ILT involved teachers rethinking the relationship between the process of learning and their role in supporting such learning' (ibid.).

Conclusion

This chapter has explored a range of teaching strategies than can be employed in college and college-related settings. Individual teachers have to try on these strategies, rather like new clothes, so see how they feel and fit, as not all the strategies listed here will suit everyone.

The culture and context of the setting in which you are teaching will also affect the extent to which you can be innovative and can take risks. Your managers may not welcome seeing you trying out something untested the week the inspectors call! Finally, your students play a key role in helping you decide which strategies to use and your relationship with them will often determine how 'safe' you are in your teaching style.

Chapter 6

Assessment and recording achievement

The role of assessment

An important and integral aspect of your work in teaching will be the assessment of your students. In England and Wales in particular, assessment has been the focus of increased interest, and indeed reform, during the past fifteen years or more. At the time of writing, the DfES has placed an emphasis on the need to streamline the assessment process in order to reduce the burden of assessment, but also to ensure that the assessment process is transparent, rigorous and consistent over time, and to emphasise the need for external assessment, thus reducing the amount of assessment undertaken through coursework.

This debate is set to run for some time since it is clear that a range of assessment strategies are necessary in order to provide sufficient evidence to confirm that learning has taken place. Within vocational programmes, for example, assessment through coursework, or other forms of practical activity, may provide more reliable evidence. As Ecclestone (2002: 3) suggests:

> The political and educational aims of assessment in these approaches resonate with growing interest amongst academic and policy based researchers in the potential power of formative and diagnostic assessment to raise standards of attainment, to motivate learners and to make them more autonomous as learners.

Assessment is not only a mandatory requirement of awarding and validating bodies for whose qualifications you are preparing students, but you will need to assess in order to maintain a record of students' progress and to assist them in planning their own learning.

At the heart of this dilemma is the need to provide accountability across a wide range of learning experiences and programmes of study, to confirm learning, to measure standards and effectiveness, as well as to contribute to the personal development of students. It is clear from this that assessment performs a range of functions:

- Providing a framework in which learning goals, aims and objectives can be set.
- Providing the benchmarks for monitoring students' progress and for planning future learning.
- Providing a framework for identifying learner needs.
- Providing a framework for designing feedback.

Assessment, then, is not simply seen as something which is used for grading work, or for processes of selection; it is increasingly recognised as an important part of the learning process.

Ecclestone (2000: 144), in a wide-ranging analysis of assessment and critical autonomy in post-compulsory education, reminds us that 'ill-formed, and often contradictory, theories of learning and motivation underpin all assessment regimes in different ways'. She gives the example of behaviourism's 'belief in the power of extrinsic motivation through externally set targets, rewards and punishments', which contrasts with the 'humanist belief in people's innate need to learn the need to cultivate intrinsic motivation'. While recognising the many debates about so-called good and bad assessment approaches, Ecclestone calls for formative and diagnostic assessment to be placed 'at the centre of teaching and learning instead of being a separate afterthought, or merely an instrumental process to generate summative targets' (ibid.: 156). In this way, teachers and learners can engage in a community of assessment, a concept which has its roots in the community of practice model described in Chapter 4. Brown (1994) suggests that, in terms of young people:

> Assessment, therefore, now has several functions including the diagnosis of causes of young people's success or failure, the motivation of them to learn, the provision of valid and meaningful accounts of what has been achieved and the evaluation of courses and teaching.
>
> (Brown, 1994: 271)

At the heart of the dilemma for the teacher is the need to provide accountability across a wide range of learning experiences and programmes of study, to confirm learning, to measure standards and effectiveness, as well as to contribute to the personal development of students. When asked, 'Why do we assess students?', a group of trainee teachers gave the following responses:

- It's a measure of feedback for students.
- It helps us to plan our teaching more effectively.
- We do it to grade students.
- Assessment is formative.
- It's for selection.

- It helps us to know if the students have understood.
- To empower the student and teacher to move forward.

The variety of responses indicates the multi-faceted nature of the assessment process. Assessment is now not so much something which is 'done unto' students but which often involves negotiations with students and sometimes with employers as well. Both its purposes and practice have changed during recent years. Some of these changes are associated with changes to the structure of qualifications and programmes. The introduction of mandatory assessment within the National Curriculum in England in the compulsory phase of schooling is mirrored by similar changes in the post-compulsory sector.

Throughout life, we are both being assessed by and assessing other people, whether it is formally as in the case of a teacher, magistrate, employer or parent, or informally as when we meet someone for the first time or attend a concert. In education and training, assessment is a powerful process, which can both empower people as well as damage them. There are many adults who carry the scars of their encounters with assessment throughout their lives. Some, for example, remember failing the 11+ examination for entry to grammar school, whereas others may never forget the agonies of oral spelling tests or being made to write their answer to an arithmetic question on the blackboard in front of the whole class. Smith (1989: 119) asserts that both the assessor and the person being assessed need to understand the nature of the assessment process and that

> The more aware both assessors and assessed become of the relationship between the outcomes of the judgement process and the sources of evidence from which they derive, and the more honest assessors become about the sources of evidence from which their judgements derive, the more equitable and generally acceptable they are likely to be.

Fitness for purpose should be the guiding principle in considering assessment design. There is a wide variety of assessment techniques. Whichever method is selected it is important to recognise the purpose of the assessment and what it is designed to measure. Different methods of assessment will be necessary to assess practical skills from those designed to assess students' ability to engage with a theoretical concept.

Reflection

The facing page shows some examples of different assessment methods, which you may have used yourself or seen used by others. Consider where, within your own particular subject area, you might use them. The first one is already completed; consider also 'fitness for purpose' issues.

	Activity	*Subject area*
Role play	Mock interviews	Business studies (Human Resources); Key skills (Communications)
Assignment		
Case study		
Short answer test		
Multi-choice questions		
Essay		
Data response		
Practical test		
Presentation		
Other examples?		

As we saw in Chapter 3, the introduction of an outcome-based model of vocational qualifications has resulted in the measurement of achievement in terms of outcomes, that is through the demonstration of competence, usually within the workplace. Here there is a danger of the assessment dominating the learning process if achievement is measured in terms of outcome and bears scant regard to the process by which these skills are acquired. Assessment for assessment's sake is unhelpful and does little to enhance the learning process. Assessment should be an integral part of learning and should help to identify evidence of achievement as well as inform the design or redesign of learning programmes.

A major contribution to the 'Assessment for Learning' debate has been made by the Assessment Reform Group. Following an extensive review of classroom practice, the group argued that:

> when carried out effectively, informal classroom assessment with constructive feedback to the student will raise levels of attainment. Although it is now fairly widely accepted that this form of assessment and feedback is important, the development of practice in this area will need a concerted policy-making push.
>
> (Assessment Reform Group, 1999: 1)

Research undertaken by Black and Wiliam (1998: 9–11) outlines some guiding principles for effective formative assessment. These stress that:

feedback should emphasise the qualities of the work and areas for improvement and not make comparisons with other students' work; students should be trained in self-assessment so that they can see what they need to achieve; students should be provided with opportunities to reflect on their performance; written work and tests should be relevant to learning aims. You may wish to reflect on these features as you begin to design your own assessment strategies.

Similarly, work on theories of learning has also influenced the debate on how we carry out assessment. We have discussed some of these in Chapter 4. Views on the ways in which individuals learn are contested. Broadly speaking, the current debate flows from two theoretical traditions, 'symbolic cognition' and 'situated cognition'. Symbolic processing, it is suggested, separates the learner from the environment, whereas theories of situated cognition place emphasis upon the contexts in which learning takes place. Learning is achieved by 'doing' as well as 'knowing' and by interacting with others through that learning process. Murphy (1999: ix) presents the difference as follows: 'The focus in understanding learning in this approach (symbolic cognition) is therefore the individual's internal mental processing and the symbolic representations of the mind. In the situated approach human knowledge and interaction are seen as inseparable from the world.'

There is insufficient space to pursue these theories in more detail here. Nevertheless, it is important to remember that in designing assessment strategies we need, as teachers, to be aware of the different ways in which our students learn. There is a wide array of assessment techniques that will be discussed in more detail in this chapter. Whichever method is selected, 'fitness for purpose' should be the guiding principle. It is important to recognise the purposes of the assessment and what it is designed to measure. Different methods of assessment will be necessary to assess practical skills from those designed to assess a student's capacity to engage with a theoretical concept. A catering student's ability to make a soufflé will ultimately have to be assessed by the production of the finished product, not by writing about it. Nevertheless, a written assignment may be used to assess the student's knowledge of the underlying food science theory, or this could be assessed by means of oral questioning. Similarly, intending teachers are assessed on their ability to convert lesson plans into practical teaching activities. Subject knowledge and classroom practice have to be assessed equally but using different techniques.

The focus of assessment should be on the student and the measurement of his or her achievement. Testing as a means of 'catching people out' does little to develop confidence or to identify real learning. Similarly, 'teaching to the test' may simply identify those with good memories or reflect a teacher's ability to spot questions. Most of us will probably remember our attempts to revise only seven out of the ten available topics for an examination, in the hope that some of them would 'come up'.

In our research for this book, one FE teacher remarked, 'Our business is to help students achieve.' This should be a guiding principle in the design of assessment procedures. Such procedures should be formative and motivational and appropriate in their design for the purpose for which they are intended. Whereas assessment will be used for the purposes of selection, it should always have a strong emphasis on the recognition of achievement. It may now be useful to consider the different types of assessment:

> The term assessment refers to all those activities undertaken by teachers, and by their students in assessing themselves, which provide information to be used as feedback to modify the teaching and learning activities in which they are engaged. Such evidence becomes 'formative assessment' when the evidence is actually used to adapt the teachingwork to meet the needs.
>
> (Black and Wiliam, 1998: 2)

Formative assessment

It is now generally recognised that assessment is most helpful when it forms an ongoing and integral part of teaching and learning so that feedback can be used at each stage in the planning/teaching/evaluation cycle. To be formative, assessment must have a *feedback* and a *feedforward* function (Brooks, 2004: 110).

The purpose of formative assessment is to provide a continuous process which charts achievement, identifies areas for development and indicates next steps for both teachers and learners. It can be either formal or informal, or a combination of both. Action planning may be a part of the formative assessment process in that students should be encouraged to reflect on what they need to do in order to move their learning on. All colleges now have continuous assessment procedures in place. Many vocational programmes require students to complete portfolios of evidence that testify to their achievement of the units of the qualification. In this way, they provide a record of achievement but they provide no real feedback on how the student is progressing. They simply record the steps along the way to achieving the full award. The same is true of NVQs. Here individual elements of competences are recorded as they are achieved. The emphasis is on the 'can do' rather than the 'will do'.

A formative assessment should consider the 'will do' in that it should help to inform the next steps of the student's development. As teachers we are constantly involved in formative assessment through informal means. For example, we will find ourselves using the chance remark, 'That's very good, but next time why don't you think about including some conclusions at the end of your report?' or 'It would be really great if you had to do something like this again, if you presented your results in the form of a bar chart.'

We should also encourage our students to reflect upon their performance. We may ask them to consider such questions as:

- In which parts of this assignment did I do well?
- In which parts of this assignment did I not do so well?
- Did I manage my time effectively?
- Are there areas which I would wish to improve?
- Do I need to access the Learning Resources Centre?
- Did I work effectively with other members of my team in completing this assignment?

Ideally, any formative assessment should involve a dialogue between student and teacher. Sometimes this may take the form of a record which may be signed by both parties. See p. 169 for an extract from a student's profile that is designed to provide formative assessment for the student. The emphasis in the student's profile is on what has been learned and on what needs to be learned in the future. The purpose of the assessment should be to improve the learning. Placing a tick or simply writing 'well done' at the end of a piece of work gives little indication of how the piece might be improved further. Tests may be useful in identifying what students know, or do not know, but unless accompanied by some feedback, they may provide no diagnosis as to the reasons why students do not know. There is always a danger too that some of the correct answers may have been arrived at through guesswork.

One of the most important uses of formative assessment is to establish a student's level of ability in the basic skills of literacy and numeracy. Research by Steve Harris, a lecturer in a college in the West Midlands, found that students on a BTEC National Diploma in Computer Studies had problems with both their written communication and basic numeracy (see Harris and Hyland, 1995). Harris followed up this research by asking delegates to a national conference on BTEC Computer Studies whether his findings were common, and found that 'Managerial and financial pressures were forcing tutors to enrol students on the BTEC Computer Studies course who, without the basic grounding, were likely to experience considerable difficulty with parts of the programme' (ibid.: 45). On the basis of his research, Harris's college decided to screen all new full-time students using a basic skills test and to offer, through its School of Learning Support, a range of support measures including courses for students with learning difficulties and basic skills' drop-in facilities (ibid.: 46–7).

It is interesting to note that within the current guidance, emphasis is placed on the importance of initial assessment in order to determine the appropriate level at which the student should prepare for key skills. Good practice dictates that this should be the starting point for any programme of study, and that appropriate guidance and induction should be provided for any student

STUDENT PROFILE

Name _____

Programme of study/course _____

Group _____

Date _____

Date of last tutorial _____

What assessed work has been completed since the last tutorial? (List)

_____

_____

What grades/marks/comments were received? (List)

_____

_____

Do these marks reflect a fair assessment of my performance?

_____

_____

In which assignments/tests did I do particularly well? (You should not just consider the overall grade, but did you make a significant improvement on previous work, or did you succeed in spite of some practical or personal difficulty?)

_____

_____

In which assignments/tests did I not do so well? (Why was this?)

_____

_____

Are there any areas in which I require help? _____

What are they? _____

_____

What do I intend to do about this? _____

_____

What do I want to achieve by the time of the next tutorial? _____

_____

How shall I achieve this? _____

_____

Signed   .... _Student_

.... _Tutor_

Figure 6.1 Student profile

embarking upon a course of further education. Inappropriate course choice can be an important factor in student retention. The recommendations for an increasingly personalised learning offer make the initial induction assessment process central to appropriate course choice and eventual successful outcome.

Brooks (2004) offers some very helpful guidance in terms of providing positive feedback to students. She suggests, for example, the importance of giving clear indication within an assignment brief of the criteria for assessment. In this way it is easy to demonstrate the extent to which these have been met and for students to plan, and later to evaluate, their work against the criteria. If you look at the qualification specifications for, say, applied A levels you will see that the assessment criteria are clearly indicated, including guidance on what would constitute achievement across the grade bands. She also stresses the importance of timely and balanced feedback – highlighting positives and drawing attention to areas for development.

Summative assessment

Summative assessment is used to ascertain whether the aims of a course or programme have been achieved, for example through the setting of a final examination. Examinations often have an important role in selecting or deselecting those for the next phase of education, for example from FE into HE or from a BTEC National programme to a Higher National programme. For this reason summative assessment is often referred to as 'high stakes' assessment because, frequently, much depends upon it. Harlen and Deakin Crick (2002) suggest that summative assessment:

- narrows the curriculum and encourages rote learning;
- widens the gap between high and low achievers;
- promotes high anxiety levels amongst students;
- erodes the self-esteem of low attainers.

Summative assessment has increasingly assumed an important accountability function for colleges, since they are required to provide detailed information on assessment outcomes. There are funding implications too in, for example, programmes such as government-supported apprenticeships where colleges receive a final payment when apprentices achieve their qualifications. Within competence-based qualifications, summative assessment is made to ensure that all units of the qualification have been achieved. In some vocational programmes, the student's portfolio is the collection of work which provides the evidence that the requirements for each unit have been met. This evidence is derived from the coursework assignments.

Reflection

In the example below a lecturer has prepared an assignment for students following AS GCE in Leisure Studies. The assignment focuses on Unit 3 of the specification, in particular 3.2: 'Operational aspects related to the leisure customer'. Read through the assignment and consider the extent to which the lecturer has provided clear guidance on what has to be achieved and by what criteria the piece will be assessed.

Unit 3 The Leisure Customer

3.2 Operational aspects related to the leisure customer

Spring Term Assignment

Background

At the end of last term, Jane Bailey, the manager of Sunny Park Leisure Centre in Boomtown, presented to the group. She outlined details of the centre's vision for customer service, along with procedures in place to ensure continued high levels of customer service. Jane also shared with us examples of customer feedback from the 'comments box' in the foyer.

Jane would like to improve the levels of customer service further and is looking for your advice!

You are required to investigate a <u>different</u> leisure organisation and <u>evaluate</u> its levels of customer service.

Using the information you obtain, you are required to prepare a report for Jane outlining your findings and making recommendations on what Sunny Park Leisure Centre can learn from the organisation you have studied.

It would help if the leisure organisation you study is involved in similar activities to Sunny Park (i.e. swimming, gymnasium etc.) although this is not essential. Please ensure you get my agreement on your choice of organisation before you start.

Please read through the next section in detail as it outlines exactly what you have to do.

Spring Term Assignment
The Leisure Customer – Operational Aspects

1   Choose a leisure organisation (preferably a fitness organisation) near to you. It may help if it is one that you or your family are familiar with.

2 Make a 'mystery visit' to the organisation. Gather in-depth information about the organisation's provision of customer service that you experienced. This should include, but is not limited to:

- quality of the service you experienced
- helpfulness of staff
- cleanliness of facilities
- access for customers, signs, etc.
- price
- opening times
- range of services on offer
- reception procedures

3 Interview the manager about how they approach customer service. <u>Review</u> any relevant documents like mission statements (often on display), or customer service training manuals or procedures. <u>Evaluate</u> whether these are effective and suitable in providing customer service.

4 Reflect on your findings and produce some key <u>learning outcomes</u> about good customer service that you can use to make recommendations for Sunny Park.

Required outputs

Your full report is required by the end <u>of this term</u>. You have 10 weeks left, so please plan your time carefully.

You will need to produce two documents:

1 a word-processed report (at least 6 pages), containing each of the four sections of the assignment;

2 a PowerPoint presentation summarising some key recommendations for Sunny Park. You should plan for a presentation of about 8–10 minutes.

Report

Section 1:   Write a section that describes the leisure organisation you have chosen, including its location, range of services and other background details. Include what sort of leisure customers the organisation is aimed at.

Section 2:   After your 'mystery visit', write up this section of the report based on the detailed notes you took during your visit. (Write a list of the areas you are going to look at <u>in advance</u>.) You are required to <u>evaluate</u> each aspect of customer service you experienced, so under each heading, make sure you write the service you experienced and how effective you felt it was. Separate the positive and negative points. This should be the longest section of the report.

Section 3:   After you have interviewed the manager and collected documents relating to customer service, write up a review of how <u>effective</u> and <u>suitable</u> they are. If you cannot get an interview, often documents such as mission statements are up on display.

Section 4: This is the conclusion. Reflect on the previous three sections and summarise the positive and negative aspects of customer service that you experienced. Where you highlight any negative aspects, try and make recommendations on how these could have been improved.

Presentation

Using your assignment report, prepare a presentation for Jane Bailey of Sunny Park Leisure Centre. Outline your key learning outcomes from the different areas of customer service you experienced and apply these to Sunny Park in the form of some recommendations.

The presentation should last for 8–10 minutes.

Assessment criteria

To gain access to the highest mark bands:

- Your report should give examples of a range of aspects of customer service you received on your mystery visit.
- You need to evaluate how successful the organisation is in serving customers. This should be possible through your conclusion as you assess its strengths and weaknesses.
- You also need to get hold of a range of documents like mission statements, training manuals, customer comments forms and comment on their effectiveness and suitability. To do this you will need to have secured an interview with the manager or other member of staff. You will also need their permission to include these.

Special notes for your assignment

- Please ensure you have agreed with me the leisure organisation you choose before you make your mystery visit.
- Before you make the mystery visit, please tell your parents/carers where you are going.
- When conducting your mystery visit, do so as part of a general 'look around' the organisation. Do not pretend to be a potential member and have a sales manager show you around as they are busy people.
- If you are unable to find a suitable leisure organisation, Jane has given the group permission to use her other local facilities which are:
  - Marsh Field Swimming Pool
  - Brook Farm Recreation Centre
  - Cherry Common Leisure Centre.

- Please do not take photographs inside any organisation unless you have prior permission. Do not take photographs inside any changing area.
- As part of this assignment you may want to interview some customers. Please make sure you ask permission from the manager first. Also – you will need to show me and the manager your questionnaire in advance.
- Remember that many organisations have their own websites. You can use these as part of your work. Please make sure you remember to include any websites visited in your references.
- Please enclose any extra resources as appendices to your work. These could include – photographs, leaflets, photocopies of mission statements or customer service policies, questionnaires, interview notes.

And finally:

- Please check your work before you hand it in for errors or for poor English.
- Please make sure all pages are numbered and that you have completed each of the four sections of the report as well as the presentation
- Please confirm this coursework is all your own work before you submit it.
- This work is due in its <u>final form</u> on <u>2 April</u>.

In the following section the lecturer provides a rationale for the assignment design. Consider how effectively he has taken into account the needs of assessment in its design.

Rationale for this assignment

This assignment was designed for the Edexcel AS GCE in Leisure Studies (Single Award) and specifically for Unit 3.2, 'Operational aspects related to the leisure customer'.

The starting point for designing any piece of coursework is the 'what you need to learn' section of the qualification specification. However, it is wise to look much further than this, as has been done in this case.

The 'Introduction' to the unit clearly states that 'theoretical and practical' activities are required, and that these should lead to 'analysis' and 'interpretation' of leisure organisations. The assumption has been made that the class time has been quite theoretical so this assignment has been designed to be wholly practical in nature, centred on a mystery visit.

The assignment has also been designed so that some points of 'analysis' are made during the visit, and that a presentation of recommendations will require 'interpretation' and 'evaluation', therefore allowing higher ability candidates to reach the highest mark bands.

As well as the specification itself, the Teacher's Guide, Mark Scheme and Examiner's Report were also studied from the Edexcel website. These also helped to guide the development of coursework and contributed to the rationale for this particular assignment.

The Teacher's Guide contains 'mock' coursework. This was a useful basis for constructing this particular assignment. It also contains examples of students' work with both teachers' comments and the examiners' comments. Again, these all help to shape an assignment which directly meets the requirements of the examiners, ensuring that the students get every opportunity to gain the highest marks possible. A good example is that only in the Teacher's Guide does it becomes clear that for section 3.2 there is only requirement for one organisation to be analysed in depth. Without viewing this, one may have created an assignment where students analysed several organisations, which would have sacrificed depth of analysis and, therefore, marks.

The Examiner's Report is a very useful resource as it is the one document written after the setting of the specification and mark scheme and, therefore, gives a very practical viewpoint on common errors of students. In the case of this assignment, the Examiner's Report was relied upon to create an assignment to help students avoid common pitfalls which result in lower marks.

In terms of the specifics of this assignment, it has been designed around a fitness/swimming establishment to which it is hoped most students would have access. The assignment has also been designed to include a talk from a leisure centre manager so the area is familiar to them.

The context of the assignment is that a real leisure manager wants 'recommendations' from each of the students. This is designed not only to motivate them, as the coursework has a real purpose outside the qualification itself, but also to make it feel more like a vocational piece of work that is not just theoretical in nature.

The assignment is also designed so that while students are encouraged to use leisure centres, there is flexibility (with the lecturer's approval). It is also acknowledged that not all students are members of, or would have access to, their own centres. For this reason agreement with the Boomtown manager has been arranged so 'sister' organisations can be visited by students if necessary without further specific permission.

The 'What you need to know' section of the specification makes it clear that a mystery visit needs to be undertaken to gain information about customer service. This is, therefore, the central theme of the assignment and the largest section of the report. In addition, the section of the specification requires understanding of 'mission statements', 'customer service policies and procedures' and 'training programmes'. Again, all these are central to the assignment to ensure that students are clear about what they need to do to access the highest mark bands.

Wherever possible, the language of the examiners is used to ensure students are encouraged to undertake the correct level of work, for example, 'evaluate', 'apply'. The assignment goes further than this, however, in being a practical piece of work requiring a final presentation to a 'real' customer with recommendations. This encourages the students to think about converting the data they have collected into information, and then evaluating this information to be able to make useful recommendations.

It is acknowledged that not every student will be able, or motivated, to obtain the highest mark bands. For this reason the assignment allows for differentiation. For example, in order to obtain mark band 3, a review of several documents needs to be undertaken. The assignment encourages students to interview a member of staff and gain access to these documents, but also encourages students who are unable, or unwilling, to do this to collect evidence such as mission statements from the public areas. This could get them to mark band 2.

The assignment spells out the key assessment criteria, in the students' own language, so the whole process of access to different mark bands is transparent.

Towards the end of the assignment, several practical issues are covered, such as parental/carer knowledge, photography in changing rooms, permission for interviewing customers, etc. It is important for assignments to contain this sort of information as it is wholly inappropriate for lecturers to set pieces of work which could encourage students to act in inappropriate ways or put themselves at risk.

The assignment provides students with an opportunity to understand customer service around the leisure customer and to experience it for themselves. It also covers all the areas detailed in the specification, and with the reality of the 'feedback presentation', it directs students towards the higher skills and, therefore, higher mark bands.

The assignment is also designed to address some areas of key skills development. The data collection is qualitative, so while there is little opportunity for application of number, the assignment is designed around several other key skills. Communication is addressed through interviewing leisure managers and, of course, through the final group presentation. IT is developed through research and through the report and presentation. Improving own learning and performance is developed through allowing the students to plan their own work schedules to complete the assignment in the allotted 10-week period.

In the case of NVQs candidates will present themselves for summative assessment whenever they consider they can demonstrate competence; that is, through the production of evidence. Evidence may take a variety of forms, for example:

- copies of documents appropriately word-processed;
- artefacts produced in practical classes;
- log books signed by supervisors testifying that certain procedures have been undertaken, for example in retailing, stock rotation.

Essentially, the purpose of the assessment is to verify that the candidate 'can do' what is described in the element.

Although summative assessment plays an important part in assessing students and, it could be argued, is the only means of assessment in competence-based qualifications, ideally, this type of assessment should always be underpinned by a diagnostic process that will help students identify how they can improve their performance next time. Competence-based qualifications attest to candidates' abilities through a series of 'can do' statements; however, there is little scope for indicating *how well* a candidate 'can do' something over a period of time. As individuals, we all know that we can perform a whole range of activities, but that we will perform some of them much better on some days than on other days, and under different sets of conditions and circumstances.

As teachers, we need to be aware of the range of assessment techniques available to us and to select those most appropriate for the piece of work we are trying to assess. In practice, we are likely to adopt a range of approaches within our teaching programmes. We now consider some of these different approaches.

Essays

There has been a considerable shift away from essay-type assessment during recent years, particularly within vocational programmes, but criticisms concerning 'lack of rigour' in assessment procedures have led to the inclusion of externally set and marked tests in both applied GCSE and applied GCE programmes. In GCSE programmes, assessment, which initially included a fair proportion of coursework, has reverted, and is now more examination-based, with a corresponding reduction in coursework. This trend is likely to continue given the proposals outlined in the recent 14–19 Implementation Plan (DfES, 2006a). The problems associated with essay-type tests are that, as Cohen and Manion (1989: 286) note, they 'are more difficult to assess reliably. With only one assessor a considerable degree of subjectivity can creep in'. In an examination constructed around essays, within a tightly regulated timeframe, there is only a limited capacity to cover the entire syllabus. This may result in some candidates being unable to show their real ability if they have 'spotted' the wrong question. In contrast, those who favour the competence-based approach would argue that this method of assessment ensures complete coverage in that the achievement of every unit must be demonstrated. The essay, on the other hand, gives only partial coverage. Nevertheless, the essay does test students' abilities to organise material, present arguments and interpret the question in their own way. It allows for a degree of creativity and individuality, though this individuality can create problems in the marking. Since no two essays will be alike, it is important to establish clear criteria, in advance, by which the resulting essays can be reliably assessed. An enormous number of candidates may sit public examinations. It is, therefore, essential that marking is standardised and that it is subject to checks and double-checks. Currently, there is significant development in the area of e-marking.

As a beginning teacher in FE, one approach is to consider what an ideal answer might look like. In setting an essay question you should ask yourself: 'What is it that I want students to be able to demonstrate?' You should also decide what marks you would want to allocate for style, grammar and syntax. Two illuminating examples spring to mind from a career in FE teaching. One chemistry candidate was referred by the external examiner because of the poor presentation of the written work, including weak spelling and punctuation. The chemistry content, when it could be disentangled from the unstructured answer, was perfectly adequate. The second example occurred during a programme review board. An HND catering student was presented as a fail, but the head of department leapt to his defence stating, 'the boy writes beautifully'. The fact that there was very little catering theory included in the answer appeared to have escaped the head's attention. These may be extreme cases but they serve to highlight the importance of setting a fixed analytic grading scheme in advance and of having a clear view of what is expected in the answer. This will avoid some of the pitfalls of impressionistic marking. It is often helpful to indicate a numerical marking scheme for students alongside the question. This will indicate the relative importance of different sections of a question.

You will notice that some assessments are given a numerical rating whereas others may receive a literal grade. The public examination results for GCSE and A level are expressed in literal terms. There is a further element of potential confusion here since what might be a B grade to one marker may be a C to another. It is necessary to have some correlation between a possible numerical score and its literal counterpart, for example 50 to 55 may equate with C. This has to be clearly stated in advance. Some vocational programmes use pass, merit and distinction as grading criteria. There is a clear indication within the specifications of the criteria for each of these levels.

In all externally set and marked examinations there is always some process of moderation. That is, an external examiner or moderator will check a sample of scripts to ensure that marking is consistent across the range of candidates and markers. One useful way of doing this for new teachers is to sample a range of scripts and to mark them according to the stated criteria, and then cross-check the results against those of the experienced teacher. Try to identify why differences have occurred.

Written tests

There are other ways of assessing students than through essay writing. These can range from simple questions requiring tick-box answers to those questions that are more unstructured or open-ended and require a student to think more deeply about a topic, to analyse, reflect and present arguments. Obviously, this form of questioning is far more suitable for some topics than for others. In mathematics, answers will be either right or wrong, but all working must be shown. For example, the key skill, Application of Number at Levels 2 and 3 is assessed through the following topics:

- interpret mathematical information
- calculate, check and generate results
- interpret, explain and present results.

(LSDA, 2001)

Here is a short-answer test, which might provide some evidence for Application of Number at the appropriate level; for example: 'Solve whole number problems involving addition and subtraction.'

Question: Here are the figures for 'Krazy Kuts' hair salon during the last week.

	Mon	Tues	Wed	Thurs	Fri	Sat
Cut and blow dry	6	10	8	16	25	20
Perm	2	3	2	5	7	10
Shampoo and set	5	8	7	13	21	20
Tints	4	2	0	4	5	16

1   How many more perms were sold on Saturday than on Tuesday?
2   How many 'cut and blow-dry' appointments were made during the week?
3   On which day were most 'shampoo and sets' carried out?
4   Which is the least popular treatment?
5   If the salon decided to close on one day of the week which day should it be? Why?

In designing such questions it is helpful to place them within the context of the students' learning. This is particularly important in the case of vocational programmes where students often find difficulty in relating the theoretical applications of topics to practical situations.

Reflection

Try to think of the opportunities presented for key skills development within your own professional subject area. This is often referred to as mapping. In order to do this, you might use the following planning matrix.

Planning matrix

Key skill	*Opportunities*
Communications	Reading, understanding and summarising information; using written communication; presenting information (orally). **Examples:**
Application of number	Interpreting mathematical information; calculating; checking and generating results; interpreting, explaining and presenting findings. **Examples:**
Information technology	Identifying sources and finding information; interpreting and exploring information; entering and developing information; presenting information. **Examples:**

Opportunities for key skills development are now signposted within all post-16 qualifications, including those offered in the 'work-based' route. Assessment of key skills has posed considerable challenges for staff, particularly for those who are more accustomed to teaching on academic programmes.

The guiding principle in the assessment of key skills is that evidence should be derived from the work which students are doing in their main programmes of study: academic, vocational, or professional: 'Key skills assignments are not literally key skills assignments at all, but are subject-based assignments that integrate the development and achievement of key skills' (LSDA, 2001: 2).

Notice the terminology: the areas are not described as mathematics or English. As a lecturer beginning your work in FE you will need to make these connections in designing your assignments for students. You may have a background in academic mathematics or English and, therefore, you will need to consider the application of your subject knowledge to new contexts. As part of the current 14–19 Curriculum and Qualification Reform, targets for the achievement of functional skills (English, mathematics and information technology) have been set for all learners up to level II. This means for example, that no one will be able to achieve a GCSE grade A*–C in English, maths or IT unless they have achieved the functional skills element. Similarly, functional skills will be a component of the proposed new diplomas (see Chapter 3). There are similar targets for functional skills within the work-based route.

Highly structured questions are, obviously, much easier to mark than unstructured questions. Multiple-choice questions are used by some awarding bodies and the answers can be precoded for ease of marking. In designing such tests care has to be taken in eliminating ambiguity from the possible answers offered since there must only be one 'right' answer. This method of testing purports to offer wide coverage of a syllabus but it offers nothing in the way of analysis or interpretation, dealing primarily with recall. Minton (1991: 194) suggests that, 'Multi-choice objective tests of the kind used by examining boards are best left to experts to compile. Few people have the skills to write them.' They can, however, provide a useful means of checking from time to time on students' learning. They can identify any misunderstandings which might have occurred. However, a balance has to be struck between the time given to testing and that given to real learning. If too much time is spent preparing for tests, including teaching to the test, then this will impede the overall learning process. It can also be demotivating for students. Testing should be seen as part of an overall learning strategy in which there are a variety of assessment methods.

In writing short-answer questions, it is important that the teacher makes absolutely clear what is required; questions should be unambiguous. It is useful to include guidance on marks awarded for each question so that a student can see the relative importance of the questions and plan the timing accordingly.

Box 6.1 (p. 182) shows a short-answer question suitable for Level 2 Business Administration. It covers the topic of Reception Duties.

Objective tests require very little judgement on the part of the marker because there may be only one correct answer. Students may be required to fill in missing words from a sentence, for example, or identify places on a map. They are reasonably easy to write and simple to do. Again they should not be used as the only means of assessment because they do not allow for creativity.

Box 6.2 shows an example of an objective test which might be used with some Level 1 Catering students.

Box 6.1 Level 2 Business Administration

'Receive and direct visitors'

1 List 3 skills/qualities required by a good receptionist

    i)   _____

    ii)   _____

    iii) _____

                                                   (3 marks)

2 What procedures should be followed when a visitor with an
   appointment arrives at your company?

   _____

   _____

   _____

                                                   (5 marks)

3 What information should be included when leaving messages for
   members of your company that have been left on the reception
   answerphone?

   _____

   _____

   _____

                                                   (5 marks)

4 Where would you find the following information?

   • a copy of the company's Annual Report _____

   • the telephone extension of the Personnel Director _____

   • the nearest first aid box _____

   • the telephone number of a local taxi company _____

   • a brochure of the company's product range _____

                                                   (5 marks)

Box 6.2 Matching pairs

Draw lines to link the type of pastry with the correct dish

Hot water crust   Apple dumplings

Choux pastry   Sausage rolls

Short crust pastry   Pork pie

Suet pastry   Eclairs

Puff pastry   Plum tart

                                   Peach crumble

                                   Yorkshire pudding

                                   Fruit cobbler

Oral tests

Oral tests are now an integral part of student assessment. Many programmes often include some form of presentation to a variety of audiences. Presentation skills are included within the specifications for key skills in Communication. At Level 2, for example, candidates would be expected to 'contribute to a discussion' or 'give a short talk'. At Level 3, the candidate would be expected to 'make a presentation about a complex subject' and would be expected to use appropriate visual aids, including 'at least one image to illustrate complex points'.

The assessment of such skills is challenging and can, of course, be highly subjective. The assessor has to be very clear about what is being tested and has to make this known to the candidates. There should be a mark sheet available and it is helpful to have another marker or moderator present in the audience. This can help to eliminate tutor bias. A sample mark sheet might look as shown in Box 6.3.

The relative weightings of the marks can be adjusted according to the purpose of the assignment. If you were assessing students' abilities in public speaking, for example, one might want to include marks for diction or, in the case of a poem, a mark for interpretation.

As with all assessment, feedback is extremely important in this type of activity and it has to be handled with great sensitivity. It is often less threatening to students if they begin by making short group presentations in which each can play a small part before asking them to embark on individual

Box 6.3

	Marks awarded	Maximum marks allowed
Content:		20
Structure:		15
Suitability of language for purpose:		10
Clarity of exposition:		15
Accuracy of information:		20
Use of visual aids:		5
Ability to handle questions:		10
Appearance:		5
		100

presentations. This requires detailed knowledge of the group and a supportive environment in which to work.

Assignments

As we saw earlier in this chapter (Sunny Park Leisure Centre), these are much longer pieces of assessed work and form a very important element in the assessment strategy of vocational qualifications. The assignment is central to the learning process and should bring together and integrate different components of the programme. Assignments should enable students to learn and develop their knowledge and to practise applying their skills in a vocational context. The assessment is based on the evidence submitted within the assignment. Designing and writing assignments is a complex task and is very different from writing essay questions or short-answer tests. In Chapter 5 we looked at the design of assignments. Every assignment should carry with it a set of grading criteria and students should be absolutely clear as to what is required.

Within qualification specifications clear grading criteria are expressed within the unit guidance in such a way that candidates know exactly what is required to achieve a pass, merit or distinction grade, or in the case of applied

GCSEs or applied A levels, a literal grade, A–E. Full details on assessment procedures for all qualifications are available from the awarding bodies and, because they are subject to revision from time to time, readers are advised to ensure that they have the latest available guidance.

The marking of assignments requires cooperation among different staff members teaching the programme. If the assignment is to be truly integrative, then it should be jointly designed and written by the course team as well as assessed by them. Coverage of the units will be cross-checked against the evidence provided in the assignment. This evidence may take a variety of forms. Within the same assignment a student may be required to:

- produce some written work, for example to write a report;
- undertake some practical activity, for example, strip down an engine;
- give a short oral presentation, for example, on work experience;
- produce a set of drawings, for example, for a design specification;
- record audio tapes;
- complete artwork.

Assessment within vocational programmes may involve using a variety of evidence and need not be done on the basis of paper-based evidence alone. Teachers have sometimes been reluctant to design assignments that will allow students to present evidence in different forms, for example, using tape-recordings, photographs or log books. This may, in part, reflect the culture of academic teaching where the only acceptable evidence is the production of written work, often under examination conditions. Group work may be seen as tantamount to 'cheating'. The issue of plagiarism raises serious concerns for the integrity of the examinations and awarding system. There is a further concern which relates to the difficulty of providing valid and reliable methods of assessing work that is not written.

In designing practical assignments it is necessary to strike a balance between the assessment of the finished product/design/result and the skills and knowledge used in achieving that result. For example, what percentage of the marks should be given to manual skills, to the selection of appropriate tools or materials, and what percentage to the final product? If a student worked with little regard to health and safety procedures should this invalidate the finished result? All these considerations need to be taken into account when drawing up the grading criteria for an assignment.

One college we visited in the English Midlands has designed an assessment procedure for NVQ Catering which involved the production of a set of photographs indicating 'standard' dishes. Students' practical outputs are then judged against the 'photographic standards'. This also helps students to identify what they are aiming for in the finished product.

It is often a useful strategy to show students examples of work which have been completed by former students, subject, of course, to their agreement.

With a teacher's help, students can be encouraged to identify the strengths and weaknesses of different approaches. This is particularly helpful in the case of adult students who may be returning to learning after a considerable break and who may be anxious about the production of assignments. You have already met some of these students in Chapter 2.

You will gather from all of this that the process of assessment and recording achievement is an extremely complex one. The teacher is required to act in a number of different roles, ranging from being purely a marker to being a guide, counsellor and mentor. Some of these roles are potentially conflicting. As a tutor you may know that a student is undergoing a series of personal difficulties, which you feel may have impinged upon the production of a good piece of work. How then are you to assess the work? In terms of a strict 'standards' methodology the work does not meet the criteria. As tutor, you are aware of the reasons why this work may not meet the standards. This brings us back to the fundamental purposes of assessment and the balance between the formative and summative elements. The tutor has to strike a balance between directing the students and 'letting the students go'. In her book, *Adults Learning*, Jenny Rogers (1992: 63) writes:

> Some teachers who rightly pride themselves on the standard of their own work, sometimes find their students' mistakes too painful to contemplate, and will often seize the work and do the difficult bits themselves, sometimes under the impression that students are grateful for such professional additions. There may be occasional students too placid to object, but most people feel cheated if someone else does all the hard work for them. They want the satisfaction and sense of achievement of learning to cope for themselves.

Students may be encouraged to involve themselves in both peer and self-assessment. Peer assessment needs to be handled very sensitively and should not be embarked upon until the teacher has a good knowledge of the group. Guidance should also be provided on the criteria to be applied in making peer assessments. Comments such as 'that was great' or 'that was rubbish' are to be avoided. On the other hand, self-evaluation is an important part of the learning process because only the individual knows his or her objectives in undertaking the programme and should, therefore, be best able to judge whether or not such objectives are being achieved. This may be a new idea to some of your students and they will require guidance in developing techniques of reflection and self-evaluation. You may wish to provide some standard form on which students can record their own evaluation or you may prefer to provide some prompts. As students become more practised they will probably be able to write a short evaluation for each assignment undertaken.

Marshall and Rowland (1993) have drawn attention to the importance of self-evaluation in the learning process and of its role in helping to provide student independence. Students should also be encouraged to discuss their assessments with tutors and there may well be a case for involving students in joint marking with tutors. This can be highly motivational.

In summarising its research findings on assessment and classroom practice, the Assessment Reform Group (1999) emphasises the following key points in ensuring that learning is central to the assessment process. Although its research focused upon learning within the compulsory education phase, the points are valid for learners of all ages:

- the provision of effective feedback to pupils;
- the active involvement of pupils in their own learning;
- adjusting teaching to take account of the results of assessment;
- a recognition of the profound influence assessment has on the motivation and self-esteem of pupils;
- the need for pupils to be able to assess themselves and understand how to improve.

(Assessment Reform Group 1999: 4–5)

Competence-based assessment

As shown in Chapter 3, in competence-based assessment the assessor must make judgements concerning the sufficiency of evidence supplied by the candidate. Evidence can take a variety of forms but the assessor needs to be assured of its validity. The assessor will want to make sure he or she has satisfactory answers to the following questions:

- Is this the candidate's own work?
- On how many occasions was this task performed?
- If a 'real-life' situation is unavailable how reliable are those results achieved through a simulation?

The following all provide legitimate forms of evidence. You may wish to consider how you would reliably assess them:

- displays and presentations
- practical demonstrations
- planning and organising events
- creative use of photographs
- making and producing models/drawings/paintings
- group work
- designing products and services
- projects undertaken by individuals or groups
- role-play work.

Evidence can be derived from observing the performance of a student within a 'real' working environment, for example, a candidate could be observed welding metal within a workshop situation. The candidate could also be assessed on a finished product. If processes cannot be directly observed by the assessor, then evidence from videotape or audiotape may also be used, providing it can be authenticated. Evidence could also be collected by questioning the candidate. There must be sufficient evidence to meet all the criteria for an element.

Often evidence collected to fulfil the criteria for one element may be relevant to and provide evidence for the achievement of other elements within the full qualification. It is not necessary to generate a separate piece of evidence for every criterion – the role of the teacher is to help students identify what evidence may count towards the achievement of those criteria.

Let us consider an example. 'Maintaining a safe and healthy working environment' is central to workplace practice and appears as a unit in the majority of occupational qualifications. The achievement of this unit cannot be assessed in isolation because sound and safe working are essential elements of good practice. Evidence of this should permeate the candidate's work across all units of a qualification. Those responsible for making assessment judgements must have regard to this across the whole qualification.

Assessment involves making judgements about the evidence which the candidate provides. This assessment may involve observing a candidate's performance in the workplace, that is watching the candidate in action. Where performance evidence cannot be assessed, supplementary evidence may be used to infer performance. For example, you may want to question a candidate about certain activities or set some form of written test. However, it should be remembered, when considering performance and supplementary evidence, that the two sorts of evidence complement each other. Activities which provide supplementary evidence do not exist in a vacuum. They are designed to support the performance evidence you have collected by confirming the knowledge and understanding of the candidate.

Competence-based assessment may be carried out by college staff within the college, even for candidates who are in employment, though sometimes college staff may go to the employers' premises to carry out assessment. Where assessment is carried out within the college it is very important that the conditions under which it is performed are as realistic as possible, that is, as far as possible under the normal conditions and pressures of the workplace and with the use of appropriate equipment and facilities. Within colleges, assessment may, therefore, be undertaken in, for example, college training restaurants, hairdressing salons, motor vehicle workshops or training offices.

For full-time students working towards NVQ accreditation, work placements have to be found so that they can demonstrate competence to workplace standards. Here assessment may be problematic since it will depend upon the goodwill and cooperation of those employers willing to provide work placements. In some sectors it is extremely difficult to access sufficient placements and there are often competing demands for them. Consistency across work placements may be variable: while some may provide excellent opportunities for candidates to demonstrate competence, others may be of a poor standard. Some colleges often have productive links with industry and provide specialist courses for employers, often tailored to the specific training requirements of the company. In return, the college may benefit from the donation of industry standard equipment.

There are some key questions upon which you may wish to reflect concerning issues of assessment within the NVQ:

- Who is assessing?
- What is being assessed?
- How valid and reliable is the evidence?
- Is there a consistency of standards across different units/elements of the qualification?
- Where is the assessment being carried out?
- What is the balance between performance evidence and supplementary evidence?
- Do the candidates understand the assessment process?
- How is evidence being recorded?

Assessing portfolios

Throughout this chapter we have been talking about the centrality of the student's portfolio in assessment within many vocational programmes. Portfolios can be confusing documents for the beginning student; navigating the apparently endless paper trail is a daunting task, particularly if its purpose is not made clear. The portfolio provides the evidence that the student can meet all the criteria set out in the specification for that programme. Let us take a specific example. Within a unit on Business Finance a student may be required to investigate a range of financial products or services suitable for different customer groups, to compare costs and evaluate the benefits. The evidence in the portfolio must demonstrate that the student has collected information from a range of financial services providers, has calculated the costs of certain products for specific customer groups and drawn conclusions from actual data. The evidence should always be suitable for the purpose for which it is provided, and authentic; in other words, it must be the student's own work. It must also be sufficient, that is, it must include all that is required to meet the criteria. If, in the example above, the student omitted to include calculations of costings, then the criteria would not have been fulfilled.

This may seem relatively straightforward. However, the organisation of the material into a coherent portfolio is often problematic. Some organisational techniques can help students to overcome the difficulties. The guiding principles are:

- appropriate induction, so that students understand clearly the purpose of the portfolio and its role in assessment;
- a clear map through the course indicating exactly where, in which units, and at what time in the programme the pieces of evidence will be produced which will go into the portfolio;
- copies of the assignment brief attached to the front of the student's assignment together with a copy of the assessor's comments and grade awarded;
- good systems which help students to organise their work, including, for example: files with dividers; tracking sheets on which students record where in the file the evidence is located, identifying the unit for which they provide evidence – signed off by assessors and dated;
- an index, which also contains relevant information about the candidate and the centre;
- keeping portfolios up to date – trying to complete them retrospectively is a recipe for disaster.

In the first instance, students' work is assessed by the appropriate tutor for the unit. All colleges offering vocational qualifications which include a portfolio assessment must appoint internal verifiers in order to ensure consistency across different markers and across programmes. This is part of the quality assurance system that is required by the awarding bodies, and ultimately by the regulators such as QCA and SQA. In addition, the awarding bodies appoint independent standards moderators to ensure that internal assessment and verification is consistent across different centres, thus ensuring national standards.

If you are involved in the delivery of vocational programmes you should ensure that you keep up to date with developments through your awarding body, or bodies, since you are likely to be teaching on qualifications offered by more than one body. All matters relating to assessment should be referred to the awarding body.

Conclusion

You will have realised that assessment is a complex and a time-consuming business. The nature and forms of assessment in FE have changed considerably during the past fifteen years. The contexts in which assessment is undertaken have also changed. It is not just a matter for the examination hall but for the workplace too and for many other settings as well.

The ways in which grades and marks are applied to assessment have also changed. There is greater emphasis on criterion referencing, that is, on what has, and what has not, been achieved, rather than on norm referencing. Norm referencing involves the measurement of an individual's achievement against the achievement of others taking the same test or exam. This is typified by the examination pass list with the marks and positions of candidates shown. You will recall the annual debates over alleged falling standards in GCSEs and A levels because too many candidates appear to be gaining higher grades. The current 14–19 reforms in England include the provision for the introduction of an A* grade at A level and a demand for more 'stretch and challenge' within the programmes available. The process of assessment has become more transparent and greater emphasis is placed upon the dialogue between the assessor and the assessed. Increasingly, assessment serves a variety of purposes. It helps to identify starting points and, in this sense, it is diagnostic. It may help to identify previous learning for which a student may wish to claim credit, as in accreditation of prior learning (APL) procedures. This type of assessment can help to inform the learning plan and avoid unnecessary duplication.

Assessment, in its formative aspects, maintains a record of ongoing progress. This type of assessment aims to improve the quality of what is being achieved and helps to structure learning. On the other hand, summative assessment may be a summary of the formative assessments already carried out of what a student can do at a given time.

In designing assessment plans for our students, we need to ensure a balance of these different types of assessment. We can collect evidence in a variety of ways and over different time periods. We can also collect evidence provided in different contexts; we all know that our students may perform differently on employers' premises from the way that they perform in our practical classes. We should also consider the motivational and personal development opportunities implicit in a negotiated record of achievement or profile.

We should not neglect the opportunities provided by assessment to review our teaching and the way in which we organise learning, and to judge their suitability for the students for whom they are intended. If we are to talk about assessment for learning, then both teachers and students are engaged in a cooperative venture that should help not only in improving the learning experiences of students but the teaching and support that we offer them. As we write, an ambitious reform programme is being rolled out in England, part of which aims to provide learners with a more personalised learning experience matched to their own particular needs (DfES, 2006b). The success of such an endeavour will depend in large part upon our ability as teachers to make critical assessment decisions when students enter programmes, throughout the course of their study, and at completion.

Part III

Professional development

Chapter 7

Evaluation, reflection and research

Introduction

> The activity of reflection is so familiar, that as teachers or trainers, we often overlook it in formal learning settings . . . reflection is a vital element in any form of learning and teachers and trainers need to consider how they can incorporate some forms of reflection in their courses.
>
> (Boud *et al.*, 1985: 8)

> Stimulated by surprise, they turn thought back on action and on the knowing which is implicit in action . . . it is this entire process of reflection-in-action which is central to the 'art' by which practitioners sometimes deal well with situations of uncertainty, instability, uniqueness and value conflict.'
>
> (Schon, 1983: 50)

In this chapter, we examine the benefits which teachers can gain from applying the concept of the 'reflective practitioner' as a means of evaluating and considering their own practice, and by helping their students use the same concept to reflect on their development as learners. Throughout this book, we have been asking you to reflect on your own learning, on some of our ideas, and on your approach to teaching. Reflection is a natural part of human life but for professionals and students, structured reflection can provide a frame-work within which they can examine their strengths and weaknesses and identify strategies for improvement. In addition, professionals can use reflection as a bridge to help span what is often regarded as a chasm between the reality of their practice as teachers and the theoretical models and concepts put forward by academics who research education.

Reflection can sometimes turn into 'navel gazing', a pleasant enough pastime for some but not one that will necessarily take the reflector any further forward or cause any changes to his or her practices! This is why we are advocating the need for reflection, whether by teachers or students, to be structured and fully incorporated within the formal framework of a course or teaching career.

Later in this chapter, we discuss ways in which teachers in colleges can build on the reflective process and begin actively to research their practice. By turning one's reflections into ideas for research projects, those reflections can be sharpened and scrutinised, and lead to real and worthwhile policies for improved practices (and policies) for both individuals and institutions.

Reflection for students

In his book, *The Enquiring Tutor*, Stephen Rowland, who has taught in both schools and HE, explains his commitment to student-centred learning:

> At the heart of this approach is the view that, both morally and practically, it is worth taking our students seriously. What they have to say about themselves provides us with the most significant information about their own learning, and thus our teaching. If we can give voice to our students' experience, we have come a long way towards understanding our own practice.
>
> (Rowland, 1993: 6)

There are many ways in which teachers can and will encourage their students to reflect on their learning but, all too often, reflection becomes confused with assessment. As we saw in Chapter 6, constructive feedback that arises out of assessment can, of course, facilitate reflection, but students need to learn how to reflect and come to regard it as a natural process in its own right.

In order to reflect, you have to ask yourself questions, some of which might be difficult or awkward. The identification of those questions may be straightforward if, for example, you have been struggling to write an essay and cannot decide how the story ends, or you may have been cooking and discover that you have left out a key ingredient from the recipe. If, however, you are reflecting on why you find it so difficult to learn how to conjugate verbs in French or how to turn what you have read in a book into a summary using your own words, then the questions you need to ask become more complex. Students, therefore, will have to practise reflection and to do that they need some guidance.

One way of helping students to reflect would be to ask them to analyse themselves as learners. They could, for example, do the exercise at the beginning of Chapter 5 in which you were asked to consider whether you were a 'good' learner. Whichever method is chosen, however, the student has to learn to reflect in a way which suits his or her own style and needs and the teacher has to create a supportive atmosphere in which this can take place:

> The open teacher, like a good therapist, establishes rapport and resonance, sensing unspoken needs, conflicts, hopes and fears. Respecting the learner

's autonomy, the teacher spends more time helping to articulate the urgent questions than demanding right answers . . . Just as you can't 'deliver' holistic health, which must start with the intention of the patient, the true teacher knows you can't impose learning. You can, as Galileo said, help the individual discover patterns and connections, foster openness to strange new possibilities, and be the midwife to ideas. The teacher is the steersman [*sic*], a catalyst, a facilitator – an agent of learning but not the first cause.

(Ferguson, 1982: 320–1)

We asked a number of students in different colleges to reflect on a recent learning experience. In the first set of examples, three 16-year-old students (two full time and one part time) give their reactions to their tutors' assessments of a piece of work:

BTEC Group Assignment: a student reflects on how the group worked together

I think the grade is fair because we all really put a lot of work into this. I mean just writing the letters and arranging the company interviews took ages. As usual, Angela did practically nothing, but I think Mrs Bennett [the tutor] knows this because she gave her a lower grade which is only fair anyway. I wasn't too happy about the marks for the oral presentation because I think we did as well as we could have done. I mean, we're not all bloomin' TV presenters! I don't see why we should have so many marks for oral presentation when it's all in the file anyway.

I think Kamal did a brilliant job with the accounts; it really helped our assignment. I am pleased he was given a higher mark for that because he really deserved it. What I especially liked about this assignment was that it really gave us a chance to get together out of college. I mean, in the evenings we used to meet up at someone's house and do all the planning – it was really great. Sharm's Dad gave us lots of help as well, like where we could find out things, and he even brought us some company brochures and reports.

I used to think people in our group were, well, sad until I got to know them through this assignment. Now I know they're OK.

An A level student reflects on the comments she received for an essay on *Hamlet*

I must say I am very disappointed with this mark. I put a lot of effort into this, practically regurgitating all the notes which we had been given. That always seemed to work at GCSE. English was my best subject. If the lecturer can't tell us the answer and give us a decent set of notes, what can he expect? He talks about critical reflection; I don't even know what he means. I don't see how he can expect me to go off and find the stuff when he hasn't told me what to look for. After all, he's paid to teach us and get us through the exam. I don't see why I should have to 'look things up'. Perhaps I should buy a set of those revision notes.

Perming hair: a hairdressing student reflects on an activity in the college's training salon

Well I think that the perm was all right. I mean, not brilliant but all right. Mrs Smith [the tutor] thought it was a pass but she said it wouldn't be fast enough in a real salon. Well it ain't a real salon anyway and the people who come here know that – that's why it's cheap. Anyway, I think Mrs Smith has got it in for me since she caught me using the mousse in the practice salon. I don't care because the gaffer [manager of the salon in which the student works when not at college] thinks I'm OK and that's what matters. He says the college don't know what they're talking about because they don't have to run a business. Anyway, college is a laugh. We have a great time and as long as I just get by that's OK. There was nothing wrong with the perm, anyway.

These reflections capture the emotional tensions which formal assessment can engender. In the first example, the experience of learning within a group structure has enabled the student to recognise the strengths and weaknesses of individual group members and to celebrate the social enjoyment to be found in working closely with colleagues. In the second and third examples, we see the students struggling to accept criticism of their work and behaviour. These students instinctively blame the tutor rather than examining their own weaknesses. They may have legitimate reasons for criticising their tutors but unless they are given opportunities to discuss the thinking behind the assessments, they may have difficulty in demonstrating their true abilities. When tutors and learners reflect together about the learning process, both parties can confront each other's level of contribution, thus identifying ways in which that process can be improved.

In the second set of examples, three mature students (one full-time and two part-time) reflect on their individual progress after six months on a course.

Adult Basic Skills student: 45-year-old Jack has been unemployed for three years

I finally started to understand where I'd been going wrong with maths when I stopped blaming myself for having failed at school. It was this week the penny dropped and I've been here nearly six months. I just sat in class on Tuesday and I heard Brenda [a fellow student] shout at our tutor. She said, 'I'm really good at some things, you know. I might not be any good at these sums you give us but I used to get good marks at school for my writing.' I thought, she's right; just because we're not much cop at maths doesn't mean we're stupid, and then I seemed to lose my fear about what Brenda calls 'sums'.

Information technology student: Frances is a 33-year-old secretary

I still don't really like coming here. I'd rather be at work but my boss wants me to learn about this stuff and I know I need to really. It's not the tutors, they're smashing. Well, I suppose it's the effort of having to concentrate on learning new things when at work I seem to get by so easily and I feel in control. When there's a test I just go to pieces and my husband says he can tell I'm worried about college because I take it out on everyone at home. I'll be glad when it's finished . . . awful isn't it? I should be grateful for the chance really.

Catering student: Edward is a 27-year-old former policeman who is now training to be a chef

If only I'd done this years ago, I would have been much happier. The course is going well but then I know I've got a good attitude, better than some of the others who are a bit up and down about the whole thing. I can't wait to get into the kitchen and the pressure doesn't bother me at all. I'm much more motivated about this than anything else I've been on and it really makes a difference to your standard of work. I never knew I could learn so fast.

In these examples, maturity helps the students reflect more deeply on their learning experience and they can relate back to earlier experiences to gain insights into their problems and successes.

Constructing a reflective journal

A 'reflective journal' can take many forms and should be a very personal record so you can be as creative as you wish. You might decide to use a typical diary format, making entries for each day or week in a notebook. You might keep a box file or shoebox in which you can store any jottings, cuttings from newspapers, cartoons, photographs and so on. Or, you might keep a very visual record using diagrams or pictures to illustrate your journey through the teaching year. If you feel happier with a more formal structure for the journal, here are some suggestions for dividing the diary into sections to include:

- a record of newly acquired knowledge, understanding and skills that are important to you;
- a commentary on your personal/professional development as you progress through the year;

- a commentary on the interesting (and perhaps contentious) issues and concepts which arise out of your professional experience;
- responses to critical incidents.

Here are two extracts from reflective journals which show how experienced college teachers record their concerns and queries about their students. The first extract records a teacher's thoughts after an induction meeting with a group of adult students on a 'two plus two' degree course:

'This seems a pleasant enough group. It's a real "mixed-bag" though. One or two obviously have the impression that they know it all and tend to dominate the rest, mainly through their attempts to monopolise the discussion and to "name drop" one or two key texts. Mrs Baker is a bit of a worry because she obviously knows quite a lot but is anxious about expressing her opinions. I must remember to let her take a more active role next time. Perhaps I should let her act as a rapporteur for feedback on group work.

'Greg seems particularly anxious. I notice he was hovering at the back afterwards waiting to catch me on my way out. Did he really need to check the time of the next class or was there something more important that he wanted to discuss? I noticed that he moved away very quickly when Tony came up.

'I must remember that Winifred is repeating this year; I need to keep her interest. I must draw on her knowledge and expertise to help me and the group, It's going to be tough for her because her son is in hospital again. I think I might suggest we plan a group get-together at the local pub or bowling alley to help establish a real group identity.'

The second extract is from a catering tutor's journal written after she assessed a group of students working in the college restaurant:

'On the whole, the group performed well with one or two notable exceptions. Ros was late and Chris didn't have his white jacket. Nevertheless, Ranjit, who was maitre d'hotel for the evening, handled the situation very well. I must remember to enter his performance under core skills in his portfolio. His communication skills were particularly appropriate.

'The main courses were well presented and service was competently handled. Must remember to tell Gill about her mistake with the cutlery although I don't think she was the only one. Lee should have noticed that the water jugs were empty before the customer had to ask. The dessert trolley was the least well handled. This group are very poor at describing the individual dishes to customers. It's not that they don't know, I think they are too scared to say. I must speak to their communications lecturer.

We need to develop some role play situations so that students can practise before they meet real customers.'

It may seem daunting to try and find the time to record observations and ideas in this way, but the two extracts above show how a number of important details can be logged by teachers in a relatively short diary-style account. In the next extract, from a trainee teacher's record of a session with a full-time vocational intermediate class that was being observed by the teacher's tutor, we see an example of how a teacher can reflect on a critical incident:

'It was a disaster, I just totally lost it. I thought I had it all planned and organised and it all went dreadfully wrong. There are some real troublemakers in this group. I should have realised that, I just wasn't prepared for it. I should have realised that the trouble was starting once the two at the front began banging the cupboard doors. I should have separated them. I can't think why I let them sit together, the whole thing just became worse and there was nothing I could do about it.

'I realise that while my attention was being taken by the troublemakers others were starting to become restless. Then those who were working well were not being given any attention. I really need to think about everyone in the group and not just concentrate on those who are causing trouble. I couldn't believe it when they started throwing the paper darts. Obviously I was an easy target. I knew then I had lost it. My real worry is how I am going to face them next week.'

The trainee teacher's tutor also recorded her own reflections on the session she had observed and provided her student with these comments:

A) Opening

Try to be on time and establish control before taking the register. What about the young lady loitering at the door, was she supposed to be in or out of the class? Close the door to show that the class has begun.

B) Introduction

You need to recap on previous class. Make sure everyone is attending before you start. What was that boy doing wandering around? You must ensure that:

- everyone understands the task and is fully prepared;
- everyone is working through the task.

Try to deal with one question at a time. You broke off in the middle of answering one boy's question to answer another. It gives the impression to the group that you are not fully in control. You must deal with the boy at the back who kept shouting. There was a lot of constructive work going on in some parts of the class, try to capitalise on this. Class eventually settled down well to the task.

C) *During lesson*

Make sure that the troublesome elements are also on the task. Don't leave people too long before checking up on them . . . the boy next to me was drawing cartoons.

D) *Feedback from activity*

Make sure all the class is ready to engage in the activity: people were still writing, others talking among themselves. You must draw the whole group together before attempting a debrief from the exercise. How should you deal with the paper darts incident? The disruption with the cupboard was very unfortunate – one strategy would have been to move the boy away from the cupboard rather than have the confrontation. The class was aware that you were losing control. It is a great pity that those who were working on the task and who had some good ideas were not used more; the disruptive students were really dominating the class. In fact, if you notice, there are only five, at the most, disruptive students, the rest of the class is fine so capitalise on them.

E) *Rounding off*

Keep your eye on the time so that you allow sufficient time to draw everything together and reinforce any key points. The lesson didn't have a proper ending but just stumbled to a close.

F) *Reflection*

* What do you feel the students learned from this class?
* How would you sum up your classroom management?
* What went well?
* What did not go well?

Put together, the two sets of reflective notes create a much more meaningful critique of the lesson than if one simply had access to just one person's account. Clearly, the trainee teacher has written his notes from a fairly acute sense of failure and, to some extent, foreboding, given that he will have to meet this same group again. His account gives the impression that the majority of students in the group were behaving badly, that the noise level was high and that he lurched from one crisis to the next. His tutor's notes provide a more coherent account (having been written from the relative calm of the back of the room) by breaking the lesson down into a chronology of pedagogical principles. We learn from this that the trainee teacher apparently arrived a little late for the lesson and so may have created the wrong impression with some students. In addition, we learn that a very small number of students caused the disruptions whereas, for the trainee teacher, it was as if they had completely taken over the proceedings. Finally, the general lack of organisation in the classroom is obviously something which the trainee teacher cannot blame entirely on' five so-called 'troublemakers'.

We are, of course, surrounded by examples of people learning, whether at home, at work, in the street, in the pub, or at the football ground. The list is endless. Try to observe your friends, relatives, colleagues and even strangers if you see them in a learning situation and record your observations in your 'reflective journal'. In fact, treat the everyday world as your research laboratory and don't forget to include yourself too!

In Chapters 4 and 5, we discussed some of the theoretical literature related to teaching and learning and tried to show how theory can inform and illuminate the teacher's role. The individual teacher should have the opportunity to contribute to and engage with the theory, and this is where the process of reflection can have real meaning and purpose. For Quicke (1996), theory needs to be balanced with reflective practice, otherwise it is in danger of putting a 'straight-jacket on teacher thought'. He gives three reasons for this:

> First, they [theories] may no longer be relevant. Although conceived originally as a way of clarifying and helping to resolve problems with which common-sense knowledge was no longer adequate to deal, they now address problems which are no longer salient. There may be new agendas in place in relation to which old theories may be obsolete. Second, theories may become reified. This problem is not so much to do with the content of a theory as with the manner in which the theory is held . . . Thirdly, theories are not so much irrelevant in terms of the issues they address but are irrelevant as theories. There may be other theories which address the same problems 'better' by constituting them differently or it's possible that common sense has already been informed by such theories. What is required is reflection on existing common sense using ideas from other aspects of common-sense knowledge.
>
> (Quicke, 1996: 21)

Teacher as researcher

The concept of the 'teacher as researcher' has been promoted for some considerable time, certainly since the 1970s when the work of Lawrence Stenhouse advocated the need for practitioners to become researchers in their own right (see Stenhouse, 1975). In the current climate of change which has swept through FE colleges, the concept should be re-examined for it has the potential to act as a vehicle for enabling college staff to investigate collaboratively the key questions and problems which concern them. Schon, as part of his advocacy of the 'reflective practitioner', insists that there needs to be a shift away from the type of educational research which appears unconcerned with the realities of practice to research, which is grounded in that practice:

> In the varied topography of professional practice, there is the high ground overlooking a swamp. On the high ground, manageable problems lend themselves to solution through the application of research-based theory and technique. In the swampy lowland, messy, confusing problems defy technical solution. The irony of this situation is that the problems of the high ground tend to be relatively unimportant to individuals or society at large, however great their technical interest may be, while in the swamp lie the problems of greatest human concern. The practitioner must choose. Shall he [sic] remain on the high ground where he can solve relatively unimportant problems according to prevailing standards of rigour, or shall he descend to the swamp of important problems and nonrigorous inquiry?
> (Schön, 1987: 3)

FE teachers are familiar with researchers, evaluators and representatives of management consultants who visit their colleges to interview students and staff, collect statistical data and observe teaching and learning. Ironically, however, the concerns of the FE teachers themselves may – though this will be rare – form the focus of this externally-generated and externally-led research activity. In the main, the teachers are left with their concerns and the external researchers move on to another set of problems. Academics in HE have, of course, their own legitimate reasons for carrying out research and play a crucial role in helping practitioners tackle the theoretical underpinning they need in furthering their understanding of and ability to examine critically the educational context in which they practise. But this relationship can be limited and much of the important work that it generates is hidden from view. There is a need, therefore, for the two communities to work much more collaboratively to ensure the following:

- that research outcomes are disseminated widely and acted upon;
- that teachers and other professionals play a more proactive part in determining the research questions to be addressed;
- that teachers contribute their professional experience and expertise to the whole of the research process rather than just a small part of it;
- that researchers are made to challenge their research practices and findings through collaborative enquiry and ongoing dialogue;

- that researchers pass on their skills to others and demystify the process of research.

This new relationship cannot, of course, be simply formed in order to meet the needs of one of the partners. It has to be recognised that university education departments are struggling to maintain adequate student numbers at postgraduate level. Gone are the days when the local education authorities and institutions would pay teachers to attend courses and give them time to study. Teachers and other professionals are having to pay their own fees and may, in some cases, be actively discouraged from attending certain courses by their managers. The pressures on college staff to meet retention and attainment targets and meet the demands of external quality assurance means that professional development becomes less of a priority.

From the colleges' point of view, a collaborative relationship with HE should not be driven solely by management priorities or imposed on staff as yet another workload clause in their contracts. Staff who are told on a Monday morning by the college chief executive that they are all to become 'researchers' are unlikely to react positively when a group of academics arrives to begin work. The considerable amount of pedagogical, curricular and policy change that has affected colleges in recent years, and the increased emphasis on the role of FE in terms of rising post-compulsory participation rates, have presented college staff with a plethora of problems and concerns to be investigated. Given the pressures of workload affecting all staff and the demands of external bodies for information about individual college performance, it will be necessary to ensure that institutions separate routine data gathering and monitoring from a more searching research programme which combines quantitative and qualitative methods and draws on a range of different research traditions and methodologies. At the same time, college staff will need to be supported over a realistic time span in their research activity by both their managers and the academics with whom they are to collaborate.

Andrew Culham sounds a realistic note in relation to teacher researchers when he writes, 'The realities of practitioner research are, in my experience, very different from the optimistic view reported by educational institutions and research journals. With all this "enthusiasm" why is it still difficult or impossible for FE practitioners to conduct research?' (Culham, 2001: 27). Culham goes on to suggest that four key factors affect practitioner research in many colleges:

- lack of time and funding;
- no 'active' research culture within FE;
- no 'value' of research within colleges;
- few opportunities for dissemination.

He calls for 'a greater understanding of the relevance and value of practitioner-based research . . . embedded within further education philosophy and policy development as part of an active promotion of a college's research effort' (ibid.: 28). Writing in the same publication as Culham, Adam Davey describes a number of strategies which his college has adopted to try and develop a research culture (Davey, 2001: 29). They include: evening meetings to hear and debate staff research presentations; a research week involving outside speakers; a teacher fellowship programme which grants teachers a term's sabbatical for research purposes; a funded internal action research programme; and research partnerships with neighbouring colleges. There are other developments in this area. University departments are seeking to accredit teacher-led research projects within their award-bearing programmes and there are opportunities for colleges and universities to apply jointly for research funding.

The difficulties facing FE teacher-researchers are, however, not to be underestimated. Anderson *et al.* (2003: 507) argue that, in the light of the 'outcome-driven culture' of many colleges, there is limited internal capacity to 'overturn the dominant paradigm of "performativity"'. Furthermore, they note that 'many colleges cannot distinguish between "criticism" and "critical voice", and can be defensive' (ibid.). Their experience has, however, enabled them to think through the different ways in which a more robust research culture might be developed across FE. For this to happen, research needs to be seen as part of a 'wider cultural change process that will make colleges fit to thrive in a changing environment . . . Teachers will share the fruits of that success through improved security and greater recognition of their professional role' (ibid.: 513).

Conclusion

Working as an FE teacher is highly demanding and it is often difficult to find time to stand back from the daily pressures to reflect and take stock. This chapter has explored some ideas to help you build on your experience, to learn from both your successes and your mistakes, and to create ways to make reflection an integral part of your working life. As discussed in Chapter 1, FE teachers come from a wide range of backgrounds and many already have had careers in other fields before coming into teaching. The process of learning to become an FE teacher will often involve the need to switch from one identity to another and, in the process, new identities will emerge. For example, the following comments come from an FE tutor in Performing Arts:

> I am an actor and also work as an actor-in-residence at a secondary school, teach Performing Arts BTEC at a college, teach a summer school on 'Shakespeare's Drama' and also teach on the PGCE/Cert Ed Performing Arts in a university. I think the duality of performers who teach is quite

complex. Firstly, there is an unspoken, inherent sense of 'failure' for a lot of performer/teachers in the self-questioning caused by the old saying 'those who can, do, those who can't, teach'. I suspect a lot of performers actually teach out of economic reality rather than any sense of 'vocation'. However, any 'negative' motivation might possibly be counteracted by the fact that performers come to the classroom with an inherent understanding of audience needs, storytelling skills, the use of dramatic effects and a tendency towards charismatic modelling that positively affect their teaching. However, it might also be true to say that performer/teachers are foremost performers and are always highly conscious of their teaching as a form of performance and are interested in monitoring its effects for their own benefit. The classroom can become a substitute stage where the teacher is the unquestioned solo actor/director and critic and if this happens, the students' learning can take second place to the gratification needs of the teacher. Teacher-led activity can take precedence over student creativity and autonomy. At best, however, teacher/performers are innate motivators who understand student's need for affirmation and praise due to their own development as 'fragile' performers. They also tend to be curious about people, open-hearted, empathetic, creative thinkers and ensemble players – all of which make them useful teachers.

From their research with teachers and nurses, Stronach *et al.* (2002) have argued for a new perspective on the concept of 'professionalism' in order to capture the plurality of the professional role. Stronach *et al.* (ibid.) found teachers and nurses constantly juggling the different aspects of their daily lives as they tried to conform to the different, and often conflicting, expectations of their work held by policymakers, managers, clients and students. In her research with schoolteachers, Watson (2006) has found that teachers find it helpful to recount their daily practice in the form of stories or narratives as these expose the way in which they have to shift their perspective to suit the changing contexts in which they work and, hence, be more aware of the different possibilities available to them.

As an FE teacher, you might find you work in a range of 'spaces' and 'places' (including, for example, teaching in classrooms and workshops or assessing students in workplaces) and this diversity of environment will also have an impact on the formation of your professional identity(ies). James and Diment's (2003) research has shown that FE staff who work away from the traditional classroom setting may need to develop different forms of practice in order to adapt to the nature of the learning environment and the needs of their students. They refer to this as 'underground' practice. Trainee FE teachers, who are on placement in a college as part of a full-time course leading to a teaching qualification, sometimes find that the realities of college life are somewhat different to the picture painted by their tutors. Bathmaker and Avis (2005) found, for example, that trainee teachers in their study in England often felt isolated from the community of practice they were seeking to join and were not, necessarily, impressed with the practices of the experienced teachers they were working alongside. Recording these different experiences in some form can help teachers make sense of the different ways in which they have to 'perform' and can also reveal how strategies that have been effective in one setting, might be transferable to another one.

Chapter 8

Professional development

Introduction

In previous chapters, we have emphasised the multi-skilled nature of the FE teacher. Given the diversity of FE life and the volatility of curricula within colleges, every FE teacher has to make plans to ensure he or she has access to relevant and appropriate professional development opportunities. Given also that teachers in FE stretch from those who concentrate on basic skills, through to those teaching at undergraduate and postgraduate level, the scope of professional development must, necessarily, be broad enough to encompass the wide range of professional needs.

In Chapter 4, we discussed the role that theory plays in developing our understanding of teaching and learning. Your initial teacher training course may have included a study of theoretical concepts and the research underpinning them, but it is important to try and maintain some connection with the developing research field. In addition, you will also need to ensure your specific professional area of expertise is kept up to date. Michael Eraut, who has made a key contribution to our understanding of professional knowledge and competence, sees the 'disposition to theorise' as the 'most important quality of the professional teacher' as once they gain this, teachers will:

> go on developing their theorising capacities throughout their teaching careers, they will be genuinely self-evaluative and they will continue to search for, invent and implement new ideas. Without it they will become prisoners of their early . . . experience, perhaps the competent teachers of today, almost certainly the ossified teachers of tomorrow.
>
> (Eraut, 1994: 71)

For Michael Tedder, writing from his experience of teaching in colleges, the concept of professionalism has many meanings in FE:

> Many of us use the term 'professional' regularly to convey a range of meanings among which might be identified the possession of a body

of knowledge and expertise, normally accredited with academic or vocational qualifications, and the awareness of a set of values or a code of conduct that governs our relationship with 'clients', the ethics of our profession. Professionalism also implies a relationship with colleagues that includes responsibility for monitoring the standards in our practice and an acceptance of responsibility or a sense of accountability to the community we serve.

(Tedder, 1994: 74)

Professional development is itself a concept in need of some clarification. A more familiar term might be staff development, but often, this will tend to refer to largely in-house, short and management-led initiatives rather than activity that is determined by the individual teacher to fulfil personal development goals. Staff development in colleges has had a mixed history. As Castling (1996) has shown, the 1970s was a period in which staff development probably meant being sent on an external course for updating related to one's teaching area, whereas in the 1980s, more emphasis was placed on colleges creating internal staff development programmes, often using ideas generated by the then Further Education Unit (FEU). Local education authorities (LEAs) also played a key role in the 1980s as they managed government funding targeted at staff development, while Her Majesty's Inspectorate (HMI) ran national conferences for staff development officers. The levels of nationally available funding gradually decreased, however, and now staff development is very much seen as a cost to be borne by colleges themselves.

Robson (1996) has pointed out the danger in assuming that terms such as professional development or staff development privilege the needs of staff, whereas in reality, the inspectors have a more college-centric outlook: 'Staffing needs will be derived from analyses of the college's objectives and staff development activities will be determined less by perceived individual need than by the college's academic and strategic plan' (Robson, 1996: 3). Thus the majority of activity which falls under the umbrella of professional development tends to be related to servicing an immediate need (for example, health and safety training, new assessment procedures, LLUK requirements, etc.) or, where it is seen as servicing a long-term goal, as Robson states above, it will be closely tied to the college's strategic plan. There is, of course, every likelihood that some of this activity will complement the professional development needs of some teaching staff, and where a college is prepared to invest large amounts of money, perhaps to retrain teachers or help them develop their professional competence in order to run courses at higher levels, then so-called staff development becomes indistinguishable from professional development.

Staff development tends to take place within the college's own campus and involve only college staff, though an outside speaker might be called upon.

Although there are clearly times when a purely internal arrangement is sufficient, there is a real danger that staff and management become too insular if all their staff development is conducted in this way. Castling warns:

> There is the risk of staff becoming bogged down in institutional problems which can obstruct progress, and there may be a lack of fresh ideas which would normally come from working with colleagues elsewhere. There might be a reluctance to resource the input by college staff as fully as that by outside experts, and indeed college staff might not command the respect which would have been accorded to visitors purely because they were from outside. The chief danger is probably insularity. The staff developer managing the programme will need to import wider views, either from their own research or by selecting colleague contributions carefully.
>
> (Castling, 1996: 80)

Perhaps, then, staff development should come with a health warning or at least those 'being developed' should recognise that the fix they gain from participating in staff development activities may be less than satisfying. Eraut reminds us that:

> Professionals continually learn on the job, because their work entails engagement in a succession of cases, problems or projects which they have to learn about. This case-specific learning, however, may not contribute a great deal to their general professional knowledge base unless the case is regarded as special rather than routine and time is set aside to deliberate upon its significance. Even then it may remain in memory as a special case without being integrated into any general theory of practice. Thus according to the disposition of individual professionals and the conditions under which they work, their knowledge base may be relatively static or developing quite rapidly. There is little research evidence to indicate the overall level of work-based learning in any profession, but individual examples of both extremes are frequently cited.
>
> (Eraut, 1994: 10)

As noted in Chapter 1, there is now a statutory requirement for FE teachers to hold a professional qualification. Many FE teachers will also hold qualifications related to their area of expertise and they may be being 'topped up' by bouts of continuing professional education (CPE) or continuing professional development (CPD). The stage at which these discipline-based professionals will add a qualification in teaching to their curriculum vitae will depend on the nature of their entry to FE. Norman Lucas has argued that this duality of professional role, that is of being at one and the same time a teacher and an expert in a professional or craft/trade area, has dogged the development of a statutory qualification structure:

> Management and staff associations have traditionally united against any statutory professional teaching qualification for further education. Historically, lecturers in further education have seen their qualification or expertise in an academic or vocational area as sufficient for teaching. This has placed specialist knowledge of subject or trade above pedagogy. Thus the notion of lecturers being seen as, or seeing themselves as professional teachers with a coherent structure of initial training and professional development has been secondary to a concentration of delivering narrow specialist expertise.
>
> (Lucas, 1996: 69)

Pathways to professional development

Clearly all colleges have their own culture and ethos that may have grown up over a number of years or that may reflect sudden changes introduced by a new senior manager or management team. The level of importance attached to the professional development needs of staff is dependent on that culture so that in some colleges staff may have to fight quite hard to get their real needs met. Jackson *et al.* (1996) stress that individual employees cannot afford to wait for their organisations to take the lead in terms of their career development:

> The trend is clearly towards increased demand on people to be proactive in looking after their own careers using their own resourcefulness. This requires continuous information-gathering and analysis, self-assessment, planning ahead for the next few years, and social skills including negotiation and self-presentation.
>
> (Jackson *et al.*, 1996: 52)

Throughout a career as a teacher in FE, you will probably want a mix of provision to satisfy your professional development needs. As discussed earlier in this chapter, some of your immediate needs might be covered in staff development activities run within the college.

One of the key mechanisms through which you will be asked to try and identify your professional development needs will be through the college's appraisal system. If the appraisal system in your college is not satisfactory in terms of helping you identify and discuss your professional development needs, you will have to find other means for this. You may, for example, be assigned a mentor. This will most likely be an experienced member of staff who provides ongoing support, advice and guidance, but in some colleges, teachers provide each other with peer mentoring. The process of mentoring has to be nurtured, especially in colleges where individuals feel under pressure to compete with each other and feel at the mercy of externally-imposed targets and inspections. From her research on the mentoring of student teachers by experienced staff in FE, Cox writes:

> There is an absence, in further education, of a culture which encourages or even allows open discussion of teaching. In order to have effective mentoring, the mentor and the student teacher must step outside the normal conventions of staffroom discourse and openly discuss, evaluate and reflect on practice. This can be difficult for both parties.
>
> (Cox, 1996: 41)

She advocates peer or collaborative mentoring because, 'In this context, the imbalance of power is less of an issue and the tension generated by the assessment function of the mentor is absent. The discussion of one's own and a collaborative colleague's teaching can be developed in a supportive atmosphere, in a constructive, private dialogue' (Cox, 1996: 42).

As well as helping you to identify and discuss your professional development needs, working with supportive colleagues will also provide tacit doses of professional development as well as enriching one's day-to-day life in college. Another strategy for considering your professional development needs involves keeping a record of your professional experience in and outside college. This record could take the form of a portfolio, diary or log and could include a combination of examples of your work with students (such as teaching plans, assessments, photographs of students' work, etc.) and more discursive accounts of your development as a teacher (for example, reflections on critical moments, ideas for new ways to teach, etc.). It might also include evidence of your activities related to your area of professional expertise or your links with the local community.

Linked to this notion of recording one's experience is the use of autobiographical writing by teachers throughout all sectors of education. Here, a teacher constructs a narrative of his or her ongoing life as a teacher and uses it to reflect on the extent to which external as well as personal influences determine one's progress and development as a professional. As Bateson argues:

> These resonances between the personal and the professional are the source of both insight and error. You avoid mistakes and distortions not so much by trying to build a wall between the observer and the observed as by observing the observer – observing yourself – as well, and bringing the personal issues into consciousness.
>
> (Bateson, 1984: 161)

By gaining a better understanding of the personal and the professional, we can then begin to 'map' out our career path and, hopefully, take more control over the nature and scope of the professional development on offer to us. In his highly creative book, *The Man Who Mistook His Wife for a Hat*, the neurologist Oliver Sacks describes a patient of his called Rebecca, a young woman whom he had known for some twelve years and who, after the death of her grandmother, appeared to emerge much more strongly as a person in her own right:

> 'I want no more classes, no more workshops,' she said. 'They do nothing for me. They do nothing to bring me together . . . I'm a sort of living carpet. I need a pattern, a design like you have on that carpet. I come apart, I unravel, unless there's a design.' I looked down at the carpet, as Rebecca said this, and found myself thinking of Sherrington's famous image, comparing the brain/mind to an 'enchanted loom', weaving patterns ever-dissolving, but always with meaning.
>
> (Sacks, 1986: 175)

Some professional development courses include biographical accounts and portfolios as part of the assessed work submitted by students. There can be problems when personal material of this nature is then used in a public context and Bloor and Butterworth (1996), in their study of the use of portfolios at the University of Greenwich, suggest that these concerns may lead to professionals being less inclined to commit themselves to paper. They stress that the ownership of portfolios must be clarified at the outset.

Clearly, if you are preparing an autobiographical account or portfolio for purely personal use, you will not have the problems of ownership. What you might want to do, however, is to use some of that material as the basis for discussions with friends or colleagues about how well you have managed to address your strengths and weaknesses. As Holloway points out, we need to have our personal constructs challenged, albeit in a gentle and supportive way: 'I know from paying close attention to myself giving accounts in a variety of different settings, that I have a stock of ready narratives to draw on which fit particular situations and which tell me nothing new unless the person I am talking to helps me produce something new' (Holloway quoted in Kehily, 1995: 28).

Apart from the personal development aspect, there are important pragmatic reasons for building a portfolio or some kind of record of your professional experience. For example, the practice of the accreditation of prior learning (APL), discussed in Chapter 6, is used in a number of HEIs and by professional bodies to give exemption from parts of programmes leading to qualifications. Also, you may find that having some physical evidence of your work will come in useful at job interviews or for promotion panels.

Once you have a 'map' or, at least, some idea of your professional development needs, you may wish to pursue a postgraduate course leading to a diploma or Masters degree, or you may become a member of a professional body that provides professional development courses. All of these may be available within your own college (if it is linked in some way to an HEI) or you may have to find a course elsewhere. Many HEIs now offer flexible ways to gain a postgraduate qualification, for example, by distance learning or residential weekend study, and, as we noted above, some have introduced APL procedures to allow experienced people to be exempted from taking the full set of course modules.

Some HEIs have also introduced a structured doctoral programme leading to the Doctorate in Education (or EdD). For this, students take a number of 'taught' modules, some of which will cover research methodology, and then produce a thesis. As noted in Chapter 7, some HEIs are developing research links with FE colleges which go beyond the traditional professional development relationship in which FE staff are merely seen as students working towards an accredited qualification. To this end, Masters and EdD programmes often encourage students to conduct action research projects, empirical studies and other forms of analysis based within their professional context.

If you are interested in developing your research potential and feel motivated enough to dedicate some three to five years to one project, you could pursue a research degree (MPhil or PhD). In this case, you would be appointed to a supervisor who has a keen interest in your research ideas and who possibly also carries out research in a similar field. Although all HEIs offer research degrees, it is advisable to gain a good impression of an institution's research rating. In addition, you should also try to find out which academics in the department in which you would be based as there may be someone who has published articles and books related to your research interests. Departments differ, too, in their provision for part-time research students in that some bring students together for seminars and social events and may provide access to information technology. A useful way to begin your investigation of an academic department in an HEI is to visit the institution's library, which will house copies of all dissertations and research degree theses. By looking at a sample of this research output for the department you are interested in, you will gain some idea of the nature and scope of projects the department is able to supervise.

If you are a member of a trade union, you should keep in touch with the professional development programmes it offers as well as conferences and discussion group meetings.

Reflection

The following questions and instructions are designed to help you evaluate and identify your professional development needs. You may find them useful during initial training as well as at different stages during your teaching career:

1   Make a list of the knowledge and skills you would like to gain (or improve) in order to be a more effective teacher. Can you acquire those skills on an in-house staff development programme?

2   Are you comfortable with the curriculum demands imposed on you? Would you feel happier if you could update your skills and knowledge in a particular area of your professional expertise? Have there been recent changes to your professional area (for example, new legislation, new inventions, changes in information technology, etc.)? Can you cope with these changes?

3   Are you aware of the different organisations which could supply you with information and ideas to support and enrich your teaching? Would you gain by joining a professional body? Are there people in neighbouring colleges, schools, HEIs, companies, government agencies and other organisations with whom you should be in contact or with whom you might work in partnership?

4   Will your management support your professional development plans? What will they expect in the form of a proposal (for example, a written proposal with costings?) and who is the best person to approach first?

5   Have you considered changing direction? There may be opportunities within the college to try a completely new field (e.g. move from teaching into student services) or to set up a new course in a related discipline, or a multi-disciplinary programme.

6   Where do you want to be in five years in terms of your career? Can you identify any professional development issues now so that you can plan your career in advance?

Chapter 9

Life beyond college

Introduction

FE colleges play a significant role in the life of their local communities and beyond; indeed, some that specialise in certain courses attract students on a national and even international basis. The range of people who come through the college doors, as we saw in Chapter 2, represents the diversity of the college's geographical, socio-economic and cultural location. Reaching out from the college, the links into the community will include outreach centres for teaching and access-related services, partnerships with local schools and HEIs, and a range of mechanisms for relating to the world of business and industry. As a college lecturer, therefore, you will be constantly aware of the wider world beyond your immediate teaching room.

Part of your duties and responsibilities as a lecturer may include liaising with community groups, representing the college on education business and lifelong learning partnership committees and so on. In this chapter, we discuss the nature of some of the organisations with whom you may be formally required to liaise, and work. We also discuss the ways in which these and other organisations can provide you with valuable support in terms of your teaching and professional development.

National and regional bodies

Prior to the 1992 FHE Act, colleges in England were affiliated to their local Regional Advisory Council (RAC), a network of which existed throughout the country. These bodies came within the remit of LEAs but were independent of each other and, although they had some activities in common such as running staff development courses, they were very different in terms of their effectiveness. Where RACs did come together was in their contribution to the work of the Further Education Unit (FEU), which was set up in 1977, under the auspices of the then Department of Education and Science, to help promote curriculum development initiatives and coordinate and disseminate good practice in teaching and learning. The FEU was particularly active in the late

1970s and early 1980s when it produced reports such as *A Basis for Choice* (1979) and *Vocational Preparation* (1981) which provided guidance and analysis for colleges in dealing with the sudden dramatic influx of recruits to the newly established government-sponsored youth training schemes. Often working alongside the national Further Education Staff College (FESC), which had been set up in 1963 at Coombe Lodge near Bristol, the FEU produced a wealth of literature, much of it based on action research projects involving colleges.

In April 1995, a new organisation, the Further Education Development Agency (FEDA), replaced both the FEU and FESC. In light of the structural changes to the post-compulsory sector described in Chapter 1, FEDA was renamed the Learning and Skills Development Agency (LSDA) in 2000, signalling that it would now represent a much wider constituency. With a head office in London, LSDA also had nine regional development offices in England and one in Wales. Each regional office of the LSDA hosted a Learning and Skills Research Network (LSRN) that brought together practitioners from organisations responsible for post-compulsory education and training in the region to share research interests and develop collaborative projects. In April 2006, LSDA was replaced by the Quality Improvement Agency (QIA) and it will be interesting to see how long this organisation lasts. Since the demise of the FEU, the subsequent agencies have been closely tied to supporting the delivery of government policy through staff development programmes and resources.

Given the incorporation of colleges in 1993 and the establishment of bodies such as FEDA, the LSDA and now QIA, the role of the RACs became confused and most have either dissolved or transformed into consultancy organisations. In Scotland, the Scottish Further Education Unit (SFEU) performs a similar role to QIA, while research on FE is also undertaken by SCRE (the Scottish Council for Research in Education).

One organisation that covers the UK and is closely related to the work of colleges is UK Skills, which organises annual competitions in a range of vocational areas. In 2011, the UK will host the World Skills Olympics. Selection trials to find competitors will be organised throughout the UK and colleges will be asked to nominate suitable candidates in the following areas: Construction and Building; Creative Arts; Engineering, Healthcare and Personal Services; Hospitality; and IT and Media.

Trade unions, professional organisation and HE

In 2006, the trade union with the largest coverage of FE lecturers in the UK, NATFHE (the National Association of Teachers in Further and Higher Education) merged with the Association of University Teachers (AUT) to form the University and College Union (UCU). The Association of Teachers and Lecturers (ATL) still exists, and in Scotland, lecturers can also join the Educational Institute Scotland (EIS). There is also a trade union in Wales covering both schools and colleges, UNAC (Undeb Cenedlaethol Athrawon Cymru). The Association for College Management (ACM) represents college staff in management positions, though some FE principals also belong to the Secondary Heads Association (SHA). Two membership organisations represent colleges in terms of promoting FE to policymakers and lobbying for change: the Association of Colleges (AoC) in England and Wales; and the Association of Scotland's Colleges. As we saw in Chapter 1, the principals of some of the largest colleges in England have recently formed the '157 Group'.

As discussed in Chapter 1, many college lecturers have a background in a profession or craft-based occupation and may find it useful to maintain a direct link through an appropriate organisation such as, for example, the Institute of Chartered Accountants or the Association of Construction Heads. Many contemporary occupations can trace their origins back to the medieval craft guilds and the City of London still boasts 107 livery companies including, for example, the Worshipful Company of Bakers and the Worshipful Company of Tylers (sic) and Bricklayers. The livery companies provide scholarships and bursaries for students and some have close links with colleges.

The Learning and Skills Research Network (LSRN) and the Scottish Further Education Unit (SFEU) are valuable sources of information for teachers in FE about developments in policy and practice. It is also worth checking if any of the universities in your area host networks to bring together teachers, employers and researchers, and, of course, colleges will have close relationships with universities for the joint delivery of degree and sub-degree programmes. Many universities open their seminars to external visitors and may also have arrangements for FE lecturers to become research associates.

Business and community-related organisations

There are many different forms of business-related organisation in the UK stretching from national bodies such as the Confederation of British Industry (CBI) and the Institute of Directors to local bodies such as Chambers of Commerce and the Round Table. The locally based organisations often have historical roots in their communities, including those which represent the interests of employees rather than those of employers, such as trades councils. The CBI has a regional network of branches that meet regularly for seminars and events at which education and training often feature. There is a wide range of community-based organisations including, for example, charities, voluntary agencies, and single issue groups.

At regional level in England, colleges will have links with one of the nine Regional Development Agencies (RDAs) established in 1999 to take forward some of the work previously done by the regional government offices. RDAs are largely responsible for the general economic regeneration of their areas and for constructing a ten-year Regional Economic Strategy (RES) in partnership with key stakeholders including business, education and local government.

RDAs control significant budgets and, given the proposals for regional assemblies in England, and the European Commission's wish to see regions gaining greater autonomy, they have an important role to play.

In England, the one organisation which will have the most direct contact and working relationship with an FE college is the Learning and Skills Council (LSC), while in Scotland, colleges will relate to one of 12 LECs as well as the SFC. In 1999, and in anticipation of its plans to harmonise the post-compulsory sector in England, the government established Lifelong Learning Partnerships analogous to what were then TEC areas. These partnerships bring together all the organisations involved in some aspect of education and training. As such, to some extent, they overlap the work of education-business partnerships (EBPs) that will include representatives from industry and commerce, the LEA, Careers Service, local HEIs, private training providers, voluntary organisations, trade unions and schools. EBPs began in 1990 at the same time the TECs were being established. At that time, most EBPs were set up and largely managed by TECs. In the mind of the, then, Employment Department, EBPs were the means to formalise the largely ad hoc and voluntaristic links between education and business which have been in existence for many years. The very notion of trying to impose a superstructure on relationships that tended to be organic rather than institutionalised has seemed to some on both sides to be too dictatorial and at odds with the concept of partnership. EBPs have, therefore, developed differently throughout the country ranging from the very successful to those which struggle to get enough people to make meetings quorate. EBPs in England, Wales and Northern Ireland belong to the National Education Business Partnership Network (NEBPN).

Where an EBP is successful, the local colleges are likely to be heavily involved. An EBP can provide college staff with an excellent forum for liaising with schools over such matters as managing an effective transition for young people transferring to college at 16 or joint initiatives to raise standards in basic skills. Useful relationships with employers can also be established through an EBP.

The following vignettes illustrate the different ways in which college staff can work together with EBPs.

Chris took over responsibility for running the Leisure and Tourism programme in her college. Although she had previously been employed in the travel business, it was some considerable time ago and she felt the need to update her knowledge of the industry. In addition, she was aware that she needed to inform herself about developments in the use of IT in the industry. Her local EBP arranged a week's placement for her with a branch of a national retail travel agent. The placement not only allowed her to gain some 'hands-on' experience of the current operation of a travel business but also enabled her to identify work placements for students.

Bob, a lecturer in engineering, was approached by the EBP about the possibility of some of his students undertaking a piece of work for a local engineering company. One of the directors of the company was chairperson of the EBP and she was anxious to improve the profile of her company, and, at the same time, improve the image of engineering in general by involving students in the company's work. Although initially reticent about the idea, Bob eventually recognised the potential benefits of the link that would allow his students to undertake real tasks to industry standards. Students were given access to the company and completed some of the tasks on site rather than in the college workshops. Bob also had the opportunity of seeing the way in which a small manufacturing company was transforming its production to match new industry standards.

Ranjeep has responsibility for teaching marketing across a range of business courses in his college. For some time, he has been interested in developing a European dimension to the work but has lacked contact with colleges or companies in Europe. The EBP was able to supply the names of several local companies that had links with Europe and the names of local schools involved in European exchanges. Ranjeep followed up these leads and made contact with a vocational school in Belgium that was happy to collaborate in a joint project involving British and Belgian business students. Assignments were developed for a unit on international marketing in which the students exchanged information about their own local economies. Students communicated by fax and e-mail. In future, Ranjeep hopes to extend the project by involving other European partners and, hopes to access some EU funding to finance student exchanges.

Because of the need for local organisations to work together to ensure they make the most of limited resources to finance education and training initiatives, EBPs and similar partnerships rely on individuals who are prepared to put their creative energies to work for the collective good.

Gravatt and Silver (2000: 121) argue that partnerships are attractive to government because:

- They bring local organisations together to deliver shared goals.
- They are a way of bridging the public and private sector and of harnessing private sector investment to deliver public goals.
- They can be formed – and dissolved – quickly.
- They make it possible to deliver new programmes without the costs of setting up new organisations or of restructuring existing ones.

Writing from their perspective as Registrar and Principal, respectively, of Lewisham College in London, Gravatt and Silver (ibid.: 123) highlight the following reasons why community and business-based partnerships work, or do not work:

Work	Don't work
Shared purpose	Forced geographically
Conscious acceptance	No trust
Voluntary	No guarantees
Respect difference	Own agendas
Shared values	Forced into frameworks
Outward-looking	Resist change
Allowed to evolve	Over-control by external audit

Gravatt and Silver (ibid.: 126) stress that colleges 'need to tread carefully in the matter of partnerships'. They continue, 'Partnerships help organizations achieve objectives and add value to their activities, but they are not a panacea for all public sector problems. Too many partnerships established too hastily with too many overlapping aims just add to the confusion and complexity that gets in the way of education and training' (ibid.).

The term 'partnership' is, of course, a contested one (see, *inter alia*, Ramsden *et al.*, 2004). Partnership suggests an equal relationship, one entered into willingly. Many of the so-called partnerships that exist in the world of education and training are simply gatherings of people who need to ensure their organisations needs and agendas are represented. As Field (2000: 26–7) argues, 'the discourse of partnership frequently cloaks a profound inequality between the so-called partners'. And the concept of partnership as envisaged by policymakers is a positivist one, that is, the partnerships exist to make the delivery of policy objectives run smoothly. It would be interesting to consider what might happen if, for example, the 'partners' at a meeting of a local Lifelong Learning Partnership decided to use their solidarity to challenge the targets and performance indicators imposed on them from on high. Mayo (2002: 199) explains that there is increasing interest in developing connections between lifelong learning and community capacity building, but such connections are particularly problematic:

> Community participants need access to appropriate education and training for capacity building, just as professionals need appropriate education and training, if they are to work with communities in empowering ways. What 'appropriateness' might mean in practice, however, depends upon how capacity-building and empowerment are defined, by whom and according to whose agendas.
>
> (ibid.)

The following example of a successful partnership between colleges and employers comes from the North West of England.

Logistics College North West (LCNW)

LCNW is a partnership between five further education colleges and the Transport and General Workers Union (TGWU) to create the largest specialist college for logistics in May 2003. City College Manchester is the lead college in the partnership, with West Cheshire, St Helens, Wigan & Leigh and Knowsley. Over 150,000 people are employed in the region in logistics, which accounts for 8 per cent of the region's output. Research highlighted a potentially critical skills shortage in the sector, prompting employers, the North West Development Agency and the Learning and Skills Council to join forces. LCNW provides training courses, delivered either on employers' sites or at its own training centres, when and where the employers want them. It's also developing new training opportunities for women, to help them break into the industry. LCNW has CoVE status.

(adapted from: www.lcnw.ac.uk)

Useful contacts and sources of support

The following organisations may prove useful at some time or other during your career in FE. We have listed them with their website addresses only as these should be more reliable than location addresses. Each of these websites will also provide links to hundreds of other organisations that may be of use but which we cannot list here for the obvious reasons!

Association of Colleges
www.aoc.org.uk
Association of Scottish Colleges
www.aosc.org.uk
Association of Northern Ireland Colleges
www.aonic.org.uk
British Educational, Communications and Technology Council (Becta)
www.becta.org.uk
Department for Children, Schools and Families
www.dcsf.gov.uk
Department of Education Northern Ireland
www.deni.gov.uk
Department for Innovation, Universities and Skills
www.dius.gov.uk
Learning and Skills Council
www.lsc.gov.uk
Learning and Skills Research Network
www.lsneducation.org.uk

National Education Business Partnership Network
www.nebpn.org.uk
Ofsted
www.ofsted.gov.uk
Qualifications and Curriculum Authority
www.qca.org.uk
Quality Improvement Agency
www.qia.org.uk
Scottish Executive
www.Scotland.gov.uk
Scottish Further Education Unit
www.sfeu.ac.uk
Scottish Qualifications Authority
www.sqa.org.uk
Trades Union Congress
www.tuc.org.uk
Welsh Assembly
www.wales.gov.uk

References

Abbott, I. and Huddleston, P. (2004) The curriculum: 14–19, in V. Brooks, I. Abbott and L. Bills, *Preparing to Teach in Secondary Schools*, Maidenhead: Open University Press.

Ainley, P. and Bailey, B. (1997) *The Business of Learning*, London, Cassell.

Ainley, P. and Vickerstaff, S. (1993) Transitions from corporatism: The privatisation of policy failure, *Contemporary Record*, 7(3): pp. 541–56.

ALI (2006) *Annual Report of the Chief Inspector 2005–6*, Coventry, Adult Learning Inspectorate.

Anderson, G., Barton, S. and Wahlberg, M. (2003) Reflection and experiences on further education research in practice, *Journal of Vocational Education and Training*, 55(4): 499–516.

AoC (2007) *Further education colleges – The sector that delivers. Submission to the Comprehensive Spending Review 2007*, London, The Association of Colleges.

Assessment Reform Group (1999) *Assessment for learning. Beyond the black box*, University of Cambridge, Assessment Reform Group.

Attwood, G., Croll, P. and Hamilton, J. (2004) Challenging students in further education: themes arising from a study of innovative FE provision for excluded and disaffected young people, *Journal of Further and Higher Education*, 28(1): 107–19.

Audit Commission/Ofsted (1993) *Unfinished Business – Full-time Educational Courses for 16–19 Year Olds*, London, HMSO.

Avis, J. (1999) Shifting identity: new conditions and the transformation of practice-teaching within post-compulsory education, *Journal of Vocational Education and Training*, 51(2): 245–64.

Avis, J. and Bathmaker, A.-M. (2006) From trainee to FE lecturer: trials and tribulations, *Journal of Vocational Education and Training*, 58(2): 171–89.

Avis, J., Bathmaker, A.-M. and Parsons, J. (2001) Reflections from a Time Log Diary: towards an analysis of the labour process within further education, *Journal of Vocational Education and Training*, 53(1): 61–80.

Bailey, B. and Robson, J. (2004) Learning Support Workers in Further Education in England: a hidden revolution?, *Journal of Further and Higher Education*, 28(4): 373–93.

Bateson, M.C. (1984) *With a Daughter's Eye*, New York, William Morrow.

Bathmaker, A.-M. and Avis, J. (2005) Is that 'tingling feeling' enough? Constructions of teaching and learning in further education, *Educational Review*, 57(1): 3–20.

Bathmaker, A.-M. and Avis, J. (2005) Becoming a lecturer in further education in England: the construction of professional identity and the role of communities of practice, *Journal of Education and Teaching*, 31(1): 47–62.

Bathmaker, A-M. and Avis, J. (2007) 'How do I cope with that?' The challenge of 'schooling' cultures in further education for trainee FE lecturers, *British Educational Research Journal*, 33(4): 509–32.

Becta (2006) *The ICT and e-Learning in FE Survey 2006*, Coventry, Becta.

Belenky, M.F., Clinchy, M.B., Goldberger, N.R. and Tarule, J.M. (1986) *Women's Ways of Knowing*, New York, Basic Books.

Berne, E. (1970) *Games People Play*, Harmondsworth: Penguin.

Betts, D. (1996) Staff appraisal and staff development in the corporate college, in J. Robson (ed.) *The Professional FE Teacher*, Aldershot, Avebury.

Billett, S. and Somerville, M. (2004) Transformations at work: identity and learning, *Studies in Continuing Education*, 26(2): 309–26.

Black, P. and Wiliam, D. (1998) *Inside the Black Box*. London, King's College.

Black, P., Harrison, C., Lee, C., Marshall, B. and Wiliam, D. (2003) *Assessment for learning: putting it into practice*, Maidenhead, Open University Press.

Bloom, B.S. (1965) *Taxonomy of Educational Objectives*, London, Longman.

Bloomer, M. (1997) *Curriculum Making in Post-16 Education. The Social Conditions ofStudentship*, London, Routledge.

Bloomer, M. and Hodkinson, P. (1997) *Moving into FE*, London, Further Education Development Agency.

Bloomer, M. and Hodkinson, P. (2000) Learning Careers: continuity and change in young people's dispositions to learning, *British Educational Research Journal*, 26(5): 583–97.

Bloor, M. and Butterworth, C, (1996) The portfolio approach to professional development, in J. Robson (ed.) *The Professional FE Teacher*, Aldershot, Avebury.

Blunkett, D. (2001) *Education into Employability: The Role of the DfEE in the Economy*, speech to the Institute of Economic Affairs, 24 January (London, Department for Education and Employment).

Boreham, N. (2002) Work process knowledge, curriculum control and the work-based route to vocational qualifications, *British Journal of Educational Studies*, 50(2): 225–37.

Boud, D., Keogh, R. and Walker, D. (1985) *Reflection: Turning Experience into Learning*, London, Kogan Page.

Bourdieu, P. and Wacquant, L. (1992) *An Invitation to Reflexive Sociology*, London, Polity Press.

Bradley, J., Dee, L. and Wilenius, F. (1994) *Students with Disabilities and/or Learning Difficulties in Further Education*, Slough, NFER.

Brandes, D. and Phillips, H. (1985) *Gamesters' Handbook*, London, Hutchinson.

Brookfield, S. (1986) *Understanding and Facilitating Adult Learning*, Milton Keynes, Open University Press.

Brooks, V. (2004) Using assessment for Formative Purposes, in V. Brooks, I. Abbott and L. Bills, *Preparing to Teach in Secondary Schools*. Maidenhead, Open University Press.

Brown, S. (1994) Assessment: a changing practice, in B. Moon and A. Shelton Mayes (eds) *Teaching and Learning in the Secondary School*, London, Open University/Routledge.

Brundage, D.H. and Mackeracher, D. (1980) *Adult Learning Principles and Their Application to Program Planning*, Toronto, Ministry of Education, Ontario.

Canning, R. (2007) Reconceptualising core skills, *Journal of Education and Work*, 20(1): 17–26.

Carr, W. (1993) Reconstructing the curriculum debate: an editorial introduction, *Curriculum Studies*, 1(1): 5–9.

Castling, A. (1996) The role of the staff development practitioner in the FE college, in J. Robson (ed.) *The Professional FE Teacher*, Aldershot, Avebury.

CEDEFOP (1994) *Determining the Need for Vocational Counselling Among Different Target Groups of Young People under 28 years of Age in the European Community*, Berlin, CEDEFOP.

City and Guilds (2005) *General units G/1, V1*, London, City and Guilds.

Clarke, J. (2002) Deconstructing domestication: women's experience and the goals of critical pedagogy, in R. Harrison, F. Reeve and J. Clarke (eds) *Supporting Lifelong Learning*, Volume 1, *Perspectives on Learning*, London, RoutledgeFalmer.

Clough, P. and Barton, L. (1995) Introduction: Self and the research act, in P. Clough and L. Barton (eds) *Making Difficulties, Research and the Construction of SEN*, London, Paul Chapman.

Coats, M. (1994) *Women's Education*, Buckingham, SRHE/Open University Press.

Coffield, F. (1999) Breaking the consensus: lifelong learning as social control, *British Educational Research Journal*, 25(4): 545–61.

Coffield, F., Moseley, D., Hall, E. and Ecclestone, K. (2004) *Should we be using learning styles? What research has to say to practice*, London, Learning and Skills Research Centre.

Coffield, F., Steer, R., Hodgson, A., Spours, K., Edward, S. and Finlay, I. (2005) A new learning and skills landscape? The central role of the Learning and Skills Council, *Journal of Education Policy*, 20(5): 631–56.

Coffield, F., Edwards, S., Finlay, I., Hodgson, A., Spours, K. and Steer, R. (2008, forthcoming) *Improving Learning and Inclusion: The Impact of Policy and Policymaking*, London, Routledge.

Cohen, L. and Manion, L. (1989) *A Guide to Teaching Practice*, 3rd edn, London, Routledge.

Cole, M. (1985) The zone of proximal development: where culture and cognition create each other, in Wertsch, J. (ed.) *Culture, Communication and Cognition. Vygotskian Perspectives*, Cambridge, Cambridge University Press.

Colley, H., James, D., Tedder, M. and Diment, K. (2003) Learning as becoming in Vocational Education and Training: class, gender and the role of vocational habitus, *Journal of Vocational Education and Training*, 55(4): 471–97.

Corbett, J. (1997) Transitions to what? Young people with special educational needs, in S. Tomlinson (ed.) *Education 14–19 Critical Perspectives*, London, The Athlone Press.

Corbett, J. and Barton, L. (1992) *A Struggle for Choice, Students with Special Needs in Transition to Adulthood*, London, Routledge.

Cox, A. (1996) Teacher as mentor: opportunities for professional development, in J. Robson (ed.) *The Professional FE Teacher*, Aldershot, Avebury.

Culham, A. (2001) Practitioner-based research in FE: realities and problems, *College Research*, 4(3): 27.

Culham, A. (2003) 'Including' permanently excluded students from pupil referral units in further education, *Journal of Further and Higher Education*, 27(4): 399–409.

Davey, A. (2001) The research culture at Cambridge Regional College, *College Research*, 4(3): 29.

Davies, P and Owen, J. (2001) *Listening to Staff*, London, Learning and Skills Development Agency.

Day, C., Kington, A., Stobart, G. and Sammons, P. (2006) The personal and the professional selves of teachers: stable and unstable identities, *British Educational Research Journal*, 32(4): 601–16.

Dearing, R. (1996) *Review of 16–19 Qualifications: Summary Report*, London, School Curriculum and Assessment Authority.

Dee, L. (1999) Inclusive learning: from rhetoric to reality, in A. Green and N. Lucas (eds) *FE and Lifelong Learning: Realigning the Sector for the 21st Century*, London.

DES/WO (1988) *Advancing A levels* (The Higginson Report), London, HMSO.

DES/ED/WO (1991) *Education and Training for the 21st Century*, London, HMSO.

Dewey, J. (1938) *Experience and Education*, New York, Collier.

DfEE (1997) *Qualifying for Success: A Consultation Paper on the Future of Post-16 Qualifications*, London, Department for Education and Employment.

DfEE (1998) *University for Industry: Pathfinder Prospectus*, Sudbury, Department for Education and Employment.

DfEE (1999) *Learning to Succeed*, Cm 4392, London, The Stationery Office.

DfES (2002) *14–19: Extending Opportunities, Raising Standards,* London, DfES.

DfES (2004a) *Five Year Strategy for Children and Learners*, Cm 6272, London, HMSO.

DfES (2004b) *Working Group on 14–19 Reform. Principles for Reform of 14–19 Learning Programmes and Qualifications*, London, DfES.

DfES (2005a) *Realising the Potential – a Review of the Future Role of Further Education Colleges (The Foster Review)*, London, DfES

DfES (2005b) *14–19 Education and Skills*, Cm 6476, London, HMSO.

DfES (2005c) *Youth Matters*, Cm 6629, London, HMSO.

DfES (2006a) *14–19 Implementation Plan*, London, DfES.

DfES (2006b) *Further Education: Raising Skills, Improving Life Chances*, Cm 6768, London, The Stationery Office.

DfES (2007) *Raising Expectations: Staying in Education and Training Post-16*, Cm 7065, London, HMSO.

Dimbleby, R. and Cooke, C. (2000) Curriculum and learning, in A. Smithers and P. Robinson (eds) *Further Education Re-formed*, London, Routledge.

Ducklin, A. and Oźga, J. (2007) Gender and management in further education in Scotland: an agenda for research, *Gender and Education*, 19(5): 627–46.

Duke, C. and Layer, G. (2005) *Widening Participation: which way forward for English higher education*, Leicester, NIACE.

Ecclestone, K. (2000) Assessment and critical autonomy in post-compulsory education in the UK, *Journal of Education and Work*, 13(2): 141–60.

Ecclestone, K. (2002) *Learning Autonomy in Post-16 Education*, London, Routledge.

Ecclestone, K. (2004) Learning or therapy? The demoralisation of education, *British Journal of Educational Studies*, 52(2), 112–37.

Edwards, A. (2001) Researching Pedagogy: a sociocultural agenda, *Pedagogy, Culture and Society*, 9(2): 161–86.

Edwards, R. (1993) Multi-skilling the flexible workforce in post-compulsory education, *Journal of Further and Higher Education*, 17(1): 44–51.

Edwards, T., Fitz-Gibbon, C., Hardman, F., Haywood, R. and Meagher, N. (1997) *Separate but Equal? A Levels and GNVQs*, London, Routledge.

Edexcel (2006) *BTEC First Certificate and First Diploma in Business: Specification*, London, Edexcel.

Education and Skills Select Committee (2007) *14–19 Diplomas*, 5th Report of House of Commons Education and Skills Select Committee, HC 249 (available from www.publications.parliament.uk).

Egan, G. (1975) *The Skilled Helper*, San Francisco, California, Wadsworth.

Eisner, E.W. (1985) *The Art of Educational Evaluation*, London, Falmer Press.

Elliott, G. (1996) *Crisis and Change in Vocational Education and Training*, London, Jessica Kingsley.

Elliott, J. (1983) A curriculum for the study of human affairs: the contribution of Lawrence Stenhouse, *Curriculum Studies*, 15(2): 105–23.

Engestrom, Y. (2001) Expansive learning at work: towards an activity – theoretical reconceptualisation, *Journal of Education and Work*, 14(1): 133–56.

Eraut, M. (1994) *Developing Professional Knowledge and Competence*, London, Falmer Press.

ESRC (2007) *Britain Today. The State of the Nation in 2007*, Swindon, Economic and Social Research Council.

Evans, K. (1998) *Shaping Futures*, Ashgate, Aldershot.

Evans, K., Hodkinson, P., Rainbird, H. and Unwin, L. (2006) *Improving Workplace Learning*, London, Routledge.

Evans, K., Kersh, N. and Sakamoto, A. (2004) Learner biographies: exploring tacit dimensions of knowledge and skills, in H, Rainbird, A. Fuller and A. Munro (eds) *Workplace Learning in Context*, London, Routledge.

FEFC (2001) *Chief Inspector's Annual Report 2000/01*, Coventry, Further Education Funding Council.

Felstead, A. and Unwin, L. (2001) Funding post compulsory education and training: a retrospective analysis of the TEC and FEFC systems and their impact on skills, *Journal of Education and Work*, 14(1): 91–111.

Ferguson, M. (1982) *The Aquarian Conspiracy: Personal and Social Transformation in the 1980s*, London, Paladin.

FEU (1979) *A Basis for Choice*, London, Further Education Unit.

FEU (1981) *Vocational Preparation*, London, Further Education Unit.

Field, J. (2000) *Lifelong Learning and the New Educational Order*, Stoke-on-Trent, Trentham Books.

Field, J. (2004) Articulation and credit transfer in Scotland: taking the highroad or a sideways step in a ghetto?, *Journal of Access Policy and Practice*, 1(2): 85–99.

Fieldhouse, R. and Associates (1996) *A History of Modern British Adult Education*, Leicester, National Institute for Adult Continuing Education.

Finegold, D., Milliband, D., Raffe, D., Spours, K. and Young, M. (1990) *A British Baccalaureate: Ending the Division between Education and Training*, London, Institute for Public Policy Research.

Finlay, I., Spours, K., Steer, R., Coffield, F., Gregson, M., Hodgson, A. and Edward, S. (2006) 'The heart of what we do'. Policies on teaching, learning and assessment in the new learning and skills sector, *Research Report 4*, London, Institute of Education, University of London.

Fisher, R. and Webb, K. (2006) Subject specialist pedagogy and initial teacher training for the learning and skills sector in England: the context, a response and some critical issues, *Journal of Further and Higher Education*, 30(4): 337–49.

Flint, C. (2005) *Staff in FE. Think Piece for the Foster Review* (available from www.dfes.gov.uk.

Freire, P. (1974) *Education: The Practice of Freedom*, London, Writers and Readers Co-operative.

Fuller, A., Hodkinson, H., Hodkinson, P. and Unwin, L. (2005) Learning as Peripheral Participation in Communities of Practice: A reassessment of key concepts in workplace learning, *British Educational Research Journal*, 31(1): 49–68.

Fuller, A. and Unwin, L. (2003) Learning as apprentices in the contemporary UK workplace: creating and managing expansive and restrictive participation, *Journal of Education and Work*, 16(4): 406–27.

Fuller, A. and Unwin, L. (2004) Expansive learning environments: integrating personal and organisational development, in H. Rainbird, A. Fuller and A. Munro (eds) *Workplace Learning in Context*, London, Routledge.

Furlong, A. and Cartmel, F. (1997) *Young People and Social Change*, Buckingham, Open University Press.

Gagne, R.M. (1988) *Principles of Instructional Design*, New York, Holt, Rinehart and Winston.

Gallacher, J. (2006) Blurring the boundaries or creating diversity? The contribution of the further education colleges to higher education in Scotland, *Journal of Further and Higher Education*, 30(1): 43–58.

Gallacher, J. and Reeve, F. (2005) *Differing national models of short cycle, work-related higher education provision in Scotland and England*, paper prepared for Centre for Research in Lifelong Learning, Glasgow Caledonian University (http://crll.gcal.ac.uk/docs/HN_FD%20comparativepaper%20final.pdf).

Gibb, J.R. (1960) Learning theory in adult education, in M. Knowles (ed.) *Handbook of Adult Education in the United States*, Washington, DC, Adult Education Association of the USA.

Giroux, H. (ed.) (1991) *Post-Modernism, Feminism and Cultural Politics: redrawing educational boundaries*, Albany, State University of New York Press.

Gleeson, D. (1996) Post-compulsory eduation in a post-industrial and post-modern age, in Avis, J., Bloomer, M., Esland, G., Gleeson, D. and Hodkinson, P. (eds) *Knowledge and Nationhood*, London, Cassell Education.

Gleeson, D. (2005) Learning for a Change in Further Education, *Journal of Vocational Education and Training*, 57(2): 239–46.

Gleeson, D. and Shain (1999) By Appointment: governance, markets and managerialism in further education, *British Educational Research Journal*, 25(4): 545–61.

Golden, S., O'Donnell, L. and Rudd, P. (2005) *Evaluation of Increased Flexibility for 14 to 16 year olds Programme: The Second Year,* Nottingham: DfES Publications.

Gravatt, J. and Silver, R. (2000) Partnerships with the Community, in Smithers, A. and Robinson, P. (eds) *Further Education Re-formed*, London, Falmer Press.

Green, A. (1997) Core skills, general education and unification in post-16 education, in Hodgson, A. and Spours, K. (eds) *Dearing and Beyond*, London, Kogan Page.

Green, A. and Lucas, N. (1999) From obscurity to crisis: the further education sector in context, in Green, A. and Lucas, N. (eds) *FE and Lifelong Learning: Realigning the Sector for the 21st Century*, London, Bedford Way Papers, Institute of Education.

Griffin, C. (1993) *Representations of Youth*, Cambridge, Polity Press.

Griffiths, M. (2003) Policy and practice proximity: the scope for college-based higher education and cross-sector collaboration in Wales, *Higher Education Quarterly*, 57 (4): 335–75.

Grubb, W.N. and Associates (1999) *Honoured But Invisible, An Inside Look at Teaching in Community Colleges*, London, Routledge.

Guile, D. (2006) What is distinctive about the knowledge economy? Implications for Education, in Lauder, H., Brown, P., Dillabough, J-A. and Halsey, A.H. (eds) *Education, Globalisation and Social Change*, Oxford, Oxford University Press.

Guile, D. and Hayton, A. (1999) Information and learning technology: the implications for teaching and learning in further education, in A. Green and N. Lucas (eds) *FE and Lifelong Learning: Realigning the Sector for the Twenty-first Century*, London, Institute of Education.

Guile, D. and Young, M. (1999) Beyond the institution of apprenticeship: towards a social theory of learning as the production of knowledge, in P. Ainley and H. Rainbird (eds) *Apprenticeship, Towards a New Paradigm for Learning*, London, Kogan Page.

Hamilton, M. (2006) Just do it: Literacies, everyday learning and the irrelevance of pedagogy, *Studies in the Education of Adults*, 38(2): 125–40.

Hardman, J. and Malcolm, R. (2005) *What Works for Learners? Case Studies of 14–16 provision in FE colleges in the West Midlands*, London: LDSA.

Harkin, J. (2005) Fragments stored against my ruin: the place of educational theory in the professional development of teachers in further education, *Journal of Vocational Education and Training*, 57(2): 165–80.

Harkin, J. (2006) Treated like adults: 14–16-year-olds in Further Education, *Research in Post-Compulsory Education*, 11(3): 319–39.

Harkin, J., Turner, G. and Dawn, T. (2001) *Teaching Young Adults*, London, Routledge/Falmer.

Harlen, W. and Deakin Crick, R. (2002) *A systematic review of the impact of summative assessment and tests on students' motivation for learning in Researching Evidence in Education Library*, London, EPPI Centre, Social Science Research Unit, Institute of Education.

Hargreaves, D. (2004) *Learning for Life*, Bristol, The Policy Press.

Harris, S. and Hyland, T. (1995) Basic Skills and Learning Support in Further Education, *Journal of Further and Higher Education*, 19(2): 42–6.

Harrow, A.J. (1972) *A Taxonomy of the Psychomotor Domain*, New York, McKay.

Harwood, J. and Harwood, D. (2006) Higher education in further education: delivering higher education in a further education context – a study of five South West colleges, *Journal of Further and Higher Education*, 28(2): 153–64.

Heathcote, G., Kempa, R. and Roberts, I. (1982) *Curriculum Styles and Strategies*, London, Further Education Unit.

Higham, J. and Yeomans, D. (2005) *Collaborative Approaches to 14–19 Provision: an Evaluation of the Second Year of the 14–19 Pathfinder Initiative*, DfES Research Report 542, Nottingham, Department for Education and Skills.

Hill, R. (2000) A study of the views of full-time FE lecturers regarding their college corporations and agencies of the FE sector, *Journal of Further and Higher Education*, 24(1): 67–76.

Hillage, J., Loukas, G., Newton, B., and Tamkin, P. (2006) *Employer Training Pilots: Final Evaluation Report*, Research Report 774, London: Department for Education and Skills.

HM Treasury (2003) *Every Child Matters*, Cm. 5860, London, HMSO.

Hochschild, A. (1983) *The Managed Heart: The Commercialization of Human Feeling*, Berkeley, The University of California Press.

Hodkinson, P. (1997) Neo-Fordism and Teacher Professionalism, *Teacher Development*, 1(1): 69–82.

Hodkinson, P. and Bloomer, M. (2000) Stokingham Sixth Form College: institutional culture and dispositions to learning, *British Journal of Sociology of Education*, 21(2): 187–200.

Hodkinson, P. and Issitt, M. (1995) *The Challenge of Competence*, London, Cassell Education.

Hodkinson, P., Sparkes, A.C. and Hodkinson, H. (1996) *Triumphs and Tears: Young People, Markets and the Transition from School to Work*, London, David Fulton.

Hodson, A. and Spours, K. (1997) *Beyond Dearing, 14–19: Qualifications, Frameworks and Systems*, London, Kogan Page.

Hodgson, A. and Spours, K. (1999) *New Labour's Educational Agenda*, London, Kogan Page.

Hodgson, A. and Spours, K. (2001) Part-time work and full-time education in the UK: the emergence of a curriculum and policy issue, *Journal of Education and Work*, 14(3): 373–8.

Hodgson, A. and Spours, K. (2003) *Beyond A Levels*, London, Kogan Page.

Honey, P. and Mumford, A. (1982) *The Manual of Learning Styles*, Maidenhead, Peter Honey.

Howieson, C., Raffe, D. and Tinklin, T. (2002) Institutional Responses to a Flexible Unified System: The Case of Scottish Colleges of Further Education, in Nijhof, W., Heikkenen, A. and Nieuwenhuis, L. (eds) *Shaping Flexibility in Vocational Education and Training*, Dordrecht, Kluwer.

Huddleston, P., Abbott, I. and Stagg, P. (1995) *Introduction to GNVQs: A Practical Guide*, London, Understanding British Industry/Employment Department.

Huddleston, P., Keep, E. and Unwin, L. (2005) *What might the Tomlinson and White Paper proposals mean for vocational education and work-based learning?* Discussion Paper 33, Nuffield Review of 14–19 Education and Training (www.nuffield1419review.org.uk/files/documents).

Hyland, T. (1994) *Competence, Education and NVQs: Dissenting Perspectives*, London, Cassell Education.

Istance, D. and Williamson, H. (1996) *16 and 17 year olds in South and Mid-Glamorgan not in Education, Training or Employment (status zero)*, Swansea, Mid-Glamorgan Training and Enterprise Council.

Jackson, C., Arnold, J., Nicholson, N. and Watts, A.G. (1996) *Managing Careers in 2000 and Beyond*, Sussex Institute of Employment Studies.

Jaques, D. (1992) *Learning in Groups*, 2nd edn, London, Croom Helm.

James, D. and Diment, K. (2003) Going underground? Learning and assessment in an ambiguous space, *Journal of Vocational Education and Training*, 55(4): 407–22.

Jarvis, P. (1987) *Adult Learning in the Social Context*, London, Croom Helm.

Jessup, G. (1994) *GNVQ An Alternative Curriculum Model*, London, NCVQ.

Johnston, R. (1999) Adult learning for citizenship: towards a reconstruction of the social purpose tradition, *International Journal of Lifelong Learning*, 18(3): 175–90.

Johnstone, J.W.C. and Rivera, R.J. (1965) *Volunteers for Learning: A Study of the Educational Pursuits of Adults*, Hawthorne, New York, Aldine.

Jones, A.M. and Hendry, C. (1994) The Learning Organisation: adult learning and organisational transformation, *British Journal of Management*, 5(2): 153–62.

Keep, E. (2005) Reflections on the curious absence of employers, labour market incentives and labour market regulation in English 14–19 policy: first signs of a change in direction?, *Journal of Education Policy*, 20(5): 533–53.

Kehily, M.J. (1995) Self-narration, autobiography and identity construction, *Gender and Education*, 7(1): 23–31.

Kennedy, H. (1997) *Learning Works: Widening Participation in Further Education*, Coventry, FEFC.

Kenway, J. (2001) The information superhighway and postmodernity: the social promise and the social price, in Paechter, C. Preedy, M., Scott, D. and Soler, J. (eds) *Knowledge, Power and Learning*, London, Paul Chapman.

Kidd, R. (1973) *How Adults Learn*, Chicago, IL, Follett.

King, E., Mann, A. and Thompson, H. (2005) *Business Planning, Income Generation, and Culture and Ethos: Think Piece for the Foster Review* (available from www.dcfs.gov.uk).

Knowles, M. (1978) *The Adult Learner: A Neglected Species*, Houston, TX, Gulf.

Knox, A.B. (1977) *Adult Development and Learning: A Handbook on Individual Growth and Competence in the Adult Years*, San Francisco, CA, Jossey-Bass.

Kolb, D.A. (1984) *Experiential Learning*, Englewood Cliffs, NJ, Prentice Hall.

Laurillard, D. (1993) *Rethinking University Teaching*, London, Routledge.

Lauzon, A.C. (1989) Educational transition: A qualitative study of full-time married male students, *International Journal of University Adult Education*, XXVIII(2): 34–46.

Lave, J. (1995) *Teaching as Learning in Practice*, Sylvia Scribner Award Lecture, American Educational Research Association Conference, San Francisco.

Lave, J. and Wenger, E. (1991) *Situated Learning*, Cambridge, Cambridge University Press.

Leitch Review (2006) *Prosperity for all in the Global Economy – World Class Skills*, London, HM Treasury.

Lipsig-Mumme, C. (1997) The politics of the new service economy, in P. James, W.F. Veit, and S. Wright (eds) *Work of the Future*, London, Allen and Unwin.

LLUK (2006) *Benchmark Role Specifications for Principals of Further Education, Sixth Form and Specialist Colleges*, London, Lifelong Learning UK.

LLUK (2007) *New Overarching Professional Standards For Teachers, Tutors And Trainers In The Lifelong Learning Sector*, London, Lifelong Learning UK.

LSDA (2001) *Key Skills, LSDA Information Pack*, London, Learning and Skills Development Agency.

Lucas, N. (1996) Teacher Training Agency: is there anyone there from further education?, *Journal of Further and Higher Education*, 20(1): 67–73.

Lucas, N. (1999) Incorporated colleges: beyond the Further Education Funding Council's Model, in A. Green and N. Lucas (eds) *FE and Lifelong Learning: Realigning the Sector for the 21st Century*, London, pp. 42–68.

Lucas, N. (2004) The 'FENTO Fandango': national standards, compulsory teaching qualifications and the growing regulation of FE college teachers, *Journal of Further and Higher Education*, 28(1): 35–51.

Lumby, J. (2001) Managing Teaching and Learning: diversity and innovation, *College Research*, 4(3): 50–2.

Lumby, J. (2007) 14–16 year olds in further education colleges: lessons for learning and leadership, *Journal of Vocational Education and Training*, 59(1): 1–18.

McGiveney, V. (1996) *Staying or leaving the course: Non-completion and retention of mature students in further and higher education*, Leicester, National Institute for Adult Continuing Education.

McLeod, J., Yates, L. and Halasa, K. (1994) Voice, difference and feminist pedagogy, *Curriculum Studies*, 2(2): 189–202.

McClure, R. (2000) Recurrent funding, in A. Smithers and P. Robinson (2000) (eds) *Further Education Re-formed*, London, Falmer Press.

Mager, R. (1962) *Preparing Instructional Objectives*, San Francisco, CA, Fearon.

Marshall, L. and Rowland, F. (1993) *A Guide to Learning Independently*, 2nd Edn, Buckingham, Open University Press.

Maslow, A (1968) *Towards a Psychology of Being*, New York, Van Nostrand.

Mayes, T. (2002) The technology of learning in a social world, in R. Harrison, F. Reeve, A. Hanson and J. Clarke (eds) *Supporting Lifelong Learning, Volume 1, Perspectives on Learning*, London, RoutledgeFalmer.

Mayo, M. (2002) Learning for active citizenship: training for and learning from participation in area regeneration, in F. Reeve, M. Cartwright and R. Edwards (eds) *Supporting Lifelong Learning*, Volume 2, *Organising Learning*, London, RoutledgeFalmer.

Miller, H.L. (1964) *Teaching and Learning in Adult Education*, New York, Macmillan.

Minton, D. (1991) *Teaching Skills in Further and Adult Education*, London, City & Guilds.

Moore, R. and Young, M. (2001) Knowledge and the Curriculum in the Sociology of Education: towards a reconceptualisation, *British Journal of Sociology of Education*, 22(4): 445–61.

Morgan-Klein, B (2003) Scottish Higher Education and the FE-HE Nexus, *Higher Education Quarterly*, 57 (4): 338–54.

Murphy, P. (1999) (ed.) *Learners, Learning and Assessment*, London, Paul Chapman/Open University.

National Council – ELWa, ACCAC and HEFCW (2003) Implementation Plan – Credit and Qualifications Framework for Wales, Cardiff, Welsh Assembly.

Neisser, U. (1983) Towards a skilful psychology, in Roghers, D. and Sloboda, J.A. (eds) *The Acquisition of Symbolic Skills*, New York, Plenum Publishing Corporation.

NIACE (2005) Meeting with Mark Haysom, Chief Executive, Learning and Skills Council, 17 January, *Policy Briefing* (available from www.niace.org.uk).

Noel, P. (2006) The secret life of teacher educators: becoming a teacher educator in the learning and skills sector, *Journal of Vocational Education and Training*, 58(2): 151–70.

NSTF (1999) *Delivering Skills for All, Second Report of the National Skills Task Force*, Sudbury, Department for Education and Employment.

OCR (2005) *GCE AS Level Applied Business*, Coventry, OCR.

Ofsted (2004) Developing new vocational pathways: final report on the introduction of new GCSEs (www.ofsted.gov.uk/assets/3674.pdf).

Osborne, R.D. (2003) Higher Education in Further Education: Northern Ireland, *Higher Education Quarterly*, 57(4): 376–95.

Parry, G. (2005) *The Higher Education Role of Further Education. Think Piece for the Foster Review* (available from: www.dfes.gov.uk).

Pearce, N. and Hillman, J. (1998) *Wasted Youth*, London: IPPR.

Perry, A. (2005) *Delivery Models. Think Piece for the Foster Review* (available from: www.dfes.gov.uk).

Piaget, J. (1970) *Genetic Epistemology*, New York, Columbia University Press.

Polanyi, M. (1967) *The Tacit Dimension*, New York, Anchor Books.

Pring, R. (1997) Aims, values and the curriculum, in S. Tomlinson (ed.) *Education 14–19 Critical Perspectives*, London, The Athlone Press.

QCA (1998) *Disapplication of the National Curriculum at Key Stage 4 Using Section 363 of the 1996 Education Act for a Wider Focus on Work-related Learning. Guidance for Schools*, London, QCA.

QCA (2001) *QCA Review of Curriculum 2000 – Report on Phase One*, July 2001, London, QCA.

Quicke, J. (1996) The reflective practitioner and teacher education: an answer to critics, *Teachers and Teaching: Theory and Practice*, 2(1): 11–22.

Raffe, D. (2003) 'Simplicity itself': the creation of the Scottish Credit and Qualifications Framework, *Journal of Education and Work*, 16(3): 239–57.

Raffe, D. (2007) Learning from 'home international' comparisons: 14–19 policy across the United Kingdom, in Raffe, D. and Spours, K. (eds) *Policymaking and Policy Learning in 14–19 Education*, London, Bedford Way Papers, Institute of Education.

Raffe, D., Spours, K., Young, M. and Howieson, C. (1998) The unification of post-compulsory education: Towards a conceptual framework, *British Journal of Educational Studies*, 4(6): 169–87.

Raggatt, P. and Williams, S. (1999) *Government, Markets and Vocational Qualifications*, London, Falmer Press.

Ramsden, M., Bennett, R.J. and Fuller, C. (2004) Short-term policy and the changing institutional landscape of post-16 education and training: the case of learning partnerships in England, Scotland and Wales, *Journal of Education and Work*, 17(2): 139–65.

Randle and Brady (1997) Further education and the new managerialism, *Journal of Further and Higher Education*, 21(2): 229–38.

RCU (2003) *Research into the Comparative Performance of Tertiary Colleges* (available at www.rcu.co.uk).

Rees, S.A. (1995) Students with emotional and behavioural difficulties: coping with a growing tide, *Journal of Further and Higher Education*, 19(2): 93–7.

Rees, G., Gorard, S., Fevre, R. and Furlong, J. (2000) Participating in the learning society: history, place and biography, in F. Coffield (ed.) *Differing Visions of a Learning Society*, volume 2, Bristol, The Policy Press.

Richardson, W., Woolhouse, J. and Finegold, D. (1993) *The Reform of Post-16 Education and Training in England and Wales*, Harlow, Longman.

Riddell, S., Litjens, L., Ahlgren, L. and Weedon, E. (2005) *Equality and Diversity in the Further Education Workforce: Final Report to the Scottish Further Education Unit*, Edinburgh, University of Edinburgh.

Riddell, S., Wilson, A. and Baron, S. (1999) Captured customers: people with learning difficulties in social markets, *British Educational Research Journal*, 25(4): 545–61.

Riding, R. and Cheema, I. (1991) Cognitive style – an overview and integration, *Educational Psychology*, 65: 113–24.

Robson, J. (ed.) (1998) *The Professional FE Teacher*, Aldershot, Avebury.

Robson, J. (1998) A profession in crisis: status, culture and identity in the further education college, *Journal of Vocational Education and Training*, 50(4): 585–607.

Robson, J., Bailey, B. and Larkin, S. (2004) Adding Value: investigating the discourse of professionalism adopted by vocational teachers in further education colleges, *Journal of Education and Work*, 17(2): 183–95.

Robson, J., Bailey, B. and Mendick, H. (2006) *An Investigation into the Roles of Learning Support Workers in the Learning and Skills Sector*, London, Learning and Skills Network.

Rogers, A. (1986) *Teaching Adults*, Milton Keynes, Open University Press.

Rogers, A. (2002) *Teaching Adults*, 3rd edn, Buckingham, Open University Press.

Rogers, J. (1992) *Adults Learning*, 3rd edn, Buckingham, Open University Press.

Rommes, E., Faulkner, W. and Van Slooten, I. (2005) Changing lives: the case for women-only technology training revisited, *Journal of Vocational Education and Training*, 57(3): 293–317.

Rowland, S. (1993) *The Enquiring Tutor*, London, Falmer Press.

Ryan, P., Gospel, H. and Lewis, P. (2007) Large employers and apprenticeship training in Britain, *British Journal of Industrial Relations*, 45(1): 127–53.

Sachs, J. (2001) Teacher professional identity: competing discourses, competing outcomes, *Journal of Education Policy*, 16(2): 149–61.

Sacks, O. (1986) *The Man Who Mistook His Wife For a Hat*, London, Pan Books.

Sanderson, B. (2001) Branding education, *RSA Journal*, 3(4): 22–5.

Satir, V. (1983) *Conjoint Family Therapy*, 3rd edn, Palo Alto, CA, Science and Behavioural Books.

Schön, D. (1983) *The Reflective Practitioner: How Professionals Think in Action*, New York, Basic Books.

Schön, D. (1987) *Educating the Reflective Practitioner*, San Francisco, CA, Jossey-Bass.

SEU (1999) *Bridging the Gap: New Opportunities for 16–18 year olds Not in Education, Employment or Training*, London, The Stationery Office.

Shattock, M. (2000) Governance and management, in A. Smithers and P. Robinson (eds) *Further Education Re-formed*, London, Falmer Press.

Silver, R. and Forrest, W. (2007) Learning to become, in Kehoe, D. (ed.) *Practice Makes Perfect: The Importance of Practical Learning*, London, The Social Market Foundation.

Simon, B. (1999) Why No Pedagogy in England?, in Leach, J. and Moon, B. (eds) *Learners and Pedagogy*, London, Paul Chapman Publishing.

Skinner, B.F. (1968) *The Technology of Teaching*, New York, Appleton-Century-Crofts.

Smith, J.J. (1989) Judgements in educational assessment, *Journal of Further and Higher Education*, 13(3): 115–19.

Smith, R.M. (1982) *Learning How to Learn: Applied Theory for Adults*, New York, Cambridge University Press.

Smith, R. and Betts, M. (2003) Partnerships and the consortia approach to United Kingdom Foundation Degrees: a case study of benefits and pitfalls, *Journal of Vocational Education and Training*, 55(2): 223–40.

Squires, G. (1987) *The Curriculum Beyond School*, London, Hodder and Stoughton.

Stanton, G. (2000) Research, in A. Smithers and P. Robinson (eds) *Further Education Reformed*, London, Falmer Press.

Stenhouse, L. (1975) *An Introduction to Curriculum Research and Development*, London, Heinemann.

Stronach, I., Corbin, B., McNamara, O., Stark, S. and Warne, T. (2002) Towards an uncertain politics of professionalism: teacher and nurse identities in flux, *Journal of Education Policy*, 17(1): 109–38.

Taubman, D. (2000) Staff relations, in A. Smithers and P. Robinson (eds) *Further Education Re-formed*, London, Falmer Press.

Tedder, M. (1994) Appraisal and professionalism in colleges, *Journal of Further and Higher Education*, 18(3): 74–82.

TES 2 (1995) Drama out of a crisis, *Times Educational Supplement,* 20 September.

THES (1998) Doubts over who foots the bill for the University of Industry, Editorial, *Times Higher Education Supplement*, 20 November.

Tomlinson, J. (1996) *Inclusive Learning: Report of the Learning Difficulties and/or Disabilities Committee*, London, The Stationery Office.

Tough, A. (1971) *The Adult's Learning Projects*, Toronto, Ontario Institute for Studies in Education.

Tuckett, A. (2005) *The Untidy Curriculum: Adult learners in Further Education, Think Piece for the Foster Review* (available at www.dcsf.gov.uk).

UDACE (1991) *What Can Graduates Do?* A Consultative Document, Leicester, UDACE.

Unwin, L. (1993) Training credits: The pilot doomed to succeed, in W. Richardson *et al.* (eds) *The Reform of Post-16 Education and Training England and Wales*, Harlow, Longman.

Unwin, L. (1995) *Staying the Course: Students' Reasons for Non-completion of Full-time Education Courses in South and East Cheshire*, Middlewich, South and East Cheshire Education-Business Partnership.

Unwin, L. (1997) Reforming the work-based route: problems and potential for change, in A. Hodgson and K. Spours (eds) *Dearing and Beyond*, London, Kogan Page.

Unwin, L. (1999) 'Flower arranging's off but floristry is on': Lifelong learning and adult education further education colleges, in A. Green and N. Lucas (eds) *FE and Lifelong Learning: Realigning the Sector for the 21st Century*, London, Bedford Way Papers.

Unwin, L. (2004) Growing Beans with Thoreau: rescuing skills and vocational education from the UK's deficit approach, *Oxford Review of Education*, 30(1): 147–60.

Unwin, L. (2008, in press) Only participate: the emergence of the 'learner' in the UK's VET system, in Keep, E., Mayhew, K., Payne, J. and Stasz, C. (eds) *Education, Skills and the Economy: The Politics of Vocational Education and Training*, Cheltenham, Edward Elgar.

Unwin, L. and Edwards, R. (1990) The tutor–learner relationship: making sense of changing contexts, *Adults Learning*, March: 197–9.

Unwin, L., Fuller, A., Turbin, J. and Young, M. (2004) *The Impact of Vocational Qualifications*, DfES Research Report 522, Nottingham: Department for Education and Skills.

Unwin, L. and Wellington, J. (2001) *Young People's Perspectives on Education, Employment and Training*, London, Kogan Page.

Usher, R., Bryant, I. and Johnston, R. (2002) Self and experience in adult learning, in R. Harrison, F. Reeve, A. Hanson and J. Clarke (eds) *Supporting Lifelong Learning*, Volume 1, London, RoutledgeFalmer.

Vygotsky, L.S. (1978) *Mind in Society*, edited by Cole, M., John-Steiner, V., Scribner, S. and Souberman, E., Cambridge, Harvard University Press.

Wahlberg, M. (2007) *What Works, What Matters? Evaluations of Centres of Vocational Excellence in FE: Full Research Report*, ESRC End of Award Report, RES-000-22-1728, Swindon, ESRC.

Wahlberg, M. and Gleeson, D. (2003) 'Doing the business': paradox and irony in vocational education – GNVQ business studies as a case in point, *Journal of Vocational Education and Training*, 55(4): 423–46.

Watson, C. (2006) Narratives of practice and the construction of identity in teaching, *Teachers and Teaching: Theory and Practice*, 12(5): 509–26.

Webb, S., Brine, J. and Jackson, J. (2005) Gender, foundation degrees and the knowledge-driven economy, *Journal of Vocational Education and Training*, 58(4): 563–76.

Wildemeersch, D. (1989) The principal meaning of dialogue for the construction and transformation of reality, in S.W. Weil and I. McGill (eds) *Making Sense of Experiential Learning*, Milton Keynes, SRHE/Open University Press.

Wilmot, M. and McLean, M. (1994) Evaluating flexible learning: A case study, *Journal of Further and Higher Education*, 18(3): 99–108.

Wolf, A. (1995) *Competence-based Assessment*, Buckingham, Open University Press.

Wolf, A. (2002) *Does Education Matter?: Myths About Education and Economic Growth*, London, Penguin.

Wolf, A., Jenkins, A. and Vignoles, A. (2006) Certifying the workforce: economic imperative or failed social policy?, *Journal of Education Policy*, 21(5): 535–65.

Young, M. (1993) A curriculum for the 21st century? Towards a new basis for overcoming academic/vocational divisions, *British Journal of Educational Studies*, 40(3): 203–22.

Young, M. (2003) National Qualifications Frameworks as a Global Phenomenon, *Journal of Education and Work*, 16(3): 223–37.

Young, M. (1998) *The Curriculum of the Future*, London, Falmer Press.

Young, M., Lucas, N., Sharp, G. and Cunningham, B. (1995) *Teacher Education for the Further Education Sector: Training the Lecturer of the Future*, London, Institute of Education, University of London.

Young, M., Guile, D., Lucas, N. and Unwin, L. (1996) Colleges as Learning Organisations: The Role of Research, Post 16 Curriculum Series Number 12, London, Institute of Education, University of London.

Young, M. and Leney, T. (1997) From A-levels to an Advanced Level curriculum of the future, in A. Hodgson and K. Spours (eds) *Dearing and Beyond*, London, Kogan Page.

Zukas, M. (2006) Pedagogic learning in the pedagogic workplace: educators' lifelong learning and learning futures, *International Journal of Pedagogies and Learning*, 2(3): 71–80.

Zukas, M. and Malcolm, J. (2002) Pedagogies for lifelong learning: Building bridges or building walls?, in R. Harrison, F. Reeve and J. Clarke (eds) *Supporting Lifelong Learning*, Volume 1, *Perspectives on Learning*), London, RoutledgeFalmer.

Further reading

PART I FURTHER EDUCATION IN CONTEXT

1 Where will I teach?

Foster, A. (2005) *Realising the Potential: A review of the future of further education colleges*, London, Department for Education and Skills.

Gallacher, J., Duncan, B., Mayes, J., Smith, L. and Watson, D. (2006) *Providing Further Education in the Community*, Glasgow, Learndirect Scotland.

2 The student body: who will I teach?

Chappell, C., Rhodes, C., Solomon, N., Tennant, M. and Yates, L. (eds) (2003) *Reconstructing the Lifelong Learner: Pedagogy and identity in individual, organisational and social change*, London, RoutledgeFalmer.

Harkin, J. (2006) Treated like adults: 14–16 year olds in further education, *Research in Post-Compulsory Education*, 11(1): 319–39.

3 Diverse curricula: what will I teach?

Bathmaker, A.-M. (2005) Hanging in or shaping a future: defining a role for vocationally related learning in a 'knowledge' society, *Journal of Education Policy*, 20(1): 81–100.

Jephcote M. and Abbott, I. (eds) (2005) *Teaching Business Education 14–19*, London, David Fulton

PART II TEACHING AND LEARNING

4 Approaches to learning

Evans, K., Hodkinson, P. and Unwin, L. (eds) (2002) *Working to Learn: Transforming workplace learning*, London, Kogan Page.

Evans, K., Hodkinson, P., Rainbird, H. and Unwin, L. (2006) *Improving Workplace Learning*, London, Routledge.

Harrison, R. *et al.* (eds) (2002) *Supporting Lifelong Learning*, Volume 1, *Perspectives on Learning*, London, Routledge.

James, D. and Biesta, G. (2007) *Improving Learning Cultures in Further Education*, London, Routledge.

Morrison, M. (2005) E-learning 'bites' for adult learners: mixed messages from research, *Research in Post-Compulsory Education*, 10(3): 403–22.

Paechter, C., Preedy, M., Scott, D. and Soler, J. (eds) (2001) *Knowledge, Power and Learning*, London, Paul Chapman.

5 Teaching strategies

Coffield, F., Moseley, D., Hall, E. and Ecclestone, K. (2004) *Learning Styles and Pedagogy in Post-16 Learning*, London: Learning and Skills Research Centre.

Edwards, R. and Smith, J (2005) Swamping and spoonfeeding: literacies for learning in Further education, *Journal of Vocational Education and Training*, 57(1): 47–59.

Harkin, J., Turner, G. and Dawn, T. (2001) *Teaching Young Adults*, London, Routledge Falmer.

Mortimore, P. (ed.) (1999) *Understanding Pedagogy and its Impact on Learning*, London, Sage.

Nixon, L., Gregson, M. and Spedding, T. (2007) Pedagogy and intuitive appeal of learning styles in post-compulsory education in England, *Journal of Vocational Education and Training*, 59(1): 39–51.

Rogers, J. (2001) *Adults Learning*, Milton Keynes, Open University Press.

Stephenson, J. (ed.) (2001) *Teaching and Learning On-line*, London, Kogan Page.

6 Assessment and recording achievement

Falchikov, N. (2004) *Improving Assessment Through Student Involvement: Practical solutions for aiding learning in higher and further education*, London, Routledge.

Irons, A. (2007) *Enhancing Learning Through Formative Assessment and Feedback*, London, Routledge.

PART III PROFESSIONAL DEVELOPMENT

7 Evaluation, reflection and research

Anderson, G., Barton, S. and Wahlberg, M. (2003) Reflections and experiences of further education research in practice, *Journal of Vocational Education and Training*, 55(4): 499–516.

Carr, W. and Kemis, S. (1986) *Becoming Critical*, London, Falmer Press.

Moon, J. (2000) *Learning Journals*, London, Kogan Page.

Somekh, B. (2006) *Action Research: A methodology for change and development*, Maidenhead, Open University Press.

Wellington, J. (2000) *Educational Research: Contemporary issues and practical approaches*, London, Continuum.

8 Professional development

Colley, H., James, D. and Diment, K. (2007) Unbecoming teachers: towards a more dynamic notion of professional participation, *Journal of Education Policy*, 22(2): 173–93.

Nasta, T. (2007) Translating national standards into practice for the initial training of further education teachers in England, *Research in Post-Compulsory Education*, 12(1): 1–17.

9 Networks and support agencies

Benefer, R. (2007) Engaging with employers in work-based learning: a foundation degree in applied technology, *Education + Training*, 49(3): 210–17.

Connolly, M., Jones, C. and Jones, N. (2007) Managing collaboration across further and higher education: a case in practice, *Journal of Further and Higher Education*, 31(2): 159–69.

Index